SOCIETY, KINSHIP AND RELIGION

SOCIETY, KINSHIP AND RELIGION

Dr. Gajanafar Alam

RANDOM
RANDOM PUBLICATIONS
NEW DELHI - 110 002 (INDIA)

Society, Kinship and Religion

ISBN 978-93-51117-35-3

Published in 2015 in India by

RANDOM PUBLICATIONS

4376-A/4B, Gali Murari Lal, Ansari Road
New Delhi-110 002
Phone: +9111-43580356, 23289044
E-mail: randomexports@gmail.com; sales@randompublications.com;
info@randompublications.com

Type Setting by: Friends Media, Delhi-110089
Printed at Thomson Press(India) Limited

Preface

Kinship is the web of social relationships that form an important part of the lives of most humans in most societies, although its exact meanings even within this discipline are often debated. Human kinship relations through marriage are commonly called "affinity" in contrast to the relationships that arise in one's group of origin, which may be called one's descent group. In some cultures, kinship relationships may be considered to extend out to people an individual has economic or political relationships with, or other forms of social connections. A religion is an organized collection of beliefs, cultural systems, and world views that relate humanity to an order of existence.

The social spheres or domains addressed by social scientists (politics, economics, religion, and kinship) are never discrete entities that operate in isolation from one another—they are interactive in every society. Kinship is the central organizational principle of many traditional societies, since it is through the kinship structure that social placement, cultural transmission and many functional necessities for life will be met. Extent of relevant kinship connection differs greatly from society to society. Kinship bonds are generally defined more broadly and extensively in traditional societies than in modern capitalist societies. Kinship is one of the universals in human society and therefore plays an important role in both the regulation of behaviour and the formation of social groups. Kinship systems depend on the social recognition and cultural implementation of relationships derived from descent and marriage and normally involve a set of kinship terms and an associated set of behavioural patterns and attitudes which, together, make up a systematic whole. All societies distinguish various categories of relationship by descent or consanguinity, and most societies distinguish relationships by marriage or affinity as well. Although dictionary definitions differentiate these relationships, it is convenient to extend the term "kinship" to cover both kinds. The resulting network of social relations may constitute almost the whole social structure in some of the simpler societies or be a relatively small part of a highly complex structure, as in modern industrial societies. In either case, however, the system of kinship and marriage plays an important role in maintaining group cohesion and solidarity and in orienting the individual members to the social maze. The use of the term "system" implies that there is a complex relation of interdependence between the component parts: the social categories and the associated rights and duties. Because of unprecedented increases in longevity, the kinship structure has been transformed. Linkages among family members have been prolonged, and the surviving generations in a family have increased in number and complexity. Today's kinship structure can be viewed in a new way: as a latent web of continually shifting linkages that provide the potential for activating and intensifying close family relationships. Kinship has very important contribution in a social structure. Kinship decides who can marry with whom and where marital relationships are taboo. It determines the rights and obligations of the members in all the sacraments and religious practices from birth to death in family life. Importance of kinship is observed on the occasion of marriage and family functions. It determines family line relationships i.e. gotra and kula.

This book is an introduction to the social anthropology of kinship to the ways in which the peoples of different cultures marry and relate to each other within and outside the family.

I thank all members of my team who have helped in the preparation of the book. My special thanks go to "Random Publications" who have published the book.

— Dr. Gajanafar Alam

Contents

Chapter 1

Society

A human society is a group of people involved in persistent interpersonal relationships, or a large social grouping sharing the same geographical or social territory, typically subject to the same political authority and dominant cultural expectations. Human societies are characterized by patterns of relationships (social relations) between individuals who share a distinctive culture and institutions; a given society may be described as the sum total of such relationships among its constituent members. In the social sciences, a larger society often evinces stratification or dominance patterns in subgroups..

Insofar as it is collaborative, a society can enable its members to benefit in ways that would not otherwise be possible on an individual basis; both individual and social (common) benefits can thus be distinguished, or in many cases found to overlap. A society can also consist of like-minded people governed by their own norms and values within a dominant, larger society. This is sometimes referred to as a subculture, a term used extensively within criminology.

More broadly, and especially within structuralist thought, a society may be illustrated as an economic, social, industrial or cultural infrastructure, made up of, yet distinct from, a varied collection of individuals. In this regard society can mean the objective relationships people have with the material world and with other people, rather than "other people" beyond the individual and their familiar social environment.

Members of a society may be from different ethnic groups. A society can be a particular ethnic group, such as the Saxons; a nation state, such as Bhutan; or a broader cultural group, such as a Western society. The word *society* may also refer to an organised voluntary association of people for religious, benevolent, cultural, scientific, political, patriotic, or other purposes. A "society" may even, though more by means of metaphor, refer to a social organism such as an ant colony or any cooperative aggregate such as, for example, in some formulations of artificial intelligence.

Etymology and Usage

***Figure:** A half-section of the 12th-century South Tang Dynasty version of* Night Revels of Han Xizai, *original by Gu Hongzhong. The painting portrays servants, musicians, monks, children, guests, and hosts all in a single social environment. It serves as an in-depth look into the Chinese social structure of the time.*

The term "society" came from the Latin word *societas*, which in turn was derived from the noun *socius* ("comrade, friend, ally"; adjectival form *socialis*) used to describe a bond or interaction between parties that are friendly, or at least civil. Without an article, the term can refer to the entirety of humanity (also: "society in general", "society at large", etc.), although those who are unfriendly or uncivil to the remainder of society in this sense may be deemed to be "antisocial". Adam Smith wrote that a society "may subsist among different men, as among different merchants, from a sense of its utility without any mutual love or affection, if only they refrain from doing injury to each other."

Used in the sense of an association, a society is a body of individuals outlined by the bounds of functional interdependence, possibly comprising characteristics such as national or cultural identity, social solidarity, language, or hierarchical structure.

Conceptions

Society, in general, addresses the fact that an individual has rather limited means as an autonomous unit. The great apes have always been more (*Bonobo*, *Homo*, *Pan*) or less (*Gorilla*, *Pongo*) social animals, so Robinson Crusoe-like situations are either fictions or unusual corner cases to the ubiquity of social context for humans, who fall between presocial and eusocial in the spectrum of animal ethology.

Human societies are most often organised according to their primary means of subsistence. Social scientists have identified hunter-gatherer societies, nomadic pastoral societies, horticulturalist or simple farming societies, and intensive agricultural societies, also called civilizations. Some consider industrial and post-industrial societies to be qualitatively different from traditional agricultural societies.

Today, anthropologists and many social scientists vigorously oppose the notion of cultural evolution and rigid "stages" such as these. In fact, much anthropological data has suggested that complexity (civilization, population growth and density, specialisation, etc.) does not always take the form of hierarchical social organisation or stratification.

Cultural relativism as a widespread approach or ethic has largely replaced notions of "primitive", better/worse, or "progress" in relation to cultures (including their material culture/technology and social organisation). According to anthropologist Maurice Godelier, one critical novelty in human society, in contrast to humanity's closest biological relatives (chimpanzees and bonobos), is the parental role assumed by the males, which supposedly would be absent in our nearest relatives for whom paternity is not generally determinable.

In Political Science

Societies may also be structured politically. In order of increasing size and complexity, there are bands, tribes, chiefdoms, and state societies. These structures may have varying degrees of political power, depending on the cultural, geographical, and historical environments that these societies must contend with. Thus, a more isolated society with the same level of technology and culture as other societies is more likely to survive than one in closer proximity to others that may encroach on their resources. A society that is unable to offer an effective response to other societies it competes with will usually be subsumed into the culture of the competing society.

In Sociology

Sociologist Gerhard Lenski differentiates societies based on their level of technology, communication, and economy: (1) hunters and gatherers, (2) simple agricultural, (3) advanced agricultural, (4) industrial, and (5) special (e.g. fishing societies or maritime societies). This is similar to the system earlier developed by anthropologists Morton H. Fried, a conflict theorist, and Elman Service, an integration theorist, who have produced a system of classification for societies in all human cultures based on the evolution of social inequality and the role of the state. This system of classification contains four categories:

- Hunter-gatherer bands (categorization of duties and responsibilities).
- Tribal societies in which there are some limited instances of social rank and prestige.

- Stratified structures led by chieftains.
- Civilizations, with complex social hierarchies and organised, institutional governments.

In addition to this there are:

- Humanity, mankind, upon which rest all the elements of society, including society's beliefs.
- Virtual society, a society based on online identity, which is evolving in the information age.

Over time, some cultures have progressed toward more complex forms of organisation and control. This cultural evolution has a profound effect on patterns of community. Hunter-gatherer tribes settled around seasonal food stocks to become agrarian villages. Villages grew to become towns and cities. Cities turned into city-states and nation-states.

Many societies distribute largess at the behest of some individual or some larger group of people. This type of generosity can be seen in all known cultures; typically, prestige accrues to the generous individual or group. Conversely, members of a society may also shun or scapegoat members of the society who violate its norms. Mechanisms such as gift-giving, joking relationships and scapegoating, which may be seen in various types of human groupings, tend to be institutionalized within a society. Social evolution as a phenomenon carries with it certain elements that could be detrimental to the population it serves.

Some societies bestow status on an individual or group of people when that individual or group performs an admired or desired action. This type of recognition is bestowed in the form of a name, title, manner of dress, or monetary reward. In many societies, adult male or female status is subject to a ritual or process of this type. Altruistic action in the interests of the larger group is seen in virtually all societies. The phenomena of community action, shunning, scapegoating, generosity, shared risk, and reward are common to many forms of society.

Types

Societies are social groups that differ according to subsistence strategies, the ways that humans use technology to provide needs for themselves. Although humans have established many types of societies throughout history, anthropologists tend to classify different societies according to the degree to which different groups within a society have unequal access to advantages such as resources, prestige, or power. Virtually all societies have developed some degree of inequality among their people through the process of social stratification, the division of members of a society into levels with unequal wealth, prestige, or power.

Sociologists place societies in three broad categories: pre-industrial, industrial, and postindustrial.

Pre-industrial Society

Pre-industrial society refers to social attributes and forms of political and cultural organisation that were prevalent before the advent of the Industrial Revolution, which occurred from 1750 to 1850. Pre-industrial is a time before there were machines and tools to help perform tasks. Pre-industrial civilization dates back to centuries ago, but the main era known as the Pre-Industrial Society occurred right before the Industrial Society. Pre-Industrial societies vary from region or region depending on the culture of a given area or history of social and political life. Europe is known for its Feudal System and Medieval era.

Attributes of the Pre-industrial Societies

- Limited production (i.e. artisanship vs. mass production)
- Primarily an agricultural economy
- Limited division of labour. In pre-industrial societies, production was relatively simple and the number of specialised crafts was limited.
- Limited variation of social classes
- Parochialism—Communications were limited between human communities in pre-industrial societies. Few had the opportunity to see or hear beyond their own village. In contrast, industrial societies grew with the help of faster means of communication, having more information at hand about the world, allowing knowledge transfer and cultural diffusion between them.
- Pre-industrial societies developed largely in rural communities. Capitalism developed largely in urban areas.
- Europe made up of numerous rural microcosms
- Populations grew at substantial rates
- Social Classes: Peasants and Lords
- The Black Plague
- Subsistence level of living
- Population dependent on peasants for food

Life in Pre-Industrial Society

- All people worked/lived in the country
- Diet included very little meat

- Most people were illiterate
- High levels of poverty and inequality
- Plagues were common as well as other extreme diseases
- War occurred often between different

Hunter-gatherer

A hunter-gatherer or forager society is a nomadic society in which most or all food is obtained from wild plants and animals, in contrast to agricultural societies, which rely mainly on domesticated species. Anthropologists have remarked that the term foraging is a more appropriate description of the predominant food source for most non-agricultural groups: Gathering is a far more important source of food than is hunting for the majority of non-agricultural societies, according to Richard Borshay Lee.

Foraging was the ancestral subsistence mode of *Homo*. As *The Cambridge Encyclopedia of Hunter-Gatherers* says: "Hunting and gathering was humanity's first and most successful adaptation, occupying at least 90 percent of human history. Until 12,000 years ago, all humans lived this way." Following the invention of agriculture, hunter-gatherers have been displaced by farming or pastoralist groups in most parts of the world. Only a few contemporary societies are classified as hunter-gatherers, and many supplement, sometimes extensively, their foraging activity with farming and/or keeping animals.

Archaeological Evidence

In the 1950s, Louis Binford suggested that early humans were obtaining meat via scavenging, not hunting. Early humans in the Lower Paleolithic lived in forests and woodlands, which allowed them to collect seafood, eggs, nuts, and fruits besides scavenging. Rather than killing large animals for meat, according to this view, they used carcasses of such animals that had either been killed by predators or that had died of natural causes. According to the endurance running hypothesis, long-distance running as in persistence hunting, a method still practiced by some hunter-gatherer groups in modern times, was likely the driving evolutionary force leading to the evolution of certain human characteristics. (This hypothesis does not necessarily contradict the scavenging hypothesis: both subsistence strategies could have been in use – sequentially, alternating or even simultaneously.)

Hunting and gathering was presumably the subsistence strategy employed by human societies beginning some 1.8 million years ago, by *Homo erectus*, and from its appearance some 0.2 million years ago by

Homo sapiens. It remained the only mode of subsistence until the end of the Mesolithic period some 10,000 years ago, and after this was replaced only gradually with the spread of the Neolithic Revolution.

Starting at the transition between the Middle to Upper Paleolithic period, some 80,000 to 70,000 years ago, some hunter-gatherers bands began to specialise, concentrating on hunting a smaller selection of (often larger than had previously been hunted) game and gathering a smaller selection of food. This specialisation of work also involved creating specialised tools, like fishing nets and hooks and bone harpoons. The transition into the subsequent Neolithic period is chiefly defined by the unprecedented development of nascent agricultural practices. Agriculture originated and spread in several different areas including the Middle East, Asia, Mesoamerica, and the Andes beginning as early as 12,000 years ago.

Forest gardening was also being used as a food production system in various parts of the world over this period. Forest gardens originated in prehistoric times along jungle-clad river banks and in the wet foothills of monsoon regions. In the gradual process of families improving their immediate environment, useful tree and vine species were identified, protected and improved, whilst undesirable species were eliminated. Eventually superior foreign species were selected and incorporated into the gardens.

Many groups continued their hunter-gatherer ways of life, although their numbers have continually declined, partly as a result of pressure from growing agricultural and pastoral communities. Many of them reside in the developing world, either in arid regions or tropical forests. Areas that were formerly available to hunter-gatherers were—and continue to be—encroached upon by the settlements of agriculturalists. In the resulting competition for land use, hunter-gatherer societies either adopted these practices or moved to other areas. In addition, Jared Diamond has blamed a decline in the availability of wild foods, particularly animal resources. In North and South America, for example, most large mammal species had gone extinct by the end of the Pleistocene—according to Diamond, because of overexploitation by humans, although the overkill hypothesis he advocates is strongly contested.

As the number and size of agricultural societies increased, they expanded into lands traditionally used by hunter-gatherers. This process of agriculture-driven expansion led to the development of the first forms of government in agricultural centres, such as the Fertile Crescent, Ancient India, Ancient China, Olmec, Sub-Saharan Africa and Norte Chico.

As a result of the now near-universal human reliance upon agriculture, the few contemporary hunter-gatherer cultures usually live in areas unsuitable for agricultural use. Archaeologists can use evidence such as stone tool use to track hunter-gatherer activities, including mobility.

Common Characteristics

Habitat and Population: Hunter-gatherer settlements may be either permanent, temporary, or some combination of the two, depending upon the mobility of the community. Mobile communities typically construct shelters using impermanent building materials, or they may use natural rock shelters, where they are available.

Social and Economic Structure

Hunter-gatherers tend to have an egalitarian social ethos, although settled hunter-gatherers (for example, those inhabiting the Northwest Coast of North America) are an exception to this rule. Nearly all African hunter-gatherers are egalitarian, with women roughly as influential and powerful as men. The egalitarianism typical of human hunters and gatherers is never perfect, but is striking when viewed in an evolutionary context. One of humanity's two closest primate relatives, chimpanzees, are anything but egalitarian, forming themselves into hierarchies that are often dominated by an alpha male. So great is the contrast with human hunter-gatherers that it is widely argued by palaeoanthropologists that resistance to being dominated was a key factor driving the evolutionary emergence of human consciousness, language, kinship and social organisation.

Some archaeologists argue that violence in hunter-gatherer societies was ubiquitous. They argue that approximately 25% to 30% of adult male deaths in these societies were due to homicide, compared to an upper estimate of 3% of all deaths in the 20th century. They claim that the cause of this is near constant tribal warfare: "From the !Kung in the Kalahari to the Inuit in the Arctic and the aborigines in Australia, two-thirds of modern hunter-gatherers are in a state of almost constant tribal warfare, and nearly 90% go to war at least once a year." However, many anthropologists, including some who have lived with hunter-gatherers, disagree with this viewpoint and claim that nomadic hunter-gatherer societies are remarkably low in violence.

Some anthropologists maintain that hunter-gatherers don't have permanent leaders; instead, the person taking the initiative at any one time depends on the task being performed. In addition to social and economic equality in hunter-gatherer societies, there is often, though not always, sexual parity as well. Hunter-gatherers are often grouped together based on kinship and band (or tribe) membership. Postmarital residence among hunter-gatherers tends to be matrilocal, at least initially. This means that young mothers can enjoy childcare support from their own mothers who continue living nearby in the same camp. The systems of kinship and descent among human hunter-gatherers were relatively flexible, although there is evidence that early human kinship in general tended to be matrilineal. A few groups, such as the Haida of present-day British Columbia, lived in such a rich environment that they could remain sedentary or semi-nomadic, like many other Native Americans of the Pacific Northwest coast.

It is easy for Western-educated scholars to fall into the trap of viewing hunter-gatherer social and sexual arrangements in the light of Western values. One common arrangement is the sexual division of labour, with women doing most of the gathering, while men concentrate on big game hunting. It might be imagined that this arrangement oppresses women, keeping them in the domestic sphere. However, according to some observers, hunter-gatherer women would not understand this interpretation. Since childcare is collective, with every baby having multiple mothers and male carers, the domestic sphere is not atomised or privatised but an empowering place to be. In all hunter-gatherer societies, women appreciate the meat brought back to camp by men. An illustrative account is Megan Biesele's study of the southern African Ju/'hoan, 'Women Like Meat'. Recent archaeological research suggests that the sexual division of labour was the fundamental organisational innovation that gave *Homo sapiens* the edge over the Neanderthals, allowing our ancestors to migrate from Africa and spread across the globe.

Figure: *A 19th century engraving of an Indigenous Australian encampment.*

To this day, most hunter-gatherers have a symbolically structured sexual division of labour, most often conceptualised through an ideology of blood. However, it is true that in a small minority of cases, women hunt the same kind of quarry as men, sometimes doing so alongside men. The best-known example are the Aeta people of the Philippines. According to one study: "About 85% of Philippine Aeta women hunt, and they hunt the same quarry as men. Aeta women hunt in groups and with dogs, and have a 31% success rate as opposed to 17% for men. Their rates are even better when they combine forces with men: mixed hunting groups have a full 41% success rate among the Aeta." It was also found among the Ju'/hoansi people of Namibia that women helped the men during hunting by helping them track down quarry.

At the 1966 "Man the Hunter" conference, anthropologists Richard Borshay Lee and Irven DeVore suggested that egalitarianism was one of several central characteristics of nomadic hunting and gathering societies because mobility requires minimization of material possessions throughout a population; therefore, there was no surplus of resources to be accumulated by any single member. Other characteristics Lee and DeVore proposed were flux in territorial boundaries as well as in demographic composition. At the same conference, Marshall Sahlins presented a paper entitled, "Notes on the Original Affluent Society", in which he challenged the popular view of hunter-gatherers living lives "solitary, poor, nasty, brutish and short," as Thomas Hobbes had put it in 1651. According to Sahlins, ethnographic data indicated that hunter-gatherers worked far fewer hours and enjoyed more leisure than typical members of industrial society, and they still ate well. Their "affluence" came from the idea that they are satisfied with very little in the material sense. This, he said, constituted a Zen economy. These people met the same requirements as their sedentary neighbours through much less complex means. Later, in 1996, Ross Sackett performed two distinct meta-analyses to empirically test Sahlin's view. The first of these studies looked at 102 time-allocation studies, and the second one analyzed 207 energy-expenditure studies. Sackett found that adults in foraging and horticultural societies work, on average, about 6.5 hours a day, where as people in agricultural and industrial societies work on average 8.8 hours a day.

Recent research also indicates that the life-expectancy of hunter-gatherers is surprisingly high. Mutual exchange and sharing of resources (i.e., meat gained from hunting) are important in the economic systems of hunter-gatherer societies. Therefore, these societies can be described as based on a "gift economy".

Variability

Hunter-gatherer societies manifest significant variability, depending on climate zone/life zone, available technology and societal structure. One way to divide hunter-gatherer groups is by their return systems. James Woodburn uses the categories "immediate return" hunter-gatherers for egalitarian and "delayed return" for nonegalitarian. Immediate return foragers consume their food within a day or two after they procure it. Delayed return foragers store the surplus food (Kelly, 31). Hunting-gathering was the common human mode of subsistence throughout the Paleolithic, but the observation of current-day hunters and gatherers does not necessarily reflect Paleolithic societies; the hunter-gatherer cultures examined today have had much contact with modern civilization and do not represent "pristine" conditions found in uncontacted peoples.

The transition from hunting and gathering to agriculture is not necessarily a one way process. It has been argued that hunting and gathering represents an adaptive strategy, which may still be exploited, if necessary, when environmental change causes extreme food stress for agriculturalists. In fact, it is sometimes difficult to draw a clear line between agricultural and hunter-gatherer societies, especially since the widespread adoption of agriculture and resulting cultural diffusion that has occurred in the last 10,000 years. This anthropological view has remained unchanged since the 1960s.

Modern and Revisionist Perspectives

Figure: *A Shoshone encampment in the Wind River Mountains of Wyoming, photographed by W. H. Jackson, 1870*

In the early 1980s, a small but vocal segment of anthropologists and archaeologists attempted to demonstrate that contemporary groups usually identified as hunter-gatherers do not, in most cases, have a continuous history of hunting and gathering, and that in many cases their ancestors were agriculturalists and/or pastoralists who were pushed into marginal areas as a result of migrations, economic exploitation, and/or violent conflict. The result of their effort has been the general acknowledgement that there has been complex interaction between hunter-gatherers and non-hunter-gatherers for millennia.

Some of the theorists who advocate this "revisionist" critique imply that, because the "pure hunter-gatherer" disappeared not long after colonial (or even agricultural) contact began, nothing meaningful can be learned about prehistoric hunter-gatherers from studies of modern ones (Kelly, 24-29)

Lee and Guenther have rejected most of the arguments put forward by Wilmsen. Doron Shultziner and others have argued that we can learn a lot about the life-styles of prehistoric hunter-gatherers from studies of contemporary hunter-gatherers—especially their impressive levels of egalitarianism.

Many hunter-gatherers consciously manipulate the landscape through cutting or burning undesirable plants while encouraging desirable ones, some even going to the extent of slash-and-burn to create habitat for game animals. These activities are on an entirely different scale to those associated with agriculture, but they are nevertheless domestication on some level. Today, almost all hunter-gatherers depend to some extent upon domesticated food sources either produced part-time or traded for products acquired in the wild.

Some agriculturalists also regularly hunt and gather (e.g. farming during the frost-free season and hunting during the winter). Still others in developed countries go hunting, primarily for leisure. In the Brazilian rainforest, those groups that recently did, or even continue to, rely on hunting and gathering techniques seem to have adopted this lifestyle, abandoning most agriculture, as a way to escape colonial control and as a result of the introduction of European diseases reducing their populations to levels where agriculture became difficult.

There are nevertheless a number of contemporary hunter-gatherer peoples who, after contact with other societies, continue their ways of life with very little external influence. One such group is the Pila Nguru (Spinifex people) of Western Australia, whose habitat in the Great Victoria Desert has proved unsuitable for European agriculture (and even pastoralism). Another are the Sentinelese of the Andaman Islands in the Indian Ocean, who live on North Sentinel Island and to date have maintained their independent existence, repelling attempts to engage with and contact them.

Americas

Evidence suggests big-game hunter gatherers crossed the Bering Strait from Asia (Eurasia) into North America over a land bridge (Beringia), that existed between 47,000–14,000 years ago. Around 18,500-15,500 years ago, these hunter-gatherers are believed to have followed herds of now-extinct Pleistocene megafauna along ice-free corridors that stretched between the Laurentide and Cordilleran ice sheets. Another route proposed is that, either on foot or using primitive boats, they migrated down the Pacific coast to South America.

Hunter-gatherers would eventually flourish all over the Americas, primarily based in the Great Plains of the United States and Canada, with offshoots as far east as the Gaspé Peninsula on the Atlantic coast, and as far south as Chile, Monte Verde. American hunter-gatherers were spread over a wide geographical area, thus there were regional variations in lifestyles. However, all the individual groups shared a common style of stone tool production, making knapping styles and progress identifiable. This early Paleo-Indian period lithic reduction tool adaptations have been found across the Americas, utilised by highly mobile bands consisting of approximately 25 to 50 members of an extended family. The Archaic period in the Americas saw a changing environment featuring a warmer more arid climate and the disappearance of the last megafauna. The majority of population groups at this time were still highly mobile hunter-gatherers; but now individual groups started to focus on resources available to them locally, thus with the passage of time there is a pattern of increasing regional generalization like, the Southwest, Arctic, Poverty, Dalton and Plano traditions. This regional adaptations would become the norm, with reliance less on hunting and gathering, with a more mixed economy of small game, fish, seasonally wild vegetables and harvested plant foods.

Pastoral Society

A pastoral society is a social group of pastoralists, whose way of life is based on pastoralism, and is typically nomadic. Daily life is centred upon the tending of herds or flocks.

Social Organisation

There is not an explicit form of social organisation associated with pastoralism. Pastoral societies are often organised in tribes, with the 'household,' often incorporating the extended family, as a basic unit for organisation of labour and expenses Lineages are often the root for property rights. Mobility allows groups of pastoralists to leave and regroup as resources permit, or as sought after with changes in social relations.

Cross-border Pastoralism

Sometimes pastoralists move their herds across international borders in search of new grazing or for trade. This cross-border activity can occasionally lead to tensions with national governments as this activity is often informal and beyond their control and regulation. In East Africa, for example, over 95% of cross-border trade is through unofficial channels and the unofficial trade of live cattle, camels, sheep and goats from Ethiopia sold to Somalia, Kenya and Djibouti generates an estimated total value of between US$250 and US$300 million annually (100 times more than the official figure). This trade helps lower food prices, increase food security, relieve border tensions and promote regional integration. However, there are also risks as the unregulated and undocumented nature of this trade runs risks, such as allow disease to spread more easily across national borders. Furthermore, governments are unhappy with lost tax revenue and foreign exchange revenues.

There have been initiatives seeking to promote cross-border trade and also document it, in order to both stimulate regional growth and food security, but also allow the effective vaccination of livestock. Initiatives include Regional Resilience Enhancement Against Drought (RREAD), the Enhanced Livelihoods in Mandera Triangle/Enhanced Livelihoods in Southern Ethiopia (ELMT/ELSE) as part of the Regional Enhanced Livelihoods in Pastoral Areas (RELPA) programme in East Africa, and the Regional Livelihoods Advocacy Project (REGLAP) funded by the European Commission Humanitarian Aid Office (ECHO).

Examples of Pastoral Societies

Traditional

North & Northeast Africa:

- Afar of the Horn of Africa
- Bedouin of North Africa and the Arabian Peninsula
- Beja of North Africa and the Horn of Africa
- Berbers of North Africa
- Oromos of the Horn of Africa

- Rendille of the Horn of Africa
- Saho of the Horn of Africa
- Somalis of the Horn of Africa
- Tigre of the Horn of Africa
- Tuareg of the north-central Sahara

Sahel:

- Fula people of Sahelian West Africa
- Toubou of Niger and Chad

Sub-Saharan Africa:

- Karimojong of Uganda
- Maasai of East Africa
- Pokot of East Africa
- Samburu of East Africa
- Turkana of East Africa

Near East:

- Kuchis of Afghanistan
- Yörük of Turkey

South Asia:

- Ahir found throughout North India
- Baghelmainly in UP and MP state of India
- Bakarwal found in Jammu and Kashmir
- Bharwad in Gujarat
- Bhutia in north India and Nepal
- Bodla found in Pakistani Punjab
- Charan in Gujarat and Rajasthan
- Chishti found in Pakistani Punjab
- Dhangar found in Maharastra, MP
- Gaddi of Himachal Pradesh
- Maldhari of Gujarat
- Muslim Gaddi
- Gaderiain UP and MP
- Gvala in Bangladesh
- Ghosi
- Gujjar found in North India, Afghanistan and Pakistan

- Kuruba found in South India
- Kurma found in South India
- Rabari of Gujarat, Rajasthan and panjab
- Ranghar found in North India and Pakistan
- Sherpa in Nepal
- Wattu found in Pakistani Punjab
- Raika found in Rajasthan

Central Asia:

- Tuvans of Mongolia

Southern Europe:

- Aromanians of Balkans
- Sarakatsani of Greece

Northern Europe:

- Komi of northern Russia
- Sami of Scandinavia

North America:

- Navajo of North America

South America:

- Quechua of The Andes region
- Aymara of The Andes and Altiplano regions

Modern

One of the consequences of the break-up of the Soviet Union and the subsequent political independence and economic collapse of its Central Asian republics is the resurgence of pastoral nomadism. Taking the Kyrgyz people as a representative example, nomadism was the centre of their economy prior to Russian colonization at the turn of the C19/C20, when they were settled into agricultural villages. The population became increasingly urbanized after World War II, but some people continued to take their herds of horses and cows to the high pasture (*jailoo*) every summer. Since the 1990s, as the cash economy shrank, unemployed relatives were absorbed back on the family farm, and the importance of this form of nomadism has increased. The symbols of nomadism, specifically the crown of the grey felt tent known as the yurt, appears on the national flag, emphasizing the centrality of their nomadic history and past in the creation of the modern nation of Kyrgyzstan.

Horticultural

Fruits and vegetables grown in garden plots that have been cleared from the jungle or forest provide the main source of food in a horticultural society. These societies have a level of technology and complexity similar to pastoral societies. Some horticultural groups use the slash-and-burn method to raise crops. The wild vegetation is cut and burned, and ashes are used as fertilizers. Horticulturists use human labour and simple tools to cultivate the land for one or more seasons. When the land becomes barren, horticulturists clear a new plot and leave the old plot to revert to its natural state. They may return to the original land several years later and begin the process again. By rotating their garden plots, horticulturists can stay in one area for a fairly long period of time. This allows them to build semipermanent or permanent villages. The size of a village's population depends on the amount of land available for farming; thus villages can range from as few as 30 people to as many as 2000.

As with pastoral societies, surplus food leads to a more complex division of labour. Specialised roles in horticultural societies include craftspeople, shamans (religious leaders), and traders. This role specialisation allows people to create a wide variety of artifacts. As in pastoral societies, surplus food can lead to inequalities in wealth and power within horticultural political systems, developed because of the settled nature of horticultural life.

Agrarian Society

An agrarian society (or agricultural society) is any society based around producing and maintaining crops and farmland. Another way to define an agrarian society is by seeing how much of a nation's total production is in agriculture. In an agrarian society cultivating the land is the primary source of wealth. Such a society may acknowledge other means of livelihood and work habits but stresses the importance of agriculture and farming. Agrarian societies have occurred in various parts of the world as far back as 10,000 years ago and continue to exist in the world today. They have been the most common form of socio-economic organisation for most of recorded human history. And thus, because of large spatial and temporal differences, there is not a homogeneous cultural, however, certain similarities and generalities occur.

History

Agrarian societies were preceded by hunter and gatherer societies and horticultural societies and transition into industrial societies. This transition, called the Neolithic Revolution, has taken place independently multiple times. Horticulture and agriculture as types of subsistence developed among humans somewhere between 10,000 and 8,000 years ago in the Fertile Crescent region of the Middle East. The reasons for the development of agriculture are debated but may have included climate change and the accumulation of food surplus for competitive gift-giving. Most certainly there was a gradual transition from hunter-gatherer to agricultural economies after a lengthy period when some crops were deliberately planted and other foods were gathered from the wild. In addition to the emergence of farming in the Fertile Crescent, agriculture appeared in: by at least 6,800 B.C.E. in East Asia (rice) and, later, in Central and South America (maize and squash). Small scale agriculture also likely arose independently in early Neolithic contexts in India (rice) and Southeast Asia (taro). . However, full dependency on domestic crops and animals, when wild resources contributed a nutritionally insignificant component to the diet, did not occur until the Bronze Age.

Agriculture allows a much greater density of population than can be supported by hunting and gathering and allows for the accumulation of excess product to keep for winter use or to sell for profit. The ability of farmers to feed large numbers of people whose activities have nothing to do with material production was the crucial factor in the rise of surplus, specialisation, advanced technology, hierarchical social structures, inequality, and standing armies. Agrarian societies thus support the emergence of a more complex social structure.

In agrarian societies, some of the simple correlations between social complexity and environment begin to disappear. One view is that humans with this technology have moved a large step toward controlling their environments, are less dependent on them, and hence show fewer correlations between environment and technology-related traits. A rather different view is that as societies become larger and the movement of goods and people cheaper, they incorporate an increasing range of environmental variation within their borders and trade system. But environmental factors may still play a strong role as variables that affect the internal structure and history of a society in complex ways. For example, the average size of agrarian states will depend on the ease of transportation, major cities will tend to be located at trade nodes, and the demographic history of a society may depend on disease episodes.

Until recent decades, the transition to farming was seen as an inherently progressive one: people learnt that planting seeds caused crops to grow, and this new improved food source led to larger populations, sedentary farm and town life, more leisure time and so to specialisation, writing, technological advances and civilization. It is now clear that agriculture was adopted despite certain disadvantages of that lifestyle. Archeological studies show that health deteriorated in populations that adopted cereal agriculture, returning to pre-agricultural levels only in modem times. This is in part attributable to the spread of infection in crowded cities, but is largely due to a decline in dietary quality that accompanied intensive cereal farming. People in many parts of the world remained hunter-gatherers until quite recently; though they were quite aware of the existence and methods of agriculture, they declined to undertake it. Many explanations have been offered, usually centred around a particular factor that forced the adoption of agriculture, such as environmental or population pressure.

In the Modern World

Agrarian societies transition into industrial societies when less than half of their population is directly engaged in agricultural production. Such societies started appearing because of the Commercial and Industrial Revolution which can be seen beginning in the Mediterranean city-states of 1000-1500 C.E. As European societies developed during the Middle Ages, classical knowledge was reacquired from scattered sources, especially the Arabs, and a new series of maritime commercial societies developed again in Europe. The initial developments were centred in Northern Italy, in the city-states of Venice, Florence, Milan, and Genoa. By about 1500 a few of these city-states probably met the requirements of having half of their populations engaged in non-agricultural pursuits and became commercial societies. These small states were highly urbanized, imported much food, and were centres of trade and manufacture to a degree quite unlike typical agrarian societies.

The culminating development, still in progress, was the development of industrial technology, the application of mechanical sources of energy to an ever increasing number of production problems. By about 1800, the agricultural population of Britain had sunk to about 1/3 of the total. . By mid-19th Century, all the countries of Western Europe, plus the United States of America had more than half their populations in non-farm occupations. Even today, the Industrial Revolution is far from completely replacing agrarianism with industrialism. Only a minority of the world's people today live in industrialized societies although most predominantly agrarian societies have a significant industrial sector.

The use of crop breeding, better management of soil nutrients, and improved weed control have greatly increased yields per unit area. At the same time, the use of mechanization has decreased labour input. The developing world generally produces lower yields, having less of the latest science, capital, and technology base. More people in the world are involved in agriculture as their primary economic activity than in any other, yet it only accounts for four percent of the world's GDP. The rapid rise of mechanization in the 20th century, especially in the form of the tractor, reduced the necessity of humans performing the demanding tasks of sowing, harvesting, and threshing. With mechanization, these tasks could be performed with a speed and on a scale barely imaginable before. These advances have resulted in a substantial increase in the yield of agricultural techniques that have also translated into a decline in the percentage of populations in developed countries that are required to work in agriculture to feed the rest of the population.

Demographics

The main demographic consequences of agrarian technology were simply a continuation of the trend toward higher population densities and larger settlements. The latter is probably a more secure consequence of agrarian technology than the former. In principle livestock compete with humans for food and in some environments, advanced horticultural techniques can probably support more people per square kilometre than agrarian techniques.

Aside from average density, agrarian technology permitted urbanization of population to a greater extent than was possible under horticulture for two reasons. First, settlement sizes grew with agrarian technology because more productive farmers freed more people for urban speciality occupations. Second, land and maritime transportation improvements made it possible to supply great cities of 1,000,000, plus inhabitants such as Rome, Baghdad, and the Chinese capital cities. Rome, for example, could draw grain and other bulk raw materials Sicily, North Africa, Egypt, and Southern France to sustain large populations, even by modern standards, using maritime transport on the Mediterranean. It is productivity per unit of labour and transport efficiency improvements of agrarian technology that had the widest impact on the more peripheral culture core features of agrarian societies.

The populations of agrarian societies also have historically fluctuated substantially around the slowly rising trend line, due to famines, disease epidemics and political disruption. At least at the high points, population densities often seem to have exceeded the level at which everyone could be productively employed at current levels of technology. Malthusian deterioration, under-employment and a decline in rural and lower-class urban standards of living, ensued.

Social Organisation

Agrarian societies are especially noted for their extremes of social classes and rigid social mobility. As land is the major source of wealth, social hierarchy develops based on landownership and not labour. The system of stratification is characterized by three coinciding contrasts: governing class versus the masses, urban minority versus peasant majority, and literatc minority versus illiterate majority. This results in two distinct subcultures the urban elite versus the peasant masses. Moreover this means that cultural differences within agrarian societies greater than differences between them. .

The landowning strata typically combine government, religious, and military institutions to justify and enforce their ownership, and support elaborate patterns of consumption, slavery, serfdom, or peonage is commonly the lot of the primary producer. Rulers of agrarian societies do not manage their empire for the common good or in the name of the public interest, but as a piece of property they own and can do with as they please. . Caste systems, as found in India, are much more typical of agrarian societies where lifelong agricultural routines depend upon a rigid sense of duty and discipline. The emphasis in the modern West on personal liberties and freedoms was in large part a reaction to the steep and rigid stratification of agrarian societies. .

Energy

Within Agrarian societies the primary source of energy is plant biomass. This means that like hunter-gatherer societies, agrarian societies are dependent on natural solar energy flows. Thus agrarian societies are characterized by their dependence on outside energy flows, low energy density, and the limited possibilities of converting one energy form into another. . Energy radiating from the sun is primarily caught and chemically fixed by plant photosynthesis. Then it is secondarily converted by animals and, finally, processed for human use. However, unlike hunter-gatherers, agrarianism's basic strategy is to control these flows. For this purpose, agrarians system mainly uses living organism which serve as food, tools, building material. Mechanical devices making use of wind or running water also can be used to convert natural energy flows. The amount of energy an agrarian society can use is restricted due to the low energy density of solar radiation and the low efficiency of technology.

In order to increase production an agrarian society must either increase the intensity of production or obtain more land to expand into. Expansion may take place either by claiming territories occupied by other communities, but expansion also may take place by claiming new ecological niches from other living species. However, societies are still limited by a diminishing margin of utility in that the best lands for farming are usually already under cultivation, forcing people to move into less and less arable lands.

Agrarianism

Agrarianism most often refers to a social philosophy which values agrarian society as superior to industrial society and stress the superiority of a simpler rural life as opposed to the complexity and chaos of urbanized, industrialized life. In this view the farmer is idealized as a self-sufficient and thus independent as opposed to the paid labourer who is vulnerable and alienated in modern society. Moreover, Agrarianism usually links working the land with morality and spirituality and links urban life, capitalism, and technology with a loss of independence and dignity while fostering vice and weakness. The agricultural community, with its fellowship of labour and cooperation, is thus the model society.

Agrarianism is similar but not identical with back-to-the-land movements. Agrarianism concentrates on the fundamental goods of the earth, communities of more limited economic and political scale than in modern society, and on simple living—even when this shift involves questioning the "progressive" character of some recent social and economic developments. Thus agrarianism is not industrial farming, with its specialisation on products and industrial scale.

Feudalism

Feudalism is a grouping of legal and military customs, prevalent in medieval Europe, which flourished between the 9th and 15th centuries, or any similar grouping of legal and military customs. Simply defined, it was a system for structuring society around relationships derived from the holding of land in exchange for service or labour.

Although derived from the Latin word *feodum* or *feudum* (fief), then in use, the term *feudalism* and the system it describes were not conceived of as a formal political system by the people living in the Middle Ages. In its classic definition, by François-Louis Ganshof (1944), *feudalism* describes a set of reciprocal legal and military obligations among the warrior nobility, revolving around the three key concepts of lords, vassals and fiefs.

A broader definition of feudalism, as described by Marc Bloch (1939), includes not only the obligations of the warrior nobility but those of all three estates of the realm: the nobility, the clergy, and the peasantry bound by manorialism; this is sometimes referred to as a "feudal society". Since the publication of Elizabeth A. R. Brown's "The Tyranny of a Construct" (1974) and Susan Reynolds's *Fiefs and Vassals* (1994), there has been ongoing inconclusive discussion among medieval historians as to whether feudalism is a useful construct for understanding medieval society. Abels notes that, "Western Civilization and World Civilization textbooks now shy away from the term 'feudalism'."

Definition

There is no commonly accepted modern definition of feudalism, at least among scholars. The adjective *feudal* was coined in the 17th century, and the noun *feudalism*, often used in a political and propaganda context, was not coined until the 19th century. By the mid-20th century, François Louis Ganshof's *Feudalism*, 3rd ed. (1964; originally published in French, 1947), became a standard scholarly definition of feudalism.

Since at least the 1960s, when Marc Bloch's *Feudal Society* (1939) was first translated into English in 1961, many medieval historians have included a broader social aspect that includes not only the nobility but all three estates of the realm, adding the peasantry bonds of manorialism and the estates of the Church; this is sometimes referred to as "feudal society" since it encompasses all members of society into the feudal system. Since the 1970s, when Elizabeth A. R. Brown published *The Tyranny of a Construct* (1974), many have re-examined the evidence and concluded that feudalism is an unworkable term and should be removed entirely from scholarly and educational discussion or at least used only with severe qualification and warning.

Outside a European context, the concept of feudalism is often used only by analogy (called *semi-feudal*), most often in discussions of feudal Japan under the shoguns and sometimes medieval and Gondarine Ethiopia. However, some have taken the feudalism analogy further, seeing feudalism (or traces of it) in places as diverse as ancient Egypt, the Parthian empire, the Indian subcontinent and the Antebellum and Jim Crow American South. The term *feudalism* has also been applied—often inappropriately or pejoratively—to non-Western societies where institutions and attitudes similar to those of medieval Europe are perceived to prevail. Some historians and political theorists believe that the term *feudalism* has been deprived of specific meaning by the many ways it has been used, leading them to reject it as a useful concept for understanding society.

Etymology

The term "feodal" was used in 17th century French legal treatises (1614) and translated into English legal treatises as an adjective, such as "feodal government".

In the 18th century, Adam Smith, seeking to describe economic systems, effectively coined the forms "feudal government" and "feudal system" in his book *Wealth of Nations* (1776). In the 19th century the adjective "feudal" evolved into a noun: "feudalism". The term *feudalism* is recent, first appearing in French in 1823, Italian in 1827, English in 1839, and in German in the second half of the 19th century.

The term "feudal" or "feodal" is derived from the medieval Latin word *feodum*. The etymology of *feodum* is complex with multiple theories, some suggesting a Germanic origin (the most widely held view) and others suggesting an Arabic origin. Initially in medieval Latin European documents, a land grant in exchange for service was called a *beneficium* (Latin). Later, the term *feudum*, or *feodum*, began to replace *beneficium* in the documents. The first attested instance of this is from 984, although more primitive forms were seen up to one-hundred years earlier. The origin of the *feudum* and why it replaced *beneficium* has not been well established, but there are multiple theories, described below.

The most widely held theory is put forth by Marc Bloch. Bloch said it is related to the Frankish term **fehu-ôd*, in which **fehu* means "cattle" and *-ôd* means "goods", implying "a moveable object of value." When land replaced currency as the primary store of value, the Germanic word **fehu-ôd* replaced the Latin word *beneficium*. This Germanic origin theory was also shared by William Stubbs in the nineteenth century.

Another theory was put forward by Archibald R. Lewis. Lewis said the origin of 'fief' is not *feudum* (or *feodum*), but rather *foderum*, the earliest attested use being in Astronomus's *Vita Hludovici* (840). In that text is a passage about Louis the Pious which says *annona militaris quas vulgo foderum vocant*, which can be translated as "Louis forbade that military provender (which they popularly call "fodder") be furnished.."

Another theory by Alauddin Samarrai suggests an Arabic origin, from *fuyû* (the plural of *fay*, which literally means "the returned", and was used especially for 'land that has been conquered from enemies that did not fight'). Samarrai's theory is that early forms of 'fief' include *feo, feu, feuz, feuum* and others, the plurality of forms strongly suggesting origins from a loanword. Indeed the first use of these terms is in Languedoc, one of the least Germanic areas of Europe and bordering Muslim Spain. Further, the earliest use of *feuum* (as a replacement for *beneficium*) can be dated to 899, the same year a Muslim base at Fraxinetum (La Garde-Freinet) in Provence was established.

It is possible, Samarrai says, that French scribes, writing in Latin, attempted to transliterate the Arabic word *fuyû* (the plural of *fay*), which was being used by the Muslim invaders and occupiers at the time, resulting in a plurality of forms - *feo, feu, feuz, feuum* and others - from which eventually *feudum* derived. Samarrai, however, also advises to handle this theory with care, as Medieval and Early Modern Muslim scribes often used etymologically "fanciful roots" in order to claim the most outlandish things to be of Arabian or Muslim origin.

History of Feudalism

Feudalism, in its various forms, usually emerged as a result of the decentralization of an empire: especially in the Japanese and Carolingian (European) empires which both lacked the bureaucratic infrastructure necessary to support cavalry without the ability to allocate land to these mounted troops. Mounted soldiers began to secure a system of hereditary rule over their allocated land and their power over the territory came to encompass the social, political, judicial, and economic spheres.

These acquired powers significantly diminished unitary power in these empires. Only when the infrastructure existed to maintain unitary power—as with the European monarchies—did Feudalism begin to yield to this new power structure and eventually disappear.

Classic (Western European) Feudalism

The classic François-Louis Ganshof version of feudalism describes a set of reciprocal legal and military obligations among the warrior nobility, revolving around the three key concepts of lords, vassals and fiefs. A lord was in broad terms a noble who held land, a vassal was a person who was granted possession of the land by the lord, and the land was known as a fief.

In exchange for the use of the fief and the protection of the lord, the vassal would provide some sort of service to the lord. There were many varieties of feudal land tenure, consisting of military and non-military service.

The obligations and corresponding rights between lord and vassal concerning the fief form the basis of the feudal relationship.

Vassalage

Figure: *Homage of Clermont-en-Beauvaisis*

Before a lord could grant land (a fief) to someone, he had to make that person a vassal. This was done at a formal and symbolic ceremony called a commendation ceremony, which was composed of the two-part act of homage and oath of fealty. During homage, the lord and vassal entered into a contract in which the vassal promised to fight for the lord at his command, whilst the lord agreed to protect the vassal from external forces. *Fealty* comes from the Latin *fidelitas* and denotes the fidelity owed by a vassal to his feudal lord. "Fealty" also refers to an oath that more explicitly reinforces the commitments of the vassal made during homage. Such an oath follows homage.

Once the commendation ceremony was complete, the lord and vassal were in a feudal relationship with agreed obligations to one another. The vassal's principal obligation to the lord was to "aid", or military service. Using whatever equipment the vassal could obtain by virtue of the revenues from the fief, the vassal was responsible to answer calls to military service on behalf of the lord. This security of military help was the primary reason the lord entered into the feudal relationship. In addition, the vassal could have other obligations to his lord, such as attendance at his court, whether manorial, baronial, both termed court baron, or at the king's court.

The phrase "feudal society" as defined by Marc Bloch expands on the definition proposed by Ganshof and includes within the feudal structure not only the warrior aristocracy bound by vassalage, but also the peasantry bound by manorialism, and the estates of the Church. Thus the entire society from top to bottom is bound by feudalism.

Historiography of Feudalism

The idea of *feudalism* was unknown and the system it describes were not conceived of as a formal political system by the people living in the Medieval Period. This section describes the history of the idea of feudalism, how the concept originated among scholars and thinkers, how it changed over time, and modern debates about its use.

Evolution of the Idea

The concept of a feudal state or period, in the sense of either a regime or a period dominated by lords who possess financial or social power and prestige, became widely held in the middle of the 18th century, as a result of works such as Montesquieu's *De L'Esprit des Lois* (1748; published in English as *The Spirit of the Laws*), and Henri de Boulainvilliers's *Histoire des anciens Parlements de France* (1737; published in English as *An Historical Account of the Antient Parliaments of France or States-General of the Kingdom*, 1739). In the 18th century, writers of the Enlightenment wrote about feudalism to denigrate the antiquated system of the *Ancien Régime*, or French monarchy. This was the Age of Enlightenment when writers valued reason and the Middle Ages were viewed as the "Dark Ages". Enlightenment authors generally mocked and ridiculed anything from the "Dark Ages" including feudalism, projecting its negative characteristics on the current French monarchy as a means of political gain. For them "feudalism" meant seigneurial privileges and prerogatives. When the French Constituent Assembly abolished the "feudal regime" in August 1789 this is what was meant.

Adam Smith used the term "feudal system" to describe a social and economic system defined by inherited social ranks, each of which possessed inherent social and economic privileges and obligations. In such a system wealth derived from agriculture, which was arranged not according to market forces but on the basis of customary labour services owed by serfs to landowning nobles.

Marx

Karl Marx also used the term in political analysis. In the 19th century, Marx described feudalism as the economic situation coming before the rise of capitalism. For Marx, what defined feudalism was that the power of the ruling class (the aristocracy) rested on their control of arable land, leading to a class society based upon the exploitation of the peasants who farm these lands, typically under serfdom. Marx thus defined feudalism primarily by its economic characteristics. Many later Marxist theorists (e.g. Eric Wolf) have applied this label to include non-European societies, grouping feudalism together with Imperial Chinese and pre-Columbian Incan societies as 'tributary.'

Later Studies

In the late 19th and early 20th centuries, John Horace Round and Frederic William Maitland, both historians of medieval Britain, arrived at different conclusions as to the character of English society before the Norman Conquest in 1066. Round argued that the Normans had brought feudalism with them to England, while Maitland contended that its fundamentals were already in place in Britain before 1066. The debate continues today, but a consensus is building: England before the Conquest had commendation, which embodied some of the personal elements in feudalism.

William the Conqueror introduced a modified northern French feudalism to England which countered decentralized aspects of feudalism abroad. In 1086 he required oaths of loyalty to the king by all, even the vassals of his principal vassals, who held by feudal tenure. Holding by feudal tenure meant that vassals must provide the quota of knights required by the king or a money payment in substitution.

In the 20th century, the historian François-Louis Ganshof was very influential on the topic of feudalism. Ganshof defined feudalism from a narrow legal and military perspective, arguing that feudal relationships existed only within the medieval nobility itself. Ganshof articulated this concept in *Feudalism* (1944). His classic definition of feudalism is the most widely known today and also the easiest to understand, simply put, when a lord granted a fief to a vassal, the vassal provided military service in return.

One of Ganshof's contemporaries, the French historian Marc Bloch, was arguably the most influential 20th century medieval historian. Bloch approached feudalism not so much from a legal and military point of view but from a sociological one. He developed his ideas in *Feudal Society* (1939–40; English 1961). Bloch characterised feudalism as a type of society that was not limited solely to the nobility. Like Ganshof, he acknowledged that there was a hierarchical relationship between lords and vassals, but Bloch also acknowledged the existence of a similar relationship between lords and peasants.

It is this radical notion that peasants were part of feudal relationship that sets Bloch apart from his peers. While the vassal performed military service in exchange for the fief, the peasant performed physical labour in return for protection. Both are a form of feudal relationship. According to Bloch, other elements of society can be seen in feudal terms; all the aspects of life were centred on "lordship", and so we can speak usefully of a feudal church structure, a feudal courtly (and anti-courtly) literature, and a feudal economy.

Although he was never formally a student in the circle of scholars around Marc Bloch and Lucien Febvre that came to be known as the Annales School, Georges Duby was an exponent of the *Annaliste* tradition. In a published version of his 1952 doctoral thesis entitled *La société aux XIe et XIIe siècles dans la région mâconnaise* (*Society in the 11th and 12th centuries in the Mâconnais region*), and working from the extensive documentary sources surviving from the Burgundian monastery of Cluny, as well as the dioceses of Mâcon and Dijon, Duby excavated the complex social and economic relationships among the individuals and institutions of the Mâconnais region and charted a profound shift in the social structures of medieval society around the year 1000. He argued that in early eleventh century, governing institutions—particularly comital courts established under the Carolingian monarchy—that had represented public justice and order in Burgundy during the ninth and tenth centuries receded and gave way to a new feudal order wherein independent aristocratic knights wielded power over peasant communities through strong-arm tactics and threats of violence.

Feudalism Revisionism

In 1974, U.S. historian Elizabeth A. R. Brown rejected the label *feudalism* as an anachronism that imparts a false sense of uniformity to the concept. Having noted the current use of many, often contradictory, definitions of *feudalism*, she argued that the word is only a construct with no basis in medieval reality, an invention of modern historians read back "tyrannically" into the historical record. Supporters of Brown have suggested that the term should be expunged from history textbooks and lectures on medieval history entirely. In *Fiefs and Vassals: The Medieval Evidence Reinterpreted* (1994), Susan Reynolds expanded upon Brown's original thesis. Although some contemporaries questioned Reynolds's methodology, other historians have supported it and her argument. Reynolds argues:

Too many models of feudalism used for comparisons, even by Marxists, are still either constructed on the sixteenth-century basis or incorporate what, in a Marxist view, must surely be superficial or irrelevant features from it. Even when one restricts oneself to Europe and to feudalism in its narrow sense it is extremely doubtful whether feudo-vassalic institutions formed a coherent bundle of institutions or concepts that were structurally separate from other institutions and concepts of the time.

The term *feudal* has also been applied to non-Western societies in which institutions and attitudes similar to those of medieval Europe are perceived to have prevailed. Japan has been extensively studied in this regard. Friday notes that in the 21st century historians of Japan rarely invoke feudalism; instead of looking at similarities, specialists attempting comparative analysis concentrate on fundamental differences. Ultimately, critics say, the many ways the term *feudalism* has been used have deprived it of specific meaning, leading some historians and political theorists to reject it as a useful concept for understanding society.

Industrial Society

In sociology, industrial society refers to a society driven by the use of technology to enable mass production, supporting a large population with a high capacity for division of labour. Such a structure developed in the west in the period of time following the Industrial Revolution, and replaced the agrarian societies of the Pre-modern, Pre-industrial age. Industrial societies are generally mass societies, and may be succeeded by an Information society. They are often contrasted to with the traditional societies.

Industrial society is characterized by the use of external energy sources, such as fossil fuels, to increase the rate and scale of production. The production of food is shifted to large commercial farms where the products of industry, such as combine harvesters and fossil fuel based fertilizers, are used to decrease required human labour while increasing production. No longer needed for the production of food, excess labour is moved into these factories where mechanization is utilised to further increase efficiency. As populations grow, and mechanization is further refined, often to the level of automation, many workers shift to expanding service industries. Industrial society makes urbanization desirable, in part so that workers can be closer to centres of production, and the service industry can provide labour to workers and those that benefit financially from them, in exchange for a piece of production profits with which they can buy goods. This leads to the rise of very large cities and surrounding suburban areas with a high rate of economic activity.

These urban centres require the input of external energy sources in order to overcome the diminishing returns of agricultural consolidation, due partially to the lack of nearby arable land, associated transportation and storage costs, and are otherwise unsustainable. This makes the reliable availability of the needed energy resources high priority in industrial government policies.

Some theoreticians—namely Ulrich Beck, Anthony Giddens and Manuel Castells—argue that we are located in the middle of a transformation or transition from industrial societies to post-modern societies. The triggering technology for the change from an agricultural to an industrial organisation was steam power, allowing mass production and reducing the agricultural work necessary. Thus many industrial cities are built around rivers. Identified as catalyst or trigger for the transition to post-modern or informational society is global information technology.

Chapter 2

Post-industrial Society

In sociology, the post-industrial society is the stage of society's development when the service sector generates more wealth than the manufacturing sector of the economy.

The concept was popularized by Daniel Bell, and is closely related to similar sociological theoretical constructs such as post-fordism, information society, knowledge economy, post-industrial economy, liquid modernity, and network society. They all can be used in economics or other social science disciplines as a general theoretical backdrop in research design.

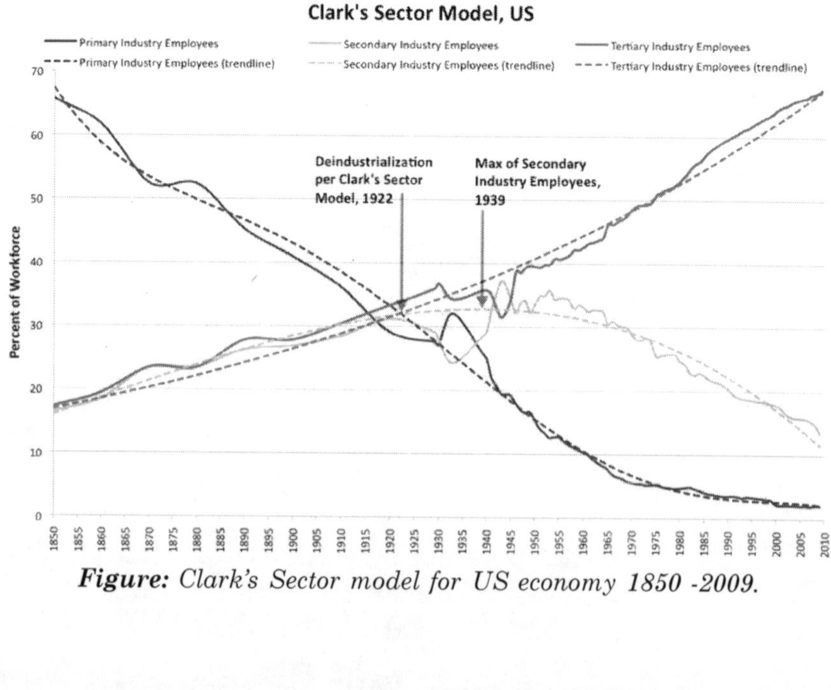

Figure: *Clark's Sector model for US economy 1850 -2009.*

Characteristics

As the term has been used, a few common themes (not limited to those below) have begun to emerge.

1. The economy undergoes a transition from the production of goods to the provision of services.
2. Knowledge becomes a valued form of capital.
3. Producing ideas is the main way to grow the economy.
4. Through processes of globalization and automation, the value and importance to the economy of blue-collar, unionized work, including manual labour (e.g., assembly-line work) decline, and those of professional workers (e.g. scientists, creative-industry professionals, and IT professionals) grow in value and prevalence.
5. Behavioural and information sciences and technologies are developed and implemented. (e.g. behavioural economics, information architecture, cybernetics, Game theory and Information theory.)

Origins

Daniel Bell popularized the term through his 1974 work *The Coming of Post-Industrial Society*. Although some have credited Bell with coining the term, it was also used extensively by social philosopher Ivan Illich in his 1973 paper *Tools for Conviviality*. It also appears occasionally in Leftist texts throughout the mid-to-late 1960s.

Recently, the term has grown and changed as it became mainstream. The term is now used by admen such as Seth Godin, public policy PhD's such as Keith Boeckelman, and sociologists such as Neil Fligstein and Ofer Sharone. President Bill Clinton even used the term to describe Chinese growth in a round-table discussion in Shanghai in 1998.

Valuation of Knowledge

The post-industrialized society is marked by an increased valuation of knowledge. This itself is unsurprising, having been foreshadowed in Daniel Bell's presumption as to how economic employment patterns will evolve in such societies. He asserts employment will grow faster in the tertiary (and quaternary) sector relative to employment in the primary and secondary sector and that the tertiary (and quaternary) sectors will take precedence in the economy. This will continue to occur such that the "impact of the expert" will expand and power will be monopolized by knowledge. As tertiary and quaternary sector positions are essentially knowledge-oriented, this will result in a restructuring of education, at least in its nuances. The "new power... of the expert" consequently gives rise to the growing role of universities and research institutes in post-industrial societies. Post-industrial societies themselves become oriented around these places of knowledge production and production of experts as their new foci. Consequently, the greatest beneficiaries in the post-industrial society are young urban professionals. As a new, educated, and politicized generation more impassioned by liberalism, social justice, and environmentalism, the shift of power into their hands, as a result of their knowledge endowments, is often cited as a good thing.

The increasing importance of knowledge in post-industrial societies results in a general increase in expertise through the economy and throughout society. In this manner, it eliminates what Alan Banks and Jim Foster identify as "undesirable work as well as the grosser forms of poverty and inequality." This effect is supplemented by the aforementioned movement of power into the hands of young educated people concerned with social justice.

Paul Romer, a professor of economics at Stanford, revolutionized the appreciation of knowledge as a valuable asset. As he says it is not just the "ingredients" (supply) that makes good food, it is the "recipe" (knowledge) that counts too. Better recipe, better food means better knowledge, more economic growth.

More recently, economists at Berkeley studied the value of knowledge as a form of capital, adding value to material capital, such as factory or a truck. Speaking along the same lines of their argument, the addition or 'production' of knowledge, could become the basis of what would undoubtedly be considered 'post-industrial' policies meant to deliver economic growth.

Creativity Culture

Similarly, post-industrial society has serviced the creative culture. Many of those most well-equipped to thrive in an increasingly technological society are young adults with tertiary education. As education itself becomes more and more oriented towards producing people capable of answering the need for self-actualization, creativity, and self-expression, successive generations become more endowed with the ability to contribute to and perpetuate such industries. This nuanced change in education, as well amongst the emerging class of young professionals, is itself initiated by what James D Wright identifies as an "unprecedented economic affluence and the satiation of basic material needs." Ellen Dunham-Jones as well observes this feature of post-industrial society where "abundant goods [are] equitably distributed [in order that] labourless leisure and self-determination" can be consumed.

The post-industrial society is repeatedly stressed to be one where knowledge is power and technology is the instrument. Naturally, where one is creatively inclined, they are advantaged by such a society. The doctrine of "speed, mobility and malleability" is well suited to a dynamic creative industry and as industries of good production decrease in precedence, the way is paved for artists, musicians, and other such types, whose skills are better utilised by the tertiary and quaternary sector. Urban geographer Trevor Barnes, in his work outlining the Vancouver experience in post-war development, evokes the post-industrial condition, citing the emergence and consolidation of a significant video games industry as a constituent of the elite service sector.

This increased faculty of the post-industrialist society with respects to the creative industry is itself reflected by the economic history of post-industrial societies. As economic activities shift from primarily primary and secondary sector-based to tertiary, and later quaternary, sector-based, cities in which this shift occurs become more open to exchanges of information. This is necessitated by the demands of a tertiary and quaternary sector: in order to better service an industry focused on finance, education, communication, management, training, engineering, and aesthetic design, the city must become points of exchange capable of providing the most updated information from across the globe. Conversely, as cities become a convergence of international ideas, the tertiary and quaternary sector can be expected to grow.

A virtual cult of 'creatives' have sprung up embodying and often describing and defending the post-industrial ethos. They argue that businesses that create intangibles have taken a more prominent role in the wake of manufacturing's decline and that in some countries.

Actor and artistic director of the Old Vic Theatre, Kevin Spacey, has argued the economic case for the arts in terms of providing jobs and being of greater importance in exports than manufacturing (as well as an educational role) in a guest column he wrote for *The Times*.

Critics

Post-industrialism is criticized for the amount of real fundamental change it produces in society, if any at all. A mild view held by Alan Banks and Jim Foster contends that representations of post-industrial society by advocates assume professional, educated elites were previously less relevant than they have become in the new social order, and that changes that have occurred are minor but greatly embellished. More critical views see the entire process as the highest evolution of capitalism, wherein the system produces commodities as opposed to practical goods and is determined privately instead of socially. This view is complemented by the assertion that "the characteristic feature of a modern [that is, post-industrial] society is that it is a technocracy." Such societies then become notable for their ability to subvert social consciousness through powers of manipulation rather than powers of coercion, reflective of the "ideology of the ruling class [as] ... predominantly managerial."

In line with the view that nothing fundamental has changed in the transition from industrial societies to post-industrial societies is the insistence of lingering problems from past development periods. Neo-Malthusian in essence, this outlook focuses on post-industrial society's continuing struggle with issues of resource scarcity, overpopulation, and environmental degradation, all of which are remnants from its industrial history. This is exacerbated by a "corporate liberalism" that seeks to continue economic growth through "the creation and satisfaction of false needs," or as Christopher Lasch more derisively refers to it, "subsidized waste."

Urban development in the context of post-industrialism is also a point of contention. In opposition to the view that the new leaders of post-industrial society are increasingly environmentally aware, this critique asserts that it rather leads to environmental degradation, this being rooted in the patterns of development. Urban sprawl, characterised behaviourally by cities "expanding at the periphery in even lower densities" and physically by "office parks, malls, strips, condo clusters, corporate campuses and gated communities," is singled out as the main issue. Resulting from a post-industrialist culture of "mobile capital, the service economy, post-Fordist disposable consumerism and banking deregulation," urban sprawl has caused post-industrialism to become environmentally and socially regressive.

Of the former, environmental degradation results from encroachment as cities meet demands on low-density habitation; the wider spread of population consumes more of the environment while necessitating more energy consumption in order to facilitate travel within the ever-growing city, incurring greater pollution. This process evokes the neo-Malthusian concerns of overpopulation and resource scarcity that inevitably lead to environmental deterioration. Of the latter, "post-industrialism's doctrine of ... mobility and malleability" encourage a disconnect between communities where social belonging falls into the category of things considered by the "post-Fordist disposable consumer[ist]" attitude as interchangeable, expendable, and replaceable.

Post-industrialism as a concept is highly Western-centric. Theoretically and effectively, it is only possible in the Global West, which its proponents assume to be solely capable of fully realising industrialization and then post-industrialization. Herman Kahn optimistically predicted the "economic growth, expanded production and growing efficiency" of post-industrial societies and the resultant "material abundance and... high quality of life" to extend to "almost all people in Western societies" and only "some in Eastern societies." This prediction is treated elsewhere by contentions that the post-industrial society merely perpetuates capitalism.

Recalling the critical assertion that all modern societies are technocracies, T. Roszak completes the analysis by stating that "all societies are moving in the direction of technocracies." From this, the foremost "suave technocracies" reside in the West, whereas all others are successively graded in descending order: "vulgar technocracies," "teratoid technocracies," and finally "comic opera technocracies." This view importantly presumes one transition and furthermore one path of transition for societies to undergo, i.e. the one that Western societies are slated to complete. Much like the Demographic Transition Model, this prediction does not entertain the idea of an Eastern or other alternative model of transitional development.

Neologism

When historians and sociologists considered the revolution that followed the agricultural society they did not call it a "post-agricultural society". "Post-industrial society" signifies only a departure, not a positive description.

One of the word's early users, Ivan Illich, prefigured this criticism and invented the term Conviviality, or the Convivial Society, to stand as a positive description of his version of a post-industrial society.

Social Critique

A group of scholars (including Allen Scott and Edward Soja) argue that industry remains at the centre of the whole process of capitalist accumulation, with services not only becoming increasingly industrialized and automated but also remaining highly dependent on industrial growth.

Some observers, including Soja (building on the theories of the French philosopher of urbanism Henri Lefebvre), suggest that although industry may be based outside of a "post-industrial" nation, that nation cannot ignore industry's necessary sociological importance.

Contemporary Usage

The term "society" is currently used to cover both a number of political and scientific connotations as well as a variety of associations.

Western World

The Western world, also known as the West and the Occident (from Latin: *occidens* "sunset, West"; as contrasted with the Orient, Greek: Äõôéêüò Êüóìïò), is a term referring to different nations depending on the context. There are many accepted definitions about what all they have in common.

The concept of the Western part of the earth has its roots in Greco-Roman civilization in Europe, and the advent of Christianity. In the modern era, Western culture has been heavily influenced by the traditions of the Renaissance, Protestant Reformation, Age of Enlightenment—and shaped by the expansive colonialism of the 15th-20th centuries. Before the Cold War era, the traditional Western viewpoint identified Western Civilization with the Western Christian (Catholic-Protestant) countries and culture. Its political usage was temporarily changed by the antagonism during the Cold War in the mid-to-late 20th Century (1947–1991).

The term originally had a literal geographic meaning. It contrasted Europe with the linked cultures and civilizations of the Middle East and North Africa, South Asia, Southeast Asia and remote Far East, which early-modern Europeans saw as the East. Today, this has little geographic relevance, since the concept of the West expanded to include the former European colonies in the Americas, Russian Northern Asia, Australia, and New Zealand. In the contemporary cultural meaning, the phrase "Western world" includes Europe, as well as many countries of European colonial origin with substantial European ancestral populations in the Americas and Oceania.

Introduction

Western culture originated in the Mediterranean basin and its vicinity; Greece and Rome are often cited as its originators. Over time, their associated empires grew first to the east and west to include the rest of Mediterranean and Black Sea coastal areas, conquering, absorbing, and being influenced by many older great civilizations of the ancient Near East (i.e., Phoenicia, Phoenician rooted Carthage, Mesopotamia and also Ancient Egypt). Later, they expanded to the north of the Mediterranean Sea to include Western, Central, and Southeastern Europe. Christianization of Bulgaria (9th century), Christianization of Kievan Rus' (Russia, Ukraine, Belarus; 10th century), Christianisation of Scandinavia (12th century) and Christianization of Lithuania (14th century) brought the rest of present-day European territory into Western civilisation.

Historians, such as Carroll Quigley in *The Evolution of Civilizations*, contend that Western civilization was born around 500 AD, after the total collapse of the Western Roman Empire, leaving a vacuum for new ideas to flourish that were impossible in Classical societies. In either view, between the fall of the Western Roman Empire and the Renaissance, the West (or those regions that would later become the heartland of the culturally "western sphere") experienced a period of first, considerable decline, and then readaptation, reorientation and considerable renewed material, technological and political development. This whole period of roughly a millennium is known as the Middle Ages, its early part forming the "Dark Ages", designations that were created during the Renaissance and reflect the perspective on history, and the self-image, of the latter period.

Figure: The School of Athens *depicts a gathering of the most prominent thinkers of classical antiquity. Fresco by Raphael, 1510–1511*

The knowledge of the ancient Western world was partly preserved during this period due to the survival of the Eastern Roman Empire and the institutions of the Catholic Church; it was also greatly expanded by the Arab importation of both the Ancient Greco-Roman and new technology through the Arabs from India and China to Europe. Since the Renaissance, the West evolved beyond the influence of the ancient Greeks and Romans and the Islamic world due to the Commercial, Scientific, and Industrial Revolutions, and the expansion of the peoples of Western and Central European empires, and particularly the globe-spanning empires of the 18th and 19th centuries. Numerous times, this expansion was accompanied by Christian missionaries, who attempted to proselytize Christianity.

Generally speaking, the current consensus would locate the West, at the very least, in the cultures and peoples of Europe, the United States, Canada, Australia, New Zealand, and parts of Latin America. There is debate among some as to whether Latin America is in a category of its own. Also, there is debate among some as to whether Central and Eastern Europe (CEE) is in a category of its own. An argument supporting Central and Eastern Europe being a part of the West is that Central European, Southeastern European and Baltic countries such as Czech Republic, Poland, Hungary, Estonia, Lithuania, Latvia, Slovakia, Slovenia, Bulgaria, Romania and Croatia are now part of the European Union and NATO, which mostly comprise Western countries. These countries were both heavily influenced by and influenced the Western World, and share sociological values and culture. The Russian culture (particularly literature, music, painting, philosophy and architecture) is classified as a part of the Western culture. Russia is often not counted politically as a part of the Western World due to contemporary political isolationism of the country.

Western Culture

The term "Western culture" is used very broadly to refer to a heritage of social norms, ethical values, traditional customs, religious beliefs, political systems, and specific artifacts and technologies.

Specifically, Western culture may imply:

- a Biblical Christian cultural influence in spiritual thinking, customs and either ethic or moral traditions, around the Post-Classical Era and after.
- European cultural influences concerning artistic, musical, folkloric, ethic and oral traditions, whose themes have been further developed by Romanticism.
- a Graeco-Roman Classical and Renaissance cultural influence, concerning artistic, philosophic, literary, and legal themes and traditions, the cultural social effects of migration period and the heritages of Celtic, Germanic, Slavic and other ethnic groups, as well as a tradition of rationalism in various spheres

of life, developed by Hellenistic philosophy, Scholasticism, Humanisms, the Scientific Revolution and Enlightenment.

The concept of Western culture is generally linked to the classical definition of the Western world. In this definition, Western culture is the set of literary, scientific, political, artistic and philosophical principles that set it apart from other civilizations. Much of this set of traditions and knowledge is collected in the Western canon.

The term has come to apply to countries whose history is strongly marked by European immigration or settlement, such as the Americas, and Oceania, and is not restricted to Europe.

Some tendencies that define modern Western societies are the existence of political pluralism, laicism, generalization of middle class, prominent subcultures or countercultures (such as New Age movements), increasing cultural syncretism resulting from globalization and human migration. The modern shape of these societies is strongly based upon the Industrial Revolution and the societies' associated social and environmental problems, such as class and pollution, as well as reactions to them, such as syndicalism and environmentalism.

Historical Divisions

The geopolitical divisions in Europe that created a concept of *East* and *West* originated in the Roman Empire. The Eastern Mediterranean was home to the highly urbanized cultures that had Greek as their common language (owing to the older empire of Alexander the Great and of the Hellenistic successors.), whereas the West was much more rural in its character and more readily adopted Latin as its common language. After the fall of the Western Roman Empire, Western and Central Europe were substantially cut off from the East where *Byzantine* Greek culture and Eastern Christianity became founding influences in the Arab/Muslim world and among the Eastern and Southern Slavic peoples. Roman Catholic Western and Central Europe, as such, maintained a distinct identity particularly as it began to redevelop during the Renaissance. Even following the Protestant Reformation, Protestant Europe continued to see itself as more tied to Roman Catholic Europe than other parts of the perceived *civilized* world.

Use of the term *West* as a specific cultural and geopolitical term developed over the course of the Age of Exploration as Europe spread its culture to other parts of the world. In the past two centuries the term *Western world* has sometimes been used synonymously with *Christian world* because of the numerical dominance of Roman

Catholicism and Protestantism compared to other Christian traditions, ancient Roman ideas, and heresies. As secularism rose in Europe and elsewhere during the 19th and 20th centuries, the term *West* came to take on less religious connotations and more political connotations, especially during the Cold War. Additionally, closer contacts between the *West* and Asia and other parts of the world in recent times have continued to cloud the use and meaning of the term.

Hellenic

The Hellenic division between the barbarians and the Greeks contrasted in many societies the Greek-speaking culture of the Greek settlements around the Mediterranean to the surrounding non-Greek cultures. Herodotus considered the Persian Wars of the early 5th century BC a conflict of Europa versus Asia (which he considered all land north and east of the Sea of Marmara, respectively). The terms "West" and "East" were not used by any Greek author to describe that conflict. The anachronistic application of those terms to that division entails a stark logical contradiction, given that, when the term "West" appeared, it was used in opposition to the Greeks and Greek-speaking culture.

Western society traces its cultural origins, at least partially, to Greek thought and Christian religion, thus following an evolution that began in ancient Greece and the Levant, continued through the Roman Empire, and spread throughout Europe. The inherently "Greek" classical ideas of history (which one might easily say they invented) and art may, however, be considered almost inviolate in the West, as their original spread of influence survived the Hellenic period of Roman classical antiquity, The Dark Ages, its resurgence during the Western Renaissance, and has managed somehow to keep and exert its pervasive influence down into the present age, with every expectation of it continuing to dominate any secular Western cultural developments.

However, the conquest of the Western parts of the Roman Empire by Germanic peoples and the subsequent dominance by the Western Christian Papacy (which held combined political and spiritual authority, a state of affairs absent from Greek civilization in all its stages), resulted in a rupture of the previously existing ties between the Latin West and Greek thought, including Christian Greek thought. The Great Schism and the Fourth Crusade confirmed this deviation.

On the other hand, the Modern West, emerging after the Renaissance as a new civilization, has been greatly influenced by (its own interpretation of) Greek thought, which was preserved in the Roman Empire and the medieval Islamic world during the Medieval West's Dark Ages and transmitted from there by emigration of Greek scholars, courtly marriages, and Latin translations. The Renaissance in the West emerged partly from currents within the Roman (Byzantine) Empire.

Roman Empire

Ancient Rome (510 BC-AD 476) was a civilization that grew from a city-state founded on the Italian Peninsula about the 9th century BC to a massive empire straddling the Mediterranean Sea. In its 12-century existence, Roman civilization shifted from a monarchy, to a republic, to an autocratic empire. It came to dominate Western, Central and Southeastern Europe and the entire area surrounding the Mediterranean Sea through conquest using the Roman legions and then through cultural assimilation by giving Roman privileges and eventually citizenship to the whole empire. Nonetheless, despite its great legacy, a number of factors led to the eventual decline of the Roman Empire.

The Western Roman Empire eventually broke into several kingdoms in the 5th century AD due to civil wars, corruption, and devastating Germanic invasions from such tribes as the Goths, the Franks and the Vandals.

The Eastern Roman Empire, governed from Constantinople, is usually referred to as the Byzantine Empire after 476, the traditional date for the "fall of the Western Roman Empire" and for the subsequent onset of the Early Middle Ages. The Eastern Roman Empire survived the fall of the West, and protected Roman legal and cultural traditions, combining them with Greek and Christian elements, for another thousand years.

The Roman Empire succeeded the about 500 year-old Roman Republic (510 BC - 1st century BC), which had been weakened by the conflict between Gaius Marius and Sulla and the civil war of Julius Caesar against Pompey and Marcus Brutus. During these struggles hundreds of senators were killed, and the Roman Senate had been refilled with loyalists of the First Triumvirate and later those of the Second Triumvirate.

Several dates are commonly proposed to mark the transition from Republic to Empire, including the date of Julius Caesar's appointment as perpetual Roman dictator (44 BC), the victory of Caesar's heir Octavian at the Battle of Actium (2, 31 September BC), and the Roman Senate's granting to Octavian the honorific *Augustus*. (16, 27 January BC). Octavian/Augustus officially proclaimed that he had saved the Roman Republic and carefully disguised his power under republican forms: Consuls continued to be elected, tribunes of the plebeians continued to offer legislation, and senators still debated in the Roman Curia. However, it was Octavian who influenced everything and controlled the final decisions, and in final analysis, had the legions to back him up, if it became necessary.

Roman expansion began long before the empire and reached its zenith under emperor Trajan with the conquest of Dacia in AD 106. During this territorial peak, the Roman Empire controlled about 5 900 000 km^2 (2,300,000 sq.mi.) of land surface and had a population of 100 million. From the time of Caesar to the Fall of the Western Roman Empire, Rome dominated Western Eurasia (as well as the Mediterranean coast of northern Africa) comprising the majority of its population, and trading with population living outside it through trade (Amber Roads). Ancient Rome has contributed greatly to the development of law, war, art, literature, architecture, technology and language in the Western world, and its history continues to have a major influence on the world today. Latin has been the base from which Roman Languages evolved and it has been the official language of the Catholic Church and all religious ceremonies all over Europe until 1967, as well as an or the official language of countries such as Poland (9th–18th centuries).

The Roman Empire is where the idea of the "West" began to emerge. Due to Rome's central location at the heart of the Empire, "West" and "East" were terms used to denote provinces West and east of the capital itself. Therefore, Iberia (Portugal and Spain), Gaul (France), Mediterranean coast of North Africa (Tunisia, Algeria, and Morocco) and Britannia were all part of the "West", while Greece, Anatolia, Syria, Egypt and Libya were part of the "East." Italy itself was considered central, until the reforms of Diocletian, with the idea of formally dividing the Empire into true two halves: Eastern and Western.

In 395, the Roman Empire formally split into a Western Roman Empire and an Eastern one, each with their own emperors, capitals, and governments, although ostensibly they still belonged to one formal Empire. The dissolution of the Western half (nominally in 476, but in truth a long process that ended by 500) left only the Eastern Roman Empire alive. For centuries, the East continued to call themselves Eastern Romans, while the West began to think in terms of Latins (those living in the old Western Empire) and Greeks (those inside the Roman remnant to the east).

Christian Schism

In the early 4th century, the Roman Emperor Constantine the Great established the city of Constantinople as the capital of the Eastern

Roman Empire. The Eastern Roman Empire included lands east of the Adriatic Sea and bordering on the Eastern Mediterranean and parts of the Black Sea. This division into Eastern and Western Roman Empires was reflected in the administration of the Christian Church, with Rome and Constantinople debating over whether either city was the capital of Christianity.

As the Eastern (Orthodox) and Western (firstly Catholic, then Protestant as well) churches spread their influence, the line between Eastern and Western Christianity was moving. Its movement was affected by the influence of the Byzantine empire and the fluctuating power and influence of the church in Rome. Beginning in the Middle Ages religious cultural hegemony slowly waned in Europe generally. This process may have prompted the geographic line of religious division to approximately follow a line of cultural divide.

Huntington argued that this cultural division still existed during the Cold War as the approximate Western boundary of those countries that were allied with the Soviet Union. Others have fiercely criticized these views arguing they confuse the Eastern Roman Empire with Russia, especially considering the fact that the country that had the most historical roots in Byzantium, Greece, expelled communists and was allied with the West during the Cold War. Still, Russia accepted Eastern Christianity from the Byzantine Empire (by the Patriarch of Constantinople: Photios I) linking Russia very close to the Eastern Roman Empire world. Later on, in 16th century Russia created its own religious centre in Moscow. Religion survived in Russia beside severe persecution carrying values alternative to the communist ideology.

Under Charlemagne, the Franks established an empire that was recognised as the Holy Roman Empire by the Pope in Rome, offending the Roman Emperor in Constantinople. The crowning of the Emperor by the Pope led to the assumption that the highest power was the papal hierarchy, establishing, until the Protestant Reformation, the civilization of West Christendom. The Latin Rite Christian Church of western and central Europe headed by the Pope split with the eastern, Greek-speaking Patriarchates during the Great Schism. Meanwhile, the extent of each expanded, as British Isles, Germanic peoples, Bohemia, Poland, Hungary, Scandinavia, Baltic peoples and the other non-Christian lands of the northwest were converted by the West Church, while Bulgaria, Romania, Russia, Belarus, Serbia, Caucasus and most of Ukraine were converted by the Eastern Church.

In this context, the Protestant reformation may be viewed as a schism within the Latin Church. Martin Luther, in the wake of precursors, broke with the pope and with the emperor, backed by many of the German princes. These changes were adopted by the Scandinavian kings. Later, the commoner Jean Cauvin (John Calvin) assumed the religio-political leadership in Geneva, a former ecclesiastical city whose prior ruler had been the bishop. The English King later improvised on the Lutheran model, but subsequently many Calvinist doctrines were adopted by popular dissenters, leading to the English Civil War.

Both royalists and dissenters colonized North America, eventually resulting in an independent United States of America.

Colonial "West"

The Reformation, and consequent dissolution of West Christendom as even a theoretical unitary political body, resulted in the Thirty Years War. The war ended in the Peace of Westphalia, which enshrined the concept of the nation-state and the principle of absolute national sovereignty in international law.

Figure: *The Industrial Revolution, which began in Great Britain in the mid 18th to early 19th century, forever modified the economy worldwide.*

These concepts of a world of nation-states, coupled with the ideologies of the Enlightenment, the coming of modernity, the Scientific Revolution, and the Industrial Revolution, produced powerful political and economic institutions that have come to influence (or been imposed upon) most nations of the world today. Historians agree that the Industrial Revolution was one of the most important events in history.

This process of influence (and imposition) began with the voyages of discovery, colonization, conquest, and exploitation of Portugal and Spain it continued with the rise of the Dutch East India Company, and the creation and expansion of the British and French colonial empires. Due to the reach of these empires, Western institutions expanded throughout the world. Even after demands for self-determination from subject peoples within Western empires were met with decolonization, these institutions persisted. One specific example was the requirement that post-colonial societies were made to form nation-states (in the Western tradition), which often created arbitrary boundaries and borders that did not necessarily represent a whole nation, people, or culture, and are often the cause of international conflicts and friction even to this day. Though the overt colonial era has passed, Western nations, as comparatively rich, well-armed, and culturally powerful states, still wield a large degree of influence throughout the world.

Although not part of Western colonization process proper, Western culture entered Japan primarily in the so-called Meiji period (1868–1912), though earlier contact with the Portuguese, the Spaniards and the Dutch were also present in the recognition of European nations as strategically important to the Japanese. The traditional Japanese society was virtually overturned into an industrial and militarist power like Western countries such as the United Kingdom, the French Third Republic, and the German Empire.

Cold War Context

During the Cold War, a new definition emerged. Earth was divided into three "worlds". The First World, analogous in this context to what was called *the West,* was composed of NATO members and other countries aligned with the United States. The Second World was the Eastern bloc in the Soviet sphere of influence, including the Soviet Union (15 republics including presently independent Estonia, Latvia, Lithuania) and Warsaw Pact countries like Poland, Bulgaria, Hungary, Romania, East Germany (now united with Germany), Czechoslovakia (now split into the Czech Republic and Slovakia).

The Third World consisted of countries, many of which were unaligned with either, and important members included India, Yugoslavia, Finland (Finlandization) and Switzerland (Swiss Neutrality); some include the People's Republic of China, though this is disputed, as the People's Republic of China is communist, had friendly relations—at certain times—with the Soviet bloc, and had a significant degree of importance in global geopolitics. Some Third World countries aligned themselves with either the US-led West or the Soviet-led Eastern bloc.

A number of countries did not fit comfortably into this neat definition of partition, including Switzerland, Sweden, Austria, and Ireland, which chose to be neutral. Finland was under the *Soviet Union's* military sphere of influence but remained neutral, was not communist, nor was it a member of the Warsaw Pact or Comecon but a member of the EFTA since 1986, and was West of the Iron Curtain. In 1955, when Austria again became a fully independent republic, it did so under the condition that it remain neutral, but as a country to the West of the Iron Curtain, it was in the *United States'* sphere of influence. Spain did not join the NATO until 1982, towards the end of the Cold War and after the death of the authoritarian Franco.

Modern Definitions

The exact scope of the Western world is somewhat subjective in nature, depending on whether cultural, economic, spiritual or political criteria are employed.

Many anthropologists, sociologists and historians oppose "the West and the Rest" in a categorical manner. The same has been done by Malthusian demographers with a sharp distinction between European and non-European family systems. Among anthropologists, this includes Durkheim, Dumont and Lévi-Strauss.

As the term "Western world" does not have a strict international definition, governments do not use the term in legislation of international treaties and instead rely on other definitions.

Cultural

From a cultural and sociological approach the Western world is defined as including all cultures that are directly derived from and influenced by European cultures, i.e. western Europe (e.g. France, Ireland, United Kingdom), central Europe (e.g. Germany, Poland, Switzerland), northern Europe (e.g. Sweden, Denmark, Finland), eastern Europe (e.g. Russia, Ukraine, Belarus), southeastern Europe (e.g. Bulgaria, Greece, Romania) and southern (or southwestern) Europe (e.g. Spain, Italy, Portugal), in the Americas (e.g. Argentina, Brazil, Canada, Chile, Costa Rica, Cuba, Mexico, United States, Uruguay, Venezuela), and Oceania (Australia and New Zealand). Together these countries constitute Western society.

In the 20th century, Christianity declined in influence in many Western countries, mostly in the northern, central and eastern parts of Europe (Sweden, Norway, Finland, Denmark, Estonia, the Czech Republic, Hungary, Romania and Bulgaria) and elsewhere. Secularism (separating religion from politics and science) increased. However, while church attendance is in decline, some western countries (i.e. Italy, Poland and Portugal) believe that religion is important, and most Westerners nominally identify themselves as Christians (e.g. 59% in the UK) and attend church on major occasions, such as Christmas and Easter. In the Americas Christianity continues to play an important societal role, though in areas such as Canada, low level of religiosity is common as a result of experiencing processes of secularization similar to European ones. The official religions of the United Kingdom and some Nordic countries are forms of Christianity, even though the majority of European countries have no official religion. Despite this, Christianity, in its different forms, remains the largest faith in most Western countries.

Modern Political

Countries of the Western world are generally considered to share certain fundamental political ideologies, including those of liberal democracy, the rule of law, human rights and gender equality (although there are notable exceptions, especially in foreign policy). Normally, all of these principles are prerequisites for a state to become a full member of both the Council of Europe and the European Union and, therefore, from a modern political point of view, all European Union member states from Western, Central and Eastern Europe are considered part of the Western world.

Economic

Though the Cold War has ended, and some members of the former Eastern Bloc make a general movement towards liberal democracy and other beliefs held in common by traditionally Western states, most of the former Soviet republics (except Baltic states) are not considered Western because of the small presence of social and political reform, as well as the significant cultural, economic and political differences to what is known today as described by the term "The West": North America (USA and Canada), Europe (EU and EFTA member states), Australia and New Zealand.

The term "Western world" is often interchangeably used with the term First World stressing the difference between First World and the Third World or developing countries. This usage occurs despite the fact that many countries that may be geographically or culturally "Western" are developing countries. In fact, most of the Americas are developing countries, which make up a significant percentage of the West. It is also used despite many developed countries not being Western (e.g., Japan, South Korea, Singapore).

The existence of "The North" implies the existence of "The South", and the socio-economic divide between North and South. The term "the North" has in some contexts replaced earlier usage of the term "the West", particularly in the critical sense, as a more robust demarcation than the terms "West" and "East". The North provides some absolute geographical indicators for the location of wealthy countries, most of which are physically situated in the Northern Hemisphere, although, as most countries are located in the northern hemisphere in general, some have considered this distinction equally unhelpful.

The 34 high-income countries in the Organisation for Economic Co-operation and Development (OECD), which include: Australia, Canada, Chile, Iceland, Israel, Japan, New Zealand, Norway, South Korea, Switzerland, the United States and the countries of the EU (except for: Bulgaria, Croatia, Cyprus, Latvia, Lithuania, Malta and Romania), are generally included in what used to be called *developed world,* although the OECD includes countries, namely, Mexico and Turkey, that are not yet fully industrial countries, but newly industrialised countries. Although Andorra, Cyprus, Hong Kong, Malta, Liechtenstein, Monaco, San Marino, Singapore, Taiwan and Vatican City, are not members of the OECD, they might also be regarded as developed countries, because their high living standards, high per capita incomes, and their social, economic and political structure are quite similar to those of the high income OECD countries.

Other views

A series of scholars of civilization, including Arnold J. Toynbee, Alfred Kroeber and Carroll Quigley have identified and analyzed "Western civilization" as one of the civilizations that have historically existed and still exist today. Toynbee entered into quite an expansive mode, including as candidates those countries or cultures who became so heavily influenced by the West as to adopt these borrowings into their very self-identity; carried to its limit, this would in practice include almost everyone within the West, in one way or another. In particular, Toynbee refers to the *intelligentsia* formed among the educated elite of countries impacted by the European expansion of centuries past. While often pointedly nationalist, these cultural and political leaders interacted within the West to such an extent as to change both themselves and the West. Yet more recently, Samuel P. Huntington has taken a far more controversial approach, forging a political science hypothesis he labelled the "The Clash of Civilizations?" in a *Foreign Affairs* article and a book. According to Huntington's hypothesis, what he calls "conflicts between civilizations" will be the primary tensions of the 21st century world. In this hypothesis, the West is based on religion, as the countries of West and Central Europe were historically influenced by the two forms of Western Christianity, namely Protestantism and Catholicism. Also, some Anglophone countries share these traits, e.g. Bermuda, Cayman Islands, British Virgin Islands, Palau, Australia and New Zealand, as well as the more heterogeneous United States and Canada. The identification of Western Civilization with the Western Christianity (Catholic-Protestant) was not Huntington's original idea, it was rather the traditional Western viewpoint and subdivision before the Cold War era.

Huntington's thesis, while influential, was by no means universally accepted; its supporters say that it explains modern conflicts, such as those in the former Yugoslavia. The thesis's detractors fear that by equating values like democracy with the concept of "Western civilization", it reinforces stereotypes that some perceive as being common within the West about non-traditionally Western societies that some may consider racist or xenophobic. Others believe that Huntington ignores the existence of non-Western democracies such as the East Asian and South-Central Asian democracies. As such, these detractors believe that it will provoke and amplify conflict rather than illuminate a way to find an accommodating world order—or, in particular cases, a commonly agreed solution.

In Huntington's narrow thesis, the historically Eastern Orthodox nations of Southeastern and Eastern Europe constitute a distinct "Euro-Asiatic civilization"; although European and mainly Christian (as well as notable Muslim influence and populations, particularly in the southeastern Europe and southern/central Russia), these nations were not, in Huntington's view, shaped by the cultural influences of the Renaissance. The Renaissance did not affect Orthodox Eastern Europe due in part to the proximity of Ottoman domination, despite the decisive influence of Greek émigré scholars on the Renaissance.

Other Views Might be Made Regarding Hungary and Russia.

The theologian and paleontologist Pierre Teilhard de Chardin conceived of the West as the set of civilizations descended from the Nile Valley Civilization of Egypt.

Palestinian-American literary critic Edward Said uses the term occident in his discussion of orientalism. According to his binary, the West, or Occident, created a romanticized vision of the East, or Orient to justify colonial and imperialist intentions. This Occident-Orient binary focuses on the Western vision of the East instead of any truths about the East. His theories are rooted in Hegel's Master-slave dialectic: The Occident would not exist without the Orient and vice versa. Further, Western writers created this irrational, feminine, weak "Other" to contrast with the rational, masculine, strong West because of a need to create a difference between the two that would justify imperialist ambitions, Said influenced Indian-American theorist Homi K. Bhabha.

The term the "West" may also be used pejoratively by certain tendencies and especially critical of the influence of the traditional West, due to the history of most of the members of the traditional West being previously involved, at one time or another, in outright imperialism and colonialism. Some of these critics also claim that the traditional West has continued to engage in what might be viewed as modern implementations of imperialism and colonialism, such as neoliberalism and globalization. (It should be noted that many Westerners who subscribe to a positive view of the traditional West are also very critical of neoliberalism and globalization, for their allegedly negative effects on both the developed and developing world.)

Allegedly, definitions of the term "Western world" that some may consider "ethnocentric" others consider "constructed" around one or another Western culture. The British writer Rudyard Kipling wrote about this contrast: *East is East and West is West and never the twain shall meet*, expressing his belief that somebody from the West "can never understand the Asian cultures" as the latter "differ too much" from the Western cultures. Some may view this alleged incompatibility as a precursor to Huntington's "clash of civilizations" theory.

Paradoxically, today Asia and Africa to varying degrees may be considered quasi-Western. Many East Asians and South Asians and Africans and others associate or even identify with the cosmopolitan cultures and international societies referred to sometimes as Western. Likewise, many in the West identify with a transcultural humanity, a notion often found in visions of the sacred.

From a very different perspective, it has also been argued that the idea of the West is, in part, a non-Western invention, deployed in the non-West to shape and define non-Western pathways through or against modernity.

Views on Latin America

By Huntington: A controversial theory of Huntington is that he considered the possibility of Latin America being a separate civilization from the West, but also mused that it might become a third part (the first two being North America and Europe, forgetting Oceania) of the West in the future. The term Latin America in itself is a French invention to denote American countries of Iberian heritage to remember them in a way of their closer linguistic and cultural relatives in Europe, and an approach to diminish the growing influence of the Anglosphere countries in the region, and some countries, such as Portuguese-speaking, largely either itself-identified or Lusophone-identified (rather than *latino*-identified, a – mostly Hispanic – strongly shared identity that generally emerges while in diaspora rather than natively), historically largely Francophile Brazil, and Marxist–Leninist, historically largely Hispanophile Cuba, do not necessarily fit more to the group in relation to other Western nations in various factors. Therefore, many believe this view would be another event of U.S. American generalizations and little knowledge on the region's cultures' and peoples' realities and their individualities.

Huntington did not present any evidence that Latin Americans see themselves as foreign in comparison to other Western cultures, or even a probably existing Western point of view of Latin Americans as foreigners in relation to Europeans and their direct descendants (though hardly for reasons other than the mixed-race descent pervasive among them, as, just like in its ruling colonial powers, both the Renaissance and the Enlightenment were strongly felt in the region). With the Latin American racial whitening policies, reflecting a still living regional tendency to the preference of imitating or prizing not only North American and European appearance, but also fashion, cultural taste and items, political values and even lexicon or given names (known as *mentalidade de colonizado*, "colonized mentality", in Portuguese), it seems more ludicrous that the reality is most often quite the reverse, i.e., that Latin Americans, especially those from Brazil and the Southern Cone, would be readily phobic about being otherized by Westerners and put in the same category as their often ridiculed or disparaged worker classes and rural people, or poorer neighbouring and close cultural relative nations, and thus, as a consequence, also phobic to being seen as collectively very "different" or "especial" in general.

Views on Turkey

By Huntington: According to Huntington, Turkey, whose political leadership has systematically tried to Westernize the country since the 1920s, is his chief example of a "torn country" that is attempting to join Western civilization. The country's elite started the Westernization efforts, beginning with Mustafa Kemal Atatürk, who took power as first president of the modern Turkish nation-state in 1923, imposed western institutions and dress, embraced the Latin alphabet, joined NATO, and are seeking to join the European Union. It should also be noted, however, that the integration of Turkey with the West can be traced back to the 18th century, during which the Ottoman Empire was actively engaged in Westernization.

By Others

In a 2010 interview given to The Times newspaper of the United Kingdom, President Abdullah Gül of Turkey stated that his country is part of the West. In a more recent interview with Zbigniew Brzezinski by the English-language Turkish daily newspaper, Today's Zaman, the former United States national security adviser also stated that Turkey is part of the West despite its religious diversity.

Information Society

An information society is a society where the creation, distribution, use, integration and manipulation of information is a significant economic, political, and cultural activity. The aim of the information society is to gain competitive advantage internationally, through using information technology (IT) in a creative and productive way. The knowledge economy is its economic counterpart, whereby wealth is created through the economic exploitation of understanding. People who have the means to partake in this form of society are sometimes called digital citizens. This is one of many dozen labels that have been identified to suggest that humans are entering a new phase of society.

The markers of this rapid change may be technological, economic, occupational, spatial, cultural, or some combination of all of these. Information society is seen as the successor to industrial society. Closely related concepts are the post-industrial society (Daniel Bell), post-fordism, post-modern society, knowledge society, telematic society, Information Revolution, liquid modernity, and network society (Manuel Castells).

Definition

There is currently no universally accepted concept of what exactly can be termed information society and what shall rather not so be termed. Most theoreticians agree that a transformation can be seen that started somewhere between the 1970s and today and is changing the way societies work fundamentally. Information technology goes beyond the internet, and there are discussions about how big the influence of specific media or specific modes of production really is.

In 2005, governments reaffirmed their dedication to the foundations of the Information Society in the Tunis Commitment and outlined the basis for implementation and follow-up in the Tunis Agenda for the Information Society. In particular, the Tunis Agenda addresses the issues of financing of ICTs for development and Internet governance that could not be resolved in the first phase.

Some people, such as Antonio Negri, characterize the information society as one in which people do immaterial labour. By this, they appear to refer to the production of knowledge or cultural artifacts. One problem with this model is that it ignores the material and essentially industrial basis of the society. However it does point to a problem for workers, namely how many creative people does this society need to function? For example, it may be that you only need a few star performers, rather than a plethora of non-celebrities, as the work of those performers can be easily distributed, forcing all secondary players to the bottom of the market. It *is* now common for publishers to promote only their best selling authors and to try to avoid the rest—even if they still sell steadily. Films are becoming more and more judged, in terms of distribution, by their first weekend's performance, in many cases cutting out opportunity for word-of-mouth development.

Considering that metaphors and technologies of information move forward in a reciprocal relationship, we can describe some societies (especially the Japanese society) as an information society because we think of it as such as letters.

The Growth of Information in Society

The growth of technologically mediated information has been quantified in different ways, including society's technological capacity to store information, to communicate information, and to compute information. It is estimated that, the world's technological capacity to store information grew from 2.6 (optimally compressed) exabytes in 1986, which is the informational equivalent to less than one 730-MB CD-ROM per person in 1986 (539 MB per person), to 295 (optimally compressed) exabytes in 2007. This is the informational equivalent of 60 CD-ROM per person in 2007 and represents a sustained annual growth rate of some 25%. The world's combined technological capacity to receive information through one-way broadcast networks was the informational equivalent of 174 newspapers per person per day in 2007.

The world's combined effective capacity to exchange information through two-way telecommunication networks was 281 petabytes of (optimally compressed) information in 1986, 471 petabytes in 1993, 2.2 (optimally compressed) exabytes in 2000, and 65 (optimally compressed) exabytes in 2007, which is the informational equivalent of 6 newspapers per person per day in 2007. The world's technological capacity to compute information with humanly guided general-purpose computers grew from 3.0 × 10^8 MIPS in 1986, to 6.4 x 10^12 MIPS in 2007, experiencing the fastest growth rate of over 60% per year during the last two decades.

James R. Beniger describes the necessity of information in modern society in the following way: "The need for sharply increased control that resulted from the industrialization of material processes through application of inanimate sources of energy probably accounts for the rapid development of automatic feedback technology in the early industrial period (1740-1830)" (p. 174) "Even with enhanced feedback control, industry could not have developed without the enhanced means to process matter and energy, not only as inputs of the raw materials of production but also as outputs distributed to final consumption."(p. 175)

Development of the Information Society Model

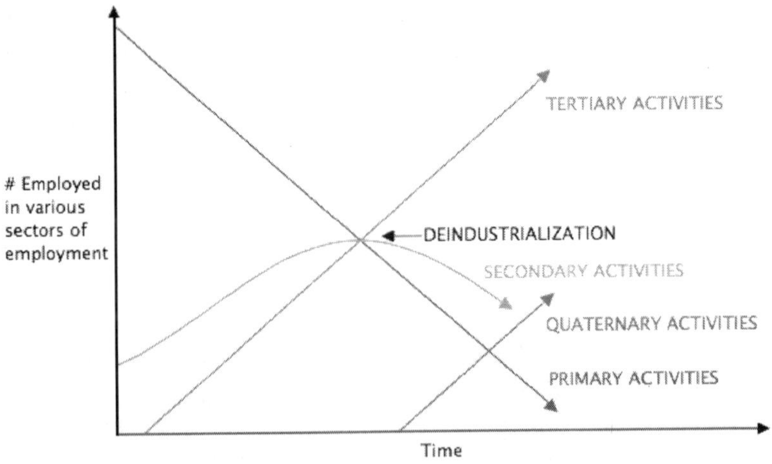

Figure: *Colin Clark's sector model of an economy undergoing technological change. In later stages, the Quaternary sector of the economy grows.*

One of the first people to develop the concept of the information society was the economist Fritz Machlup. In 1933, Fritz Machlup began studying the effect of patents on research. His work culminated in the study *The production and distribution of knowledge in the United States* in 1962. This book was widely regarded and was eventually translated into Russian and Japanese. The Japanese have also studied the information society (or *johoka shakai*, Å'1XS>yO).

The issue of technologies and their role in contemporary society have been discussed in the scientific literature using a range of labels and concepts. This section introduces some of them. Ideas of a knowledge or information economy, post-industrial society, postmodern society, network society, the information revolution, informational capitalism, network capitalism, and the like, have been debated over the last several decades.

Fritz Machlup (1962) introduced the concept of the knowledge industry. He distinguished five sectors of the knowledge sector: education, research and development, mass media, information technologies, information services. Based on this categorization he calculated that in 1959 29% per cent of the GNP in the USA had been produced in knowledge industries.

Economic Transition

Peter Drucker has argued that there is a transition from an economy based on material goods to one based on knowledge. Marc Porat distinguishes a primary (information goods and services that are directly used in the production, distribution or processing of information) and a secondary sector (information services produced for internal consumption by government and non-information firms) of the information economy.

Porat uses the total value added by the primary and secondary information sector to the GNP as an indicator for the information economy. The OECD has employed Porat's definition for calculating the share of the information economy in the total economy (e.g. OECD 1981, 1986). Based on such indicators, the information society has been defined as a society where more than half of the GNP is produced and more than half of the employees are active in the information economy.

For Daniel Bell the number of employees producing services and information is an indicator for the informational character of a society. "A post-industrial society is based on services. (...) What counts is not raw muscle power, or energy, but information. (...) A post industrial society is one in which the majority of those employed are not involved in the production of tangible goods".

Alain Touraine already spoke in 1971 of the post-industrial society. "The passage to postindustrial society takes place when investment results in the production of symbolic goods that modify values, needs, representations, far more than in the production of material goods or even of 'services'. Industrial society had transformed the means of production: post-industrial society changes the ends of production, that is, culture. (...) The decisive point here is that in postindustrial society all of the economic system is the object of intervention of society upon itself. That is why we can call it the programmed society, because this phrase captures its capacity to create models of management, production, organisation, distribution, and consumption, so that such a society appears, at all its functional levels, as the product of an action exercised by the society itself, and not as the outcome of natural laws or cultural specificities" (Touraine 1988: 104). In the programmed society also the area of cultural reproduction including aspects such as information, consumption, health, research, education would be industrialized. That modern society is increasing its capacity to act upon itself means for Touraine that society is reinvesting ever larger parts of production and so produces and transforms itself. This makes Touraine's concept substantially different from that of Daniel Bell who focused on the capacity to process and generate information for efficient society functioning.

Jean-François Lyotard has argued that "knowledge has become the principle [*sic*] force of production over the last few decades". Knowledge would be transformed into a commodity. Lyotard says that postindustrial society makes knowledge accessible to the layman because knowledge and information technologies would diffuse into society and break up Grand Narratives of centralized structures and groups. Lyotard denotes these changing circumstances as postmodern condition or postmodern society.

Similarly to Bell, Peter Otto and Philipp Sonntag (1985) say that an information society is a society where the majority of employees work in information jobs, i.e. they have to deal more with information, signals, symbols, and images than with energy and matter. Radovan Richta (1977) argues that society has been transformed into a scientific civilization based on services, education, and creative activities. This transformation would be the result of a scientific-technological transformation based on technological progress and the increasing importance of computer technology. Science and technology would become immediate forces of production (Aristovnik 2014: 55).

Nico Stehr (1994, 2002a, b) says that in the knowledge society a majority of jobs involves working with knowledge. "Contemporary society may be described as a knowledge society based on the extensive penetration of all its spheres of life and institutions by scientific and technological knowledge" (Stehr 2002b: 18). For Stehr, knowledge is a capacity for social action. Science would become an immediate productive force, knowledge would no longer be primarily embodied in machines, but already appropriated nature that represents knowledge would be rearranged according to certain designs and programs (Ibid.: 41-46). For Stehr, the economy of a knowledge society is largely driven not by material inputs, but by symbolic or knowledge-based inputs (Ibid.: 67), there would be a large number of professions that involve working with knowledge, and a declining number of jobs that demand low cognitive skills as well as in manufacturing (Stehr 2002a).

Also Alvin Toffler argues that knowledge is the central resource in the economy of the information society: "In a Third Wave economy, the central resource – a single word broadly encompassing data, information, images, symbols, culture, ideology, and values – is actionable knowledge" (Dyson/Gilder/Keyworth/Toffler 1994).

At the end of the twentieth century, the concept of the network society gained importance in information society theory. For Manuel Castells, network logic is besides information, pervasiveness, flexibility, and convergence a central feature of the information technology paradigm (2000a: 69ff). "One of the key features of informational society is the networking logic of its basic structure, which explains the use of the concept of 'network society'" (Castells 2000: 21). "As an historical trend, dominant functions and processes in the Information Age are increasingly organised around networks. Networks constitute the new social morphology of our societies, and the diffusion of networking logic substantially modifies the operation and outcomes in processes of production, experience, power, and culture" (Castells 2000: 500). For Castells the network society is the result of informationalism, a new technological paradigm.

Jan Van Dijk (2006) defines the network society as a "social formation with an infrastructure of social and media networks enabling its prime mode of organisation at all levels (individual, group/ organisational and societal). Increasingly, these networks link all units or parts of this formation (individuals, groups and organisations)" (Van Dijk 2006: 20). For Van Dijk networks have become the nervous system of society, whereas Castells links the concept of the network society to capitalist transformation, Van Dijk sees it as the logical result of the increasing widening and thickening of networks in nature and society. Darin Barney uses the term for characterizing societies that exhibit two fundamental characteristics: "The first is the presence in those societies of sophisticated – almost exclusively digital – technologies of networked communication and information management/distribution, technologies which form the basic infrastructure mediating an increasing array of social, political and economic practices. (...) The second, arguably more intriguing, characteristic of network societies is the reproduction and institutionalization throughout (and between) those societies of networks as the basic form of human organisation and relationship across a wide range of social, political and economic configurations and associations".

Critiques

The major critique of concepts such as information society, knowledge society, network society, postmodern society, postindustrial society, etc. that has mainly been voiced by critical scholars is that they create the impression that we have entered a completely new type of society. "If there is just more information then it is hard to understand why anyone should suggest that we have before us something radically new" (Webster 2002a: 259). Critics such as Frank Webster argue that these approaches stress discontinuity, as if contemporary society had nothing in common with society as it was 100 or 150 years ago. Such assumptions would have ideological character because they would fit with the view that we can do nothing about change and have to adopt to existing political realities (Webster 2002b: 267).

These critics argue that contemporary society first of all is still a capitalist society oriented towards accumulating economic, political, and cultural capital. They acknowledge that information society theories stress some important new qualities of society (notably globalization and informatization), but charge that they fail to show that these are attributes of overall capitalist structures. Critics such as Webster insist on the continuities that characterise change. In this way Webster distinguishes between different epochs of capitalism: laissez-faire capitalism of the 19th century, corporate capitalism in the 20th century, and informational capitalism for the 21st century (Webster 2006).

For describing contemporary society based on a dialectic of the old and the new, continuity and discontinuity, other critical scholars have suggested several terms like:

- transnational network capitalism, transnational informational capitalism (Christian Fuchs 2008, 2007): "Computer networks are the technological foundation that has allowed the emergence of global network capitalism, that is, regimes of accumulation, regulation, and discipline that are helping to increasingly base the accumulation of economic, political, and cultural capital on transnational network organisations that make use of cyberspace and other new technologies for global coordination and communication. [...] The need to find new strategies for executing corporate and political domination has resulted in a restructuration of capitalism that is characterized by the emergence of transnational, networked spaces in the economic, political, and cultural system and has been mediated by cyberspace as a tool of global coordination and communication. Economic, political, and cultural space have been restructured; they have become more fluid and dynamic, have enlarged their borders to a transnational scale, and handle the inclusion and exclusion of nodes in flexible ways. These networks are complex due to the high number of nodes (individuals, enterprises, teams, political actors, etc.) that can be involved and the high speed at which a high number of resources is produced and transported within them. But global network capitalism is based on structural inequalities; it is made up of segmented spaces in which central hubs (transnational corporations, certain political actors, regions, countries, Western lifestyles, and worldviews) centralize the production, control, and flows of economic, political, and cultural capital (property, power, definition capacities). This segmentation is an expression of the overall competitive character of contemporary society." (Fuchs 2008: 110+119).

- digital capitalism (Schiller 2000, cf. also Peter Glotz): "networks are directly generalizing the social and cultural range of the capitalist economy as never before" (Schiller 2000: xiv)
- virtual capitalism: the "combination of marketing and the new information technology will enable certain firms to obtain higher profit margins and larger market shares, and will thereby promote greater concentration and centralization of capital" (Dawson/John Bellamy Foster 1998: 63sq),
- high-tech capitalism or informatic capitalism (Fitzpatrick 2002) – to focus on the computer as a guiding technology that has transformed the productive forces of capitalism and has enabled a globalized economy.

Other scholars prefer to speak of information capitalism (Morris-Suzuki 1997) or informational capitalism (Manuel Castells 2000, Christian Fuchs 2005, Schmiede 2006a, b). Manuel Castells sees informationalism as a new technological paradigm (he speaks of a mode of development) characterized by "information generation, processing, and transmission" that have become "the fundamental sources of productivity and power" (Castells 2000: 21). The "most decisive historical factor accelerating, channelling and shaping the information technology paradigm, and inducing its associated social forms, was/is the process of capitalist restructuring undertaken since the 1980s, so that the new techno-economic system can be adequately characterized as informational capitalism" (Castells 2000: 18). Castells has added to theories of the information society the idea that in contemporary society dominant functions and processes are increasingly organised around networks that constitute the new social morphology of society (Castells 2000: 500). Nicholas Garnham is critical of Castells and argues that the latter's account is technologically determinist because Castells points out that his approach is based on a dialectic of technology and society in which technology embodies society and society uses technology (Castells 2000: 5sqq). But Castells also makes clear that the rise of a new "mode of development" is shaped by capitalist production, i.e. by society, which implies that technology isn't the only driving force of society.

Antonio Negri and Michael Hardt argue that contemporary society is an Empire that is characterized by a singular global logic of capitalist domination that is based on immaterial labour. With the concept of immaterial labour Negri and Hardt introduce ideas of information society discourse into their Marxist account of contemporary capitalism. Immaterial labour would be labour "that creates immaterial products, such as knowledge, information, communication, a relationship, or an emotional response" (Hardt/Negri 2005: 108; cf. also 2000: 280-303), or services, cultural products, knowledge (Hardt/Negri 2000: 290). There would be two forms: intellectual labour that produces ideas, symbols, codes, texts, linguistic figures, images, etc.; and affective labour that produces and manipulates affects such as a feeling of ease, well-being, satisfaction, excitement, passion, joy, sadness, etc. (Ibid.).

Overall, neo-Marxist accounts of the information society have in common that they stress that knowledge, information technologies, and computer networks have played a role in the restructuration and globalization of capitalism and the emergence of a flexible regime of accumulation (David Harvey 1989). They warn that new technologies are embedded into societal antagonisms that cause structural unemployment, rising poverty, social exclusion, the deregulation of the welfare state and of labour rights, the lowering of wages, welfare, etc.

Concepts such as knowledge society, information society, network society, informational capitalism, postindustrial society, transnational network capitalism, postmodern society, etc. show that there is a vivid discussion in contemporary sociology on the character of contemporary society and the role that technologies, information, communication, and co-operation play in it. Information society theory discusses the role of information and information technology in society, the question which key concepts shall be used for characterizing contemporary society, and how to define such concepts. It has become a specific branch of contemporary sociology.

Second and Third Nature

Information society is the means of getting information from one place to another (Wark, 1997, p. 22). As technology has advanced so too has the way people have adapted in sharing this information with each other.

"Second nature" refers a group of experiences that get made over by culture (Wark, 1997, p. 23). They then get remade into something else that can then take on a new meaning. As a society we transform this process so it becomes something natural to us, i.e. second nature. So, by following a particular pattern created by culture we are able to recognise how we use and move information in different ways. From sharing information via different time zones (such as talking online) to information ending up in a different location (sending a letter overseas) this has all become a habitual process that we as a society take for granted (Wark, 1997, p. 21).

However, through the process of sharing information vectors have enabled us to spread information even further. Through the use of these vectors information is able to move and then separate from the initial things that enabled them to move (Wark, 1997, p. 24). From here, something called "third nature" has developed. An extension of second nature, third nature is in control of second nature. It expands on what second nature is limited by. It has the ability to mould information in new and different ways. So, third nature is able to 'speed up, proliferate, divide, mutate, and beam in on us from else where (Wark, 1997, p.25). It aims to create a balance between the boundaries of space and time.

This can be seen through the telegraph, it was the first successful technology that could send and receive information faster than a human being could move an object (Wark, 1997, p.26). As a result different vectors of people have the ability to not only shape culture but create new possibilities that will ultimately shape society.

Therefore, through the use of second nature and third nature society is able to use and explore new vectors of possibility where information can be moulded to create new forms of interaction (Wark, 1997, p.28).

Sociological Uses

In sociology, *informational society* refers to a post-modern type of society. Theoreticians like Ulrich Beck, Anthony Giddens and Manuel Castells argue that since the 1970s a transformation from industrial society to informational society has happened on a global scale.

As steam power was the technology standing behind industrial society, so information technology is seen as the catalyst for the changes in work organisation, societal structure and politics occurring in the late 20th century.

In the book *Future Shock,* Alvin Toffler used the phrase super-industrial society to describe this type of society. Other writers and thinkers have used terms like "post-industrial society" and "post-modern industrial society" with a similar meaning.

Related Terms

A number of terms in current use emphasize related but different aspects of the emerging global economic order. The Information Society intends to be the most encompassing in that an economy is a subset of a society. The Information Age is somewhat limiting, in that it refers to a 30-year period between the widespread use of computers and the knowledge economy, rather than an emerging economic order. The knowledge era is about the nature of the content, not the socioeconomic processes by which it will be traded.

The computer revolution, and knowledge revolution refer to specific revolutionary transitions, rather than the end state towards which we are evolving. The Information Revolution relates with the well known terms agricultural revolution and industrial revolution.

- The information economy and the knowledge economy emphasize the content or intellectual property that is being traded through an information market or knowledge market, respectively. Electronic commerce and electronic business emphasize the nature of transactions and running a business, respectively, using the Internet and World-Wide Web. The digital economy focuses on trading bits in cyberspace rather than atoms in physical space. The network economy stresses that businesses will work collectively in webs or as part of business ecosystems rather than as stand-alone units. Social networking refers to the process of collaboration on massive, global scales. The internet economy focuses on the nature of markets that are enabled by the Internet.

- Knowledge services and knowledge value put content into an economic context. Knowledge services integrates Knowledge management, within a Knowledge organisation, that trades in a Knowledge market. In order for individuals to receive more knowledge, surveillance is used. This relates to the use of Drones as a tool in order to gather knowledge on other individuals. Although seemingly synonymous, each term conveys more than nuances or slightly different views of the same thing. Each term represents one attribute of the likely nature of economic activity in the emerging post-industrial society. Alternatively, the new economic order will incorporate all of the above plus other attributes that have not yet fully emerged.
- In connection with the development of the information society, appeared information pollution, evolving information ecology - associated with information hygiene.

Intellectual Property Considerations

One of the central paradoxes of the information society is that it makes information easily reproducible, leading to a variety of freedom/ control problems relating to intellectual property. Essentially, business and capital, whose place becomes that of producing and selling information and knowledge, seems to require control over this new resource so that it can effectively be managed and sold as the basis of the information economy.

However, such control can prove to be both technically and socially problematic. Technically because copy protection is often easily circumvented and socially *rejected* [1] because the users and citizens of the information society can prove to be unwilling to accept such absolute commodification of the facts and information that compose their environment.

Responses to this concern range from the Digital Millennium Copyright Act in the United States (and similar legislation elsewhere) which make copy protection circumvention illegal, to the free software, open source and copyleft movements, which seek to encourage and disseminate the "freedom" of various information products (traditionally both as in "gratis" or free of cost, and liberty, as in freedom to use, explore and share).

Caveat: Information society is often used by politicians meaning something like "we all do internet now"; the sociological term information society (or informational society) has some deeper implications about change of societal structure.

Knowledge Society

A knowledge society generates, processes, shares and makes available to all members of the society knowledge that may be used to improve the human condition. A knowledge society differs from an information society in that the former serves to transform information into resources that allow society to take effective action while the latter only creates and disseminates the raw data. The capacity to gather and analyze information has existed throughout human history. However, the idea of the present-day knowledge society is based on the vast increase in data creation and information dissemination that results from the innovation of information technologies. The UNESCO World Report addresses the definition, content and future of knowledge societies.

Information and Communication Technology

The growth of Information and communication technology (ICT) has significantly increased the world's capacity for creation of raw data and the speed at which it is produced. The advent of the internet delivered unheard of quantities of information to people. The evolution of the internet from Web 1.0 to Web 2.0 offered individuals tools to connect with each other worldwide as well as become content users and producers. Innovation in digital technologies and mobile devices offers individuals a means to connect anywhere anytime where digital technologies are accessible. Tools of ICT have the potential to transform education, training, employment and access to life-sustaining resources for all members of society.

However, this capacity for individuals to produce and use data on a global scale does not necessarily result in knowledge creation. Contemporary media delivers seemingly endless amounts of information and yet, the information alone does not create knowledge. For knowledge creation to take place, reflection is required to create awareness, meaning and understanding. The improvement of human circumstances requires critical analysis of information to develop the knowledge that assists humankind. Absent reflection and critical thinking, information can actually become "non-knowledge", that which is false or inaccurate. The anticipated Semantic Web 3.0 and Ubiquitous Web 4.0 will move both information and knowledge creation forward in their capacities to use intelligence to digitally create meaning independent of user-driven ICT.

Social Theory

The social theory of a knowledge society explains how knowledge is fundamental to the politics, economics, and culture of modern society.

Associated ideas include the knowledge economy created by economists and the learning society created by educators. Knowledge is a commodity to be traded for economic prosperity. In a knowledge society, individuals, communities, and organisations produce knowledge-intensive work.

Peter Drucker viewed knowledge as a key economic resource and coined the term knowledge worker in 1969. Fast forward to present-day, and in this knowledge-intensive environment, knowledge begets knowledge, new competencies develop, and the result is innovation.

A knowledge society promotes human rights and offers equal, inclusive, and universal access to all knowledge creation. The UNESCO World Report establishes four principles that are essential for development of an equitable knowledge society:

- Cultural diversity
- Equal access to education
- Universal access to information (in the public domain)
- Freedom of expression

However, they acknowledge that the digital divide is an obstacle to achievement of genuine knowledge societies. Access to the internet is available to 39 percent of the world's population. This statistic represents growth as well as a continued gap. Among the many challenges that contribute to a global digital divide are issues regarding economic resources, geography, age, gender, language, education, social and cultural background, employment and disabilities.

Politics

To reduce the span of the digital divide, leaders and policymakers worldwide must first develop and understanding of knowledge societies and second, create and deploy initiatives that will universally benefit all populations. The public expects politicians and public institutions to act rationally and rely on relevant knowledge for decision-making. Yet, in many cases, there are no definitive answers for some of the issues that impact humankind. Science is no longer viewed as the provider of unquestionable knowledge and sometimes raises more uncertainty in its search for knowledge. The very advancement of knowledge creates the existence of increased ignorance or non-knowledge. This means that public policy must learn to manage doubt, probability, risk and uncertainty while making the best decisions possible.

To confront the uncertainty that comes from an increase in both knowledge and the resulting lack of knowledge, members of a society disagree and make decisions using justification and observation of consequences. Public policy may operate with the intent to prevent the worst possible outcome versus find the perfect solution. Democratization of expert knowledge occurs when a knowledge society produces and relies on more experts.

Expert knowledge is no longer exclusive to certain individuals, professional or organisations. If in a knowledge society, knowledge is a public good to which all people have access, any individual may also serve as a creator of knowledge and receive credit as an expert. Since politicians rely on expert knowledge for decision making, the layperson who may lack specialised knowledge might hold a view that serves as expertise to the political process.

Education

As technologies are deployed to improve global information access, the role of education will continue to grow and change. Education is viewed as a basic human right. For a society where reading and counting are a requisite for daily living, skills in reading, writing, and basic arithmetic are critical for future learning.

However, in a knowledge society, education is not restricted to school. The advent of ICT allows learners to seek information and develop knowledge at any time and any place where access is available and unrestricted. In these circumstances, the skill of learning to learn is one of the most important tools to help people acquire formal and informal education. In a knowledge society supported by ICT, the ability to locate, classify and sort information is essential. Equipped with this skill, the use of ICT becomes an active versus a passive endeavour and integral to literacy and lifelong learning.

One marker of a knowledge society is continuous innovation that demands lifelong learning, knowledge development, and knowledge sharing. The institution of education will need to become responsive to changing demands. Education professionals will need to learn along with everyone else, and as leaders of changing designs in learning, they will serve as a bridge between technology and teaching. The ability to individually reflect on personal learning requirements and seek knowledge in whatever method is appropriate characterizes lifelong learning.

One model that supports this type of learning is the W. Edwards Deming Plan-do-check-act cycle that promotes continuous improvement. Educational professionals will need to prepare learners to be accountable for their own lifelong learning.

Other Uses

People of many nations united by common political and cultural traditions, beliefs, or values are sometimes also said to form a society (such as Judeo-Christian, Eastern, and Western). When used in this context, the term is employed as a means of contrasting two or more "societies" whose members represent alternative conflicting and competing worldviews.

Some academic, professional, and scientific associations describe themselves as *societies* (for example, the American Mathematical Society, the American Society of Civil Engineers, or the Royal Society).

In some countries, e.g. the United States, France, and Latin America, the term "society' is used in commerce to denote a partnership between investors or the start of a business. In the United Kingdom, partnerships are not called societies, but co-operatives or mutuals are often known as societies (such as friendly societies and building societies).

Chapter 3

Religion

A religion is an organised collection of beliefs, cultural systems, and world views that relate humanity to an order of existence. Many religions have narratives, symbols, and sacred histories that are intended to explain the meaning of life and/or to explain the origin of life or the Universe. From their beliefs about the cosmos and human nature, people derive morality, ethics, religious laws or a preferred lifestyle. According to some estimates, there are roughly 4,200 religions in the world.

Many religions may have organised behaviours, clergy, a definition of what constitutes adherence or membership, holy places, and scriptures. The practice of a religion may also include rituals, sermons, commemoration or veneration of a deity, gods or goddesses, sacrifices, festivals, feasts, trance, initiations, funerary services, matrimonial services, meditation, prayer, music, art, dance, public service or other aspects of human culture. Religions may also contain mythology.

The word *religion* is sometimes used interchangeably with *faith*, *belief system* or sometimes *set of duties*; however, in the words of Émile Durkheim, religion differs from private belief in that it is "something eminently social".

A global 2012 poll reports that 59% of the world's population is religious, and 36% are not religious, including 13% who are atheists, with a 9% decrease in religious belief from 2005. On average, women are more religious than men. Some people follow multiple religions or multiple religious principles at the same time, regardless of whether or not the religious principles they follow traditionally allow for syncretism.

Etymology

Religion (from O.Fr. *religion* "religious community," from L. *religionem* (nom. *religio*) "respect for what is sacred, reverence for the gods," "obligation, the bond between man and the gods") is derived from the Latin *religiô*, the ultimate origins of which are obscure. One possibility is an interpretation traced to Cicero, connecting *lego* "read", i.e. *re* (again) + *lego* in the sense of "choose", "go over again" or "consider carefully". Modern scholars such as Tom Harpur and Joseph Campbell favour the derivation from *ligare* "bind, connect", probably from a prefixed *re-ligare*, i.e. *re* (again) + *ligare* or "to reconnect," which was made prominent by St. Augustine, following the interpretation of Lactantius. The medieval usage alternates with *order* in designating bonded communities like those of monastic orders: "we hear of the 'religion' of the Golden Fleece, of a knight 'of the religion of Avys'".

According to the philologist Max Müller, the root of the English word "religion", the Latin *religio*, was originally used to mean only "reverence for God or the gods, careful pondering of divine things, piety" (which Cicero further derived to mean "diligence"). Max Müller characterized many other cultures around the world, including Egypt, Persia, and India, as having a similar power structure at this point in history. What is called ancient religion today, they would have only called "law".

Many languages have words that can be translated as "religion", but they may use them in a very different way, and some have no word for religion at all. For example, the Sanskrit word dharma, sometimes translated as "religion", also means law. Throughout classical South Asia, the study of law consisted of concepts such as penance through piety and ceremonial as well as practical traditions. Medieval Japan at first had a similar union between "imperial law" and universal or "Buddha law", but these later became independent sources of power.

There is no precise equivalent of "religion" in Hebrew, and Judaism does not distinguish clearly between religious, national, racial, or ethnic identities. One of its central concepts is "halakha", sometimes translated as "law"", which guides religious practice and belief and many aspects of daily life.

The use of other terms, such as obedience to God or Islam are likewise grounded in particular histories and vocabularies.

Definitions

There are numerous definitions of religion and only a few are stated here. The typical dictionary definition of religion refers to a "belief in, or the worship of, a god or gods" or the "service and worship of God or the supernatural". However, writers and scholars have expanded upon the "belief in god" definitions as insufficient to capture the diversity of religious thought and experience.

Peter Mandaville and Paul James define religion as "a relatively-bounded system of beliefs, symbols and practices that addresses the nature of existence, and in which communion with others and Otherness is *lived* as if it both takes in and spiritually transcends socially-grounded ontologies of time, space, embodiment and knowing". This definition is intended, they write, to get away from the modernist dualisms or dichotomous understandings of immanence/transcendence, spirituality/materialism, and sacredness/secularity.

Figure: *Urarina shaman, Peru, 1988*

Edward Burnett Tylor defined religion as "the belief in spiritual beings". He argued, back in 1871, that narrowing the definition to mean the belief in a supreme deity or judgment after death or idolatry and so on, would exclude many peoples from the category of religious, and thus "has the fault of identifying religion rather with particular developments than with the deeper motive which underlies them". He also argued that the belief in spiritual beings exists in all known societies.

The anthropologist Clifford Geertz defined religion as a "system of symbols which acts to establish powerful, pervasive, and long-lasting moods and motivations in men by formulating conceptions of a general order of existence and clothing these conceptions with such an aura of factuality that the moods and motivations seem uniquely realistic." Alluding perhaps to Tylor's "deeper motive", Geertz remarked that "we have very little idea of how, in empirical terms, this particular miracle is accomplished. We just know that it is done, annually, weekly, daily, for some people almost hourly; and we have an enormous ethnographic literature to demonstrate it". The theologian Antoine Vergote also emphasized the "cultural reality" of religion, which he defined as "the entirety of the linguistic expressions, emotions and, actions and signs that refer to a supernatural being or supernatural beings"; he took the term "supernatural" simply to mean whatever transcends the powers of nature or human agency.

The sociologist Durkheim, in his seminal book The Elementary Forms of the Religious Life, defined religion as a "unified system of beliefs and practices relative to sacred things". By sacred things he meant things "set apart and forbidden—beliefs and practices which unite into one single moral community called a Church, all those who adhere to them". Sacred things are not, however, limited to gods or spirits. On the contrary, a sacred thing can be "a rock, a tree, a spring, a pebble, a piece of wood, a house, in a word, anything can be sacred". Religious beliefs, myths, dogmas and legends are the representations that express the nature of these sacred things, and the virtues and powers which are attributed to them.

In his book The Varieties of Religious Experience, the psychologist William James defined religion as "the feelings, acts, and experiences of individual men in their solitude, so far as they apprehend themselves to stand in relation to whatever they may consider the divine". By the term "divine" James meant "any object that is god*like*, whether it be a concrete deity or not" to which the individual feels impelled to respond with solemnity and gravity.

Echoes of James' and Durkheim's definitions are to be found in the writings of, for example, Frederick Ferré who defined religion as "one's way of valuing most comprehensively and intensively". Similarly, for the theologian Paul Tillich, faith is "the state of being ultimately concerned", which "is itself religion. Religion is the substance, the ground, and the depth of man's spiritual life." Friedrich Schleiermacher in the late 18th century defined religion as *das schlechthinnige Abhängigkeitsgefühl*, commonly translated as "a feeling of absolute dependence". His contemporary Hegel disagreed thoroughly, defining religion as "the Divine Spirit becoming conscious of Himself through the finite spirit." When religion is seen in terms of "sacred", "divine", intensive "valuing", or "ultimate concern", then it is possible to understand why scientific findings and philosophical criticisms (e.g. Richard Dawkins) do not necessarily disturb its adherents.

Theories About Religions

Sociological and anthropological theories about religion generally attempt to answer at least two interrelated questions: what is the origin of religion and what is its function. These theories, for the most part, attempt to explain certain universal characteristics of religious belief and practice.

History

Thinkers have proposed prescientific theories about religion since presocratic times. Herodotus (484 – 425 BCE) saw the gods of Greece as the same as the gods of Egypt. Euhemerus (about 330 – 264 BCE) regarded gods as excellent historical persons whom admirers eventually came to worship.

Theorizing beyond mere speculation became possible after data from tribes and peoples all over the world became available in the 18th and 19th centuries. Max Müller (1823–1900) has the reputation of having founded the scientific study of religion; he advocated comparative religion. Later, Geertz and others raised serious doubts about whether one can formulate a general theory of all religions.

Classification

Theories of religion can be classified into:

- Substantive (or essentialist) theories that focus on the contents of religions and the meaning the contents have for people. This approach asserts that people have faith because beliefs make sense insofar as they hold value and are comprehensible. The theories by Tylor and Frazer (focusing on the explanatory value of religion for its adherents), by Rudolf Otto (focusing on the importance of religious experience, more specifically experiences that are both fascinating and terrifying) and by Mircea Eliade (focusing on the longing for otherworldly perfection, the quest for meaning, and the search for patterns in mythology in various religions) offer examples of substantive theories.
- Functional (and in a stronger form reductionist) theories that focuses on the social or psychological functions that religion

has for a group or a person. In simple terms, the functional approach sees religion as "performing certain functions for society". Theories by Karl Marx (role of religion in capitalist and pre-capitalist societies), Sigmund Freud (psychological origin of religious beliefs), Émile Durkheim (social function of religions), and the theory by Stark and Bainbridge exemplify functional theories. This approach tends to be static, with the exception of Marx' theory, and unlike e.g. Weber's approach, which treats of the interaction and dynamic processes between religions and the rest of societies.

Other dichotomies according to which theories or descriptions of religions can be classified include:

- "insider" versus "outsider" perspectives (roughly corresponding to emic versus etic descriptions)
- individualist versus social views
- evolutionist versus relativist views

Methodologies

Most sociologists and anthropologists who tend to see religion as inseparable from and determined by the social context resort to what is called "methodological atheism". When explaining religion they reject divine or supernatural explanations for the status or origins of religions because they are not testable.

The anthropologist E. E. Evans-Pritchard preferred detailed ethnographical study of a tribe and their religion to untestable speculation over the origins of religions by, for example, Müller, Tylor, and Durkheim, and what he termed "armchair anthropologist".

Karl Marx

The social philosopher Karl Marx (1818–1883) held a strictly materialist world view and saw economics, including class distinctions, as the determining factor of society. He saw the human mind and human consciousness as part of matter. According to Marx, the dynamics of society were fuelled by economics, according to the Hegelian concept of theses, anti-theses and synthese. False consciousness is a term used by Marx' collaborator Friedrich Engels (1820–1895), not by Marx. He saw religion originating from alienation and aiding the persistence of alienation. He saw religion as supportive as the status quo, in correspondence with his famous saying that religion is opium of the people. This view is however contradicted by the existence of certain religious groups, like the liberation theology. Marx saw religion as a source of happiness, though illusory and temporary, or at least a source of comfort. Marx saw religion as an unnecessary part of human culture. These claims were limited, however, to his analysis of the historical relationship between European cultures, political institutions, and their Christian religious traditions.

Marxist views strongly influenced individuals' comprehension and conclusions about society, among others the anthropological school of cultural materialism.

Marx' explanations for all religions, always, in all forms, and everywhere have never been taken seriously by many experts in the field, though a substantial fraction accept that Marx' views possibly explain some aspects of religions. Some recent work has suggested that, while the standard account of Marx's analysis of religion is true, it is also only one side of a dialectical account, which takes seriously the disruptive, as well as the passifying moments of religion

Edward Burnett Tylor and James George Frazer

The anthropologist Edward Burnett Tylor (1832–1917) defined religion as belief in supernatural beings and stated that this belief originated as explanations to the world. Belief in supernatural being grew out of attempts to explain life and death. Primitive people used human dreams in which spirits seemed to appear as an indication that the human mind could exist independent of a body. They used this by extension to explain life and death, and belief in the after life. Myths and deities to explain natural phenomena originated out of an analogy and an extension of these explanations. His theory assumed that the psyche of all peoples of all times are more or less the same and that explanations in cultures and religions tend to grow more sophisticated via monotheist religions, like Christianity and eventually to science. Tylor saw backwards practices and beliefs in modern societies as *survivals*, but he did not explain why they survived.

James George Frazer (1854–1941) followed Tylor's theories to a great extent in his book The Golden Bough, but he distinguished between magic and religion. Magic is used to influence the natural world in the primitive man's struggle for survival. He asserted that magic relied on an uncritical belief of primitive people in contact and imitation. For example, precipitation may be invoked by the primitive man by sprinkling water on the ground. He asserted that according to them magic worked through laws. In contrast religion is faith that the natural world is ruled by one or more deities with personal characteristics with whom can be pleaded, not by laws.

The method that Tylor and Frazer used was seeking similar beliefs and practices in all societies, especially the more primitive ones, more or less regardless of time and place. They relied heavily on reports made by missionaries, discoverers, and colonial civil servants.

Their theory has been criticized as one-sided for focusing on mere intellectual aspects of religions, while neglecting social aspects of religion, among others by the anthropologist E. E. Evans-Pritchard. Tylor's anthropological method has been criticized as out-of-context comparisons of practices in different cultures and times. Tylor's and Frazer's view on the origin of religion has been classified as unverifiable speculation. The view that monotheism is a more evolved than polytheism has been disconfirmed by evidence: monotheism is more prevalent in hunter societies than in agricultural societies. The view that societies' views and practices grow more evolved over time in a uniform way has been criticized as unverifiable and contradicted by data from anthropological studies, among others by the writer Andrew Lang (1844–1912) and E. E. Evans-Pritchard. The individualist, intellectual view of religion, as proposed by Tylor and Frazer, is still considered worthwhile by many contemporary experts of the field, among others by the anthropologist Robin Horton.

Émile Durkheim and Functionalism

Functionalism may be seen "as a general approach functionalism explains the existence of social institutions such as religion in terms of the needs that the institutions would meet in society." The main proponent of this theory, Émile Durkheim (1858–1917) saw the concept of the sacred as the defining characteristic of religion, not faith in the supernatural. He saw religion as a reflection of the concern for society. He based his view on recent research regarding totemism among the Australian aboriginals. With totemism he meant that each of the many clans had a different object, plant, or animal that they held sacred and that symbolizes the clan. Durkheim saw totemism as the original and simplest form of religion. According to Durkheim, the analysis of this simple form of religion could provide the building blocks for more complex religions. He asserted that moralism cannot be separated from religion. The sacred i.e. religion reinforces group interest that clash very often with individual interests. Durkheim held the view that the function of religion is group cohesion often performed by collectively attended rituals. He asserted that these group meeting provided a special kind of energy, which he called effervescence, that made group members lose their individuality and to feel united with the gods and thus with the group. Differing from Tylor and Frazer, he saw magic not as religious, but as an individual instrument to achieve something. Durkheim's proposed method for progress and refinement is first to carefully study religion in its simplest form in one contemporary society and then the same in another society and compare the religions then and only between societies that are the same. The empirical basis for Durkheim's view has been severely criticized when more detailed studies of the Australian aboriginals surfaced. More specifically, the definition of religion as dealing with the sacred only, regardless of the supernatural, is not supported by studies of these aboriginals. The view that religion has a social aspect, at the very least, introduced in a generalized very strong form by Durkheim has become influential and uncontested.

Durkheim's approach gave rise to functionalist school in sociology and anthropology Functionalism is a sociological paradigm that originally attempted to explain social institutions as collective means to fill individual biological needs, focusing on the ways in which social institutions fill social needs, especially social stability. Thus because Durkheim viewed society as an "organismic analogy of the body, wherein all the parts work together to maintain the equilibrium of the whole, religion was understood to be the glue that held society together."

The anthropologist Bronis³aw Malinowski (1884–1942) was strongly influenced by the functionalist school and argued that religion originated from coping with death. He saw science as practical knowledge that every society needs abundantly to survive and magic as related to this practical knowledge, but generally dealing with phenomena that humans cannot control.

Max Weber

Max Weber (1864–1920) thought that the truth claims of religious movement were irrelevant for the scientific study of the movements. He portrayed each religion as rational and consistent in their respective societies. Weber acknowledged that religion had a strong social component, but diverged from Durkheim by arguing, for example in his book The Protestant Ethic and the Spirit of Capitalism that religion can be a force of change in society. In the book Weber wrote that modern capitalism spread quickly partially due to the Protestant worldly ascetic morale. Weber's main focus was not on developing a theory of religion but on the interaction between society and religion, while introducing concepts that are still widely used in the sociology of religion. These concept include

- Church sect typology, Weber distinguished between sects and churches by stating that membership of a sect is a personal choice and church membership is determined by birth. The typology later developed more extensively by his friend Ernst Troeltsch and others. According to the typology, churches, ecclesia, denomination, and sects form a continuum with decreasing influence on society. Sects are protest break away groups and tend to be in tension with society.

- Ideal type, a hypothetical "pure" or "clear" form, used in typologies
- Charismatic authority Weber saw charisma as a volatile form or authority that depends on the acceptance of unique quality of a person by this person's followers. Charisma can be a revolutionary force and the authority can either be routinized (change into other forms of authority) or disappear upon the death of the charismatic person.

Somewhat differing from Marx, Weber dealt with status groups, not with class. In status groups the primary motivation is prestige and social cohesion. Status groups have differing levels of access to power and prestige and indirectly to economic resources. In his 1920 treatment of the religion in China he saw Confucianism as helping a certain status group, i.e. the educated elite to maintain access to prestige and power. He asserted that Confucianism opposition against both extravagance and thrift made it unlikely that capitalism could have originated in China.

He used the concept of *Verstehen* (German for "understanding") to describe his method of interpretation of the intention and context of human action.

Sigmund Freud

Sigmund Freud (1856–1939) saw religion as an illusion, a belief that people very much wanted to be true. Unlike Tylor and Frazer, Freud attempted to explain why religion persists in spite of the lack of evidence for its tenets. Freud asserted that religion is a largely unconscious neurotic response to repression. By repression Freud meant that civilized society demands that we not fulfill all our desires immediately, but that they have to be repressed. Rational arguments to a person holding a religious conviction will not change the neurotic response of a person. This is in contrast to Tylor and Frazer, who saw religion as a rational and conscious, though primitive and mistaken, attempt to explain the natural world.

In his 1913 book *Totem and Taboo* he developed a speculative story about how all monotheist religions originated and developed. In the book he asserted that monotheistic religions grew out of a homicide in a clan of a father by his sons. This incident was subconsciously remembered in human societies.

In *Moses and Monotheism*, Freud proposed that Moses had been a priest of Akhenaten who fled Egypt after the pharaoh's death and perpetuated monotheism through a different religion.

Freud's view on religion was embedded in his larger theory of psychoanalysis, which has been criticized as unscientific. Although Freud's attempt to explain the historical origins of religions have not been accepted, his generalized view that all religions originate from unfulfilled psychological needs is still seen as offering a credible explanation in some cases.

Rudolf Otto

The theologian Rudolf Otto (1869–1937) focused on religious experience, more specifically moments that he called numinous which means "Wholly Other". He described it as *mysterium tremendum* (terrifying mystery) and *mysterium fascinans* (awe inspiring, fascinating mystery). He saw religion as emerging from these experiences.

He asserted that these experiences arise from a special, non-rational faculty of the human mind, largely unrelated to other faculties, so religion cannot be reduced to culture or society Some of his views, among others that the experience of the numinous was caused by a transcendental reality, are untestable and hence unscientific. His ideas strongly influenced phenomenologists and Mircea Eliade.

Mircea Eliade

Mircea Eliade's (1907–1986) approach grew out of the phenomenology of religion. Like Otto, he saw religion as something special and autonomous, that cannot be reduced to the social, economical or psychological alone. Like Durkheim, he saw the sacred as central to religion, but differing from Durkheim, he views the sacred as often dealing with the supernatural, not with the clan or society. The daily life of an ordinary person is connected to the sacred by the appearance of the sacred, called hierophany. Theophany (an appearance of a god) is a special case of it. In *The Myth of the Eternal Return* Eliade wrote that archaic men wish to participate in the sacred, and that they long to return to lost paradise outside the historic time to escape meaninglessness. The primitive man could not endure that his struggle to survive had no meaning. According to Eliade, man had a nostalgia (longing) for an otherworldly perfection. Archaic man wishes to escape the *terror of time* and saw time as cyclic. Historical religions like Christianity and Judaism revolted against this older concept of cyclic time. They provided meaning and contact with the sacred *in* history through the god of Israel.

Eliade sought and found patterns in myth in various cultures, e.g. a sky god. Zeus is an example of a sky god.

Eliade's methodology was studying comparative religion of various cultures and societies more or less regardless of other aspects of these societies, often relying on second hand reports. He also used some personal knowledge of other societies and cultures for his theories, among others his knowledge of Hindu folk religion.

He has been criticized for vagueness in defining his key concepts. Like Frazer and Tylor he has also been accused of out-of-context comparisons of religious beliefs of very different societies and cultures. He has also been accused of having a pro-religious bias (Christian and Hindu), though this bias does not seem essential for his theory.

E. E. Evans-Pritchard

The anthropologist Edward Evan Evans-Pritchard (1902–1973) did extensive ethnographic studies among the Azande and Nuer peoples who were considered "primitive" by society and earlier scholars. Evans-Pritchard saw these people as different, but not primitive.

Unlike the previous scholars, Evans-Pritchard did not propose a grand universal theory and he did extensive long-term fieldwork among "primitive" peoples, studying their culture and religion, among other among the Azande. Not just passing contact, like Eliade.

He argued that the religion of the Azande (witchcraft and oracles) can not be understood without the social context and its social function. Witchcraft and oracles played a great role in solving disputes among the Azande. In this respect he agreed with Durkheim, though he acknowledged that Frazer and Tylor were right that their religion also had an intellectual explanatory aspect. The Azande's faith in witchcraft and oracles was quite logical and consistent once some fundamental tenets were accepted. Loss of faith in the fundamental tenets could not be endured because of its social importance and hence they had an elaborate system of explanations (or excuses) against disproving evidence. Besides an alternative system of terms or school of thought did not exist.

He was heavily critical about earlier theorists of primitive religion with the exception of Lucien Lévy-Bruhl, asserting that they made statements about primitive people without having enough inside knowledge to make more than a guess. In spite of his praise of Bruhl's works, Evans-Pritchard disagreed with Bruhl's statement that a member of a "primitive" tribe saying "I am the moon" is prelogical, but that this statement makes perfect sense within their culture if understood metaphorically.

Apart from the Azande, Evans-Pritchard, also studied the neighbouring, but very different Nuer people. The Nuer had an abstract monotheistic faith, somewhat similar to Christianity and Judaism, though it included lesser spirits. They had also totemism, but this was a minor aspect of their religion and hence a corrective to Durkheim's generalizations should be made. Evans-Pritchard did not propose a theory of religions, but only a theory of the Nuer religion.

Clifford Geertz

The anthropologist Clifford Geertz (1926–2006) made several detailed ethnography studies in Javanese villages, a more complex and multi-religious society than Evans-Pritchard had studied. He avoided the subjective and vague concept of group attitude as used by Ruth Benedict by using the analysis of society as proposed by Talcott Parsons who in turn had adapted it from Max Weber. Parsons' adaptation distinguished all human groups on three levels i.e. *1.* an individual level that is controlled by *2.* a social system that is in turn controlled by *3.* a cultural system. Geertz followed Weber when he wrote that "man is an animal suspended in webs of significance he himself has spun and the analysis of it to be therefore not an experimental science in search of law but an interpretive one in search of meaning". Geertz held the view that mere explanations to describe religions and cultures are not sufficient: interpretations are needed too. He advocated what he called *thick descriptions* to interpret symbols by observing them in use. He therefore held the view that the anthropologist must be both empirically rigorous and a good interpreter. In 1972 he wrote that "cultural analysis is (or should be) guessing at meanings, assessing the guesses and drawing explanatory conclusions from the better guesses."

Geertz Saw Religion as One of the Cultural Systems of a Society. He Defined Religion as

(1) a system of symbols

(2) which acts to establish powerful, pervasive and long-lasting moods and motivations in men

(3) by formulating conceptions of a general order of existence and

(4) clothing these conceptions with such an aura of factuality that

(5) the moods and motivations seem uniquely realistic.

With symbols Geertz meant a carrier that embodies a conception, because he saw religion and culture as systems of communication.

This definition emphasizes the mutual reinforcement between world view and ethics.

Though he used more or less the same methodology as Evans-Pritchard, he did not share Evans-Pritchard's hope that a theory of religion could ever be found. Geertz proposed methodology was not the scientific method of the natural science, but the method of historians studying history.

Rational Choice Theory

The rational choice theory has been applied to religions, among others by the sociologists Rodney Stark (1934 –) and William Sims Bainbridge (1940 –). They see religions as systems of "compensators", and view human beings as "rational actors, making choices that she or he thinks best, calculating costs and benefits". Compensators are a body of language and practices that compensate for some physical lack or frustrated goal. They can be divided into specific compensators (compensators for the failure to achieve specific goals), and general compensators (compensators for failure to achieve any goal). They define religion as a system of compensation that relies on the supernatural. The main reasoning behind this theory is that the compensation is what controls the choice, or in other words the choices which the "rational actors" make are "rational in the sense that they are centred on the satisfaction of wants".

It has been observed that social or political movements that fail to achieve their goals will often transform into religions. As it becomes clear that the goals of the movement will not be achieved by natural means (at least within their lifetimes), members of the movement will look to the supernatural to achieve what cannot be achieved naturally. The new religious beliefs are compensators for the failure to achieve the original goals. Examples of this include the counterculture movement in America: the early counterculture movement was intent on changing society and removing its injustice and boredom; but as members of the movement proved unable to achieve these goals they turned to Eastern and new religions as compensators.

Most religions start out their lives as cults or sects, i.e. groups in high tension with the surrounding society, containing different views and beliefs contrary to the societal norm. Over time, they tend to either die out, or become more established, mainstream and in less tension with society. Cults are new groups with a new novel theology, while sects are attempts to return mainstream religions to (what the sect views as) their original purity. Mainstream established groups are called denominations. The comments below about cult formation apply equally well to sect formation.

There are four models of cult formation: the Psychopathological Model, the Entrepreneurial Model, the Social Model and the Normal Revelations model.

- Psychopathological model: religions are founded during a period of severe stress in the life of the founder. The founder suffers from psychological problems, which they resolve through the founding of the religion. (The development of the religion is for them a form of self-therapy, or self-medication.)
- Entrepreneurial model: founders of religions act like entrepreneurs, developing new products (religions) to sell to consumers (to convert people to). According to this model, most founders of new religions already have experience in several religious groups before they begin their own. They take ideas from the pre-existing religions, and try to improve on them to make them more popular.
- Social model: religions are founded by means of social implosions. Members of the religious group spend less and less time with people outside the group, and more and more time with each other within it. The level of affection and emotional bonding between members of a group increases, and their emotional bonds to members outside the group diminish. According to the social model, when a social implosion occurs, the group will naturally develop a new theology and rituals to accompany it.
- Normal revelations: religions are founded when the founder interprets ordinary natural phenomena as supernatural; for instance, ascribing his or her own creativity in inventing the religion to that of the deity.

Some religions are better described by one model than another, though all apply to differing degrees to all religions. Once a cult or sect has been founded, the next problem for the founder is to convert new members to it. Prime candidates for religious conversion are those with an openness to religion, but who do not belong or fit well in any existing religious group. Those with no religion or no interest in religion are difficult to convert, especially since the cult and sect beliefs are so extreme by the standards of the surrounding society. But those already happy members of a religious group are difficult to convert as well, since they have strong social links to their preexisting religion and are unlikely to want to sever them in order to join a new one. The best candidates for religious conversion are those who are members of or have been associated with religious groups (thereby showing an interest or openness to religion), yet exist on the fringe of these groups, without strong social ties to prevent them from joining a new group.

Potential converts vary in their level of social connection. New religions best spread through pre-existing friendship networks. Converts who are marginal with few friends are easy to convert, but having few friends to convert they cannot add much to the further growth of the organisation. Converts with a large social network are harder to convert, since they tend to have more invested in mainstream society; but once converted they yield many new followers through their friendship network.

Cults initially can have quite high growth rates; but as the social networks that initially feed them are exhausted, their growth rate falls quickly. On the other hand, the rate of growth is exponential (ignoring the limited supply of potential converts): the more converts you have, the more missionaries you can have out looking for new converts. But nonetheless it can take a very long time for religions to grow to a large size by natural growth. This often leads to cult leaders giving up after several decades, and withdrawing the cult from the world.

It is difficult for cults and sects to maintain their initial enthusiasm for more than about a generation. As children are born into the cult or sect, members begin to demand a more stable life. When this happens, cults tend to lose or de-emphasise many of their more radical beliefs, and become more open to the surrounding society; they then become denominations.

The theory of religious economy sees different religious organisations competing for followers in a religious economy, much like the way businesses compete for consumers in a commercial economy. Theorists assert that a true religious economy is the result of religious pluralism, giving the population a wider variety of choices in religion. According to the theory, the more religions there are, the more likely the population is to be religious and hereby contradicting the secularization thesis.

Evolutionary Theories

Evolutionary theories view religion as either an adaptation or a byproduct. Adaptationist theories view religion as being of adaptive value to the survival of Pleistocene humans. Byproduct theories view religion as spandrels.

Comparative Religion

Comparative religion is the branch of the study of religions concerned with the systematic comparison of the doctrines and practices of the world's religions. In general the comparative study of religion yields a deeper understanding of the fundamental philosophical concerns of religion such as ethics, metaphysics and the nature and form of salvation. Studying such material is meant to give one a richer and more sophisticated understanding of human beliefs and practices regarding the sacred, numinous, spiritual and divine.

In the field of comparative religion, a common geographical classification of the main world religions includes Middle Eastern religions (including Zoroastrism and Iranian religions), Indian religions, East Asian religions, African religions, American religions, Oceanic religions, and classical Hellenistic religions.

Geographical Classification

According to Charles Joseph Adams, in the field of comparative religion, a common geographical classification discerns the main world religions as follows:

1. Middle Eastern religions, including Judaism, Christianity, Islam, Zoroastrianism, and a variety of ancient cults;
2. East Asian religions, comprising the religious communities of China, Japan, and Korea, and consisting of Confucianism, Daoism, the various schools of Mahayana ("Greater Vehicle") Buddhism, and Shintô;
3. Indian religions, including early Buddhism, Hinduism, Jainism, and Sikhism, and sometimes also the Theravada ("Way of the Elders") Buddhism and the Hindu- and Buddhist-inspired religions of South and Southeast Asia;
4. African religions, or the cults of the tribal peoples of Sub-Saharan Africa, but excluding ancient Egyptian religion, which is considered to belong to the ancient Middle East;
5. American religions, consisting of the beliefs and practices of the Indian peoples indigenous to the two American continents;
6. Oceanic religions—i.e., the religious systems of the peoples of the Pacific islands, Australia, and New Zealand; and
7. Classical religions of ancient Greece and Rome and their Hellenistic descendants.

Middle Eastern Religions

Abrahamic or Western Asian religions: In the study of comparative religion, the category of Abrahamic religions consists of the three monotheistic religions, Christianity, Islam and Judaism, which claim Abraham (Hebrew *Avraham* àÇáÀøÈäÈí ; Arabic *Ibrahim* ÅÈÑÇåíã) as a part of their sacred history. Other religions (such as the Bahá'í Faith) that fit this description are sometimes included but are often omitted.

The original belief in the One God of Abraham eventually became present-day Rabbinic Judaism. Christians believe that Christianity is the fulfillment and continuation of the Jewish Old Testament. Christians believe that Jesus (Hebrew *Yeshua* éÅùÑåÌòÇ) is the Messiah (Christ) foretold in the Old Testament prophecy, and believe in subsequent New Testament revelations based on the divine authority of Jesus in Christian belief (as the Incarnation of God). Islam believes the present Christian and Jewish scriptures have been corrupted over time and are no longer the original divine revelations as given to Moses, Jesus, and other prophets. For Muslims, the Qur'an is the final, complete revelation from God (Arabic Çáåå *Allah*), who believe it to have been revealed to Muhammad, who is believed by Muslims to be the final prophet of Islam.

Christianity and Judaism are two closely related Abrahamic religions that in some ways parallel each other and in other ways diverge in theology and practice.

The historical interaction of Islam and Judaism started in the 7th century CE with the origin and spread of Islam. There are many common aspects between Islam and Judaism, and as Islam developed, it gradually became the major religion closest to Judaism. As opposed to Christianity, which originated from interaction between ancient Greek and Hebrew cultures, Judaism is very similar to Islam in its fundamental religious outlook, structure, jurisprudence and practice. There are many traditions within Islam originating from traditions within the Hebrew Bible or from post-biblical Jewish traditions. These practices are known collectively as the *Isra'iliyat*.

The historical interaction between Christianity and Islam connects fundamental ideas in Christianity with similar ones in Islam. Islam accepts many aspects of Christianity as part of its faith - with some differences in interpretation - and rejects other aspects. Islam believes the Qur'an is the final revelation from God and a completion of all previous revelations, including the Bible.

Iranian Religions

Several important religions and religious movements originated in Greater Iran, that is, among speakers of various Iranian languages and hence with an Iranian cultural background. They include Mithraism, Zoroastrianism, Zurvanism, Mandaeism, Manichaeism and Mazdakism.

Indian Religions

Indian religions refers to a number of religions that have originated on the Indian subcontinent. They encompass Hinduism, Buddhism, Jainism, and Sikhism.

Buddhism and modern Hinduism are both post-Vedic religions. Gautama Buddha is mentioned as an Avatar of Vishnu in the Puranic texts of Hinduism. Some Hindus believe the Buddha accepted and incorporated many tenets of Hinduism in his doctrine, however, Buddhists disagree and state there was no such thing as Hinduism at the time of Buddha and in fact, "Indeed, it absorbed so many Buddhist traits that it is virtually impossible to distinguish the latter in medieval and later Hinduism." Prominent Hindu reformers such as Gandhi and Vivekananda acknowledge Buddhist influence. Gandhi, like Hindus, did not believe Buddha established a non-Hindu tradition. He writes, "I do not regard Jainism or Buddhism as separate from Hinduism."

East Asian or Taoic Religions

A Taoic religion is a religion, or religious philosophy, that focuses on the East Asian concept of *Tao* ("The Way"). This forms a large group of religions including Taoism, Confucianism, Jeung San Do, Shinto, I-Kuan Tao, Chondogyo, Chen Tao and Cao Dai. In large parts of East Asia, Buddhism has taken on some taoic features.

Tao can be roughly stated to be the flow of the universe, or the force behind the natural order. It is believed to be the influence that keeps the universe balanced and ordered and is associated with nature, due to a belief that nature demonstrates the *Tao*. The flow of *Ch'i*, as the essential energy of action and existence, is compared to the universal order of *Tao*. Following the *Tao* is also associated with a "proper" attitude, morality and lifestyle. This is intimately tied to the complex concept of *De*, or literally "virtue" or "power." *De* is the active expression of *Tao*.

Taoism and Ch'an Buddhism for centuries had a mutual influence on each other in China, Korea and Vietnam. These influences were inherited by Zen Buddhism when Ch'an Buddhism arrived in Japan and adapted as Zen Buddhism.

Types

Categories: Some scholars classify religions as either *universal religions* that seek worldwide acceptance and actively look for new converts, or *ethnic religions* that are identified with a particular ethnic group and do not seek converts. Others reject the distinction, pointing out that all religious practices, whatever their philosophical origin, are ethnic because they come from a particular culture.

In the 19th and 20th centuries, the academic practice of comparative religion divided religious belief into philosophically defined categories called "world religions." However, some recent scholarship has argued that not all types of religion are necessarily separated by mutually exclusive philosophies, and furthermore that the utility of ascribing a practice to a certain philosophy, or even calling a given practice religious, rather than cultural, political, or social in nature, is limited. The current state of psychological study about the nature of religiousness suggests that it is better to refer to religion as a largely invariant phenomenon that should be distinguished from cultural norms (i.e. "religions").

Some academics studying the subject have divided religions into three broad categories:

1. world religions, a term which refers to transcultural, international faiths;
2. indigenous religions, which refers to smaller, culture-specific or nation-specific religious groups; and
3. new religious movements, which refers to recently developed faiths.

Interfaith Cooperation

Because religion continues to be recognised in Western thought as a universal impulse, many religious practitioners have aimed to band together in interfaith dialogue, cooperation, and religious peacebuilding. The first major dialogue was the Parliament of the World's Religions at the 1893 Chicago World's Fair, which remains notable even today both in affirming "universal values" and recognition of the diversity of practices among different cultures. The 20th century has been especially fruitful in use of interfaith dialogue as a means of solving ethnic, political, or even religious conflict, with Christian–Jewish reconciliation representing a complete reverse in the attitudes of many Christian communities towards Jews.

Recent interfaith initiatives include "A Common Word", launched in 2007 and focused on bringing Muslim and Christian leaders together, the "C1 World Dialogue", the "Common Ground" initiative between Islam and Buddhism, and a United Nations sponsored "World Interfaith Harmony Week".

Religious Groups

The list of still-active religious movements given here is an attempt to summarize the most important regional and philosophical influences on local communities, but it is by no means a complete description of every religious community, nor does it explain the most important elements of individual religiousness.

The five largest religious groups by world population, estimated to account for 5 billion people, are Christianity, Islam, Buddhism, Hinduism (with the relative numbers for Buddhism and Hinduism dependent on the extent of syncretism) and Chinese folk religion.

Five largest religions	*2012 (billion)*	*2012 (%)*	*2000 (billion)*	*2000 (%)*	*Demographics*
Christianity	*2.2*	*32%*	*2.0*	*33%*	*Christianity by country*
Islam	1.6	23%	1.2	19.6%	Islam by country
Hinduism	1.0	15%	0.811	13.4%	Hinduism by country
Buddhism	0.5	7%	0.360	5.9%	Buddhism by country
Chinese folk religion	0.4	6%	0.385	6.4%	Chinese folk religion
Total	6.9	100%	6.15	100%	

Abrahamic

Abrahamic religions are monotheistic religions which believe they descend from Abraham.

- Judaism is the oldest Abrahamic religion, originating in the people of ancient Israel and Judea. Judaism is based primarily on the Torah, a text which some Jews believe was handed down to the people of Israel through the prophet Moses. This along with the rest of the Hebrew Bible and the Talmud are the central texts of Judaism. The Jewish people were scattered after the destruction of the Temple in Jerusalem in 70 CE. Today there are about 13 million Jews, about 40 per cent living in Israel and 40 per cent in the United States.
- Christianity is based on the life and teachings of Jesus of Nazareth (1st century) as presented in the New Testament. The Christian faith is essentially faith in Jesus as the Christ, the Son of God, and as Savior and Lord. Almost all Christians believe in the Trinity, which teaches the unity of Father, Son (Jesus Christ), and Holy Spirit as three persons in one Godhead. Most Christians can describe their faith with the Nicene Creed. As the religion of Byzantine Empire in the first millennium and of

Western Europe during the time of colonization, Christianity has been propagated throughout the world. The main divisions of Christianity are, according to the number of adherents:

- o Catholic Church, headed by the Pope in Rome, is a communion of the Western church and 22 Eastern Catholic churches.
- o Protestantism, separated from the Catholic Church in the 16th-century Reformation and split in many denominations,
- o Eastern Christianity, which include Eastern Orthodoxy, Oriental Orthodoxy, and the Church of the East.

There are other smaller groups, such as Jehovah's Witnesses and the Latter Day Saint movement, whose inclusion in Christianity is sometimes disputed.

- Islam is based on the Quran, one of the holy books considered by Muslims to be revealed by God, and on the teachings (hadith) of the Islamic prophet Muhammad, a major political and religious figure of the 7th century CE. Islam is the most widely practiced religion of Southeast Asia, North Africa, Western Asia, and Central Asia, while Muslim-majority countries also exist in parts of South Asia, Sub-Saharan Africa, and Southeast Europe. There are also several Islamic republics, including Iran, Pakistan, Mauritania, and Afghanistan.
  - o Sunni Islam is the largest denomination within Islam and follows the Quran, the hadiths which record the sunnah, whilst placing emphasis on the sahabah.
  - o Shia Islam is the second largest denomination of Islam and its adherents believe that Ali succeeded Muhammad and further places emphasis on Muhammad's family.
  - o Ahmadiyya adherents believe that the awaited Imam Mahdi and the Promised Messiah has arrived, believed to be Mirza Ghulam Ahmad by Ahmadis.
  - o Other denominations of Islam include Nation of Islam, Ibadi, Sufism, Quranism, Mahdavia, and non-denominational Muslims. Wahhabism is the dominant Muslim schools of thought in the Kingdom of Saudi Arabia.
- The Bahá'v Faith is an Abrahamic religion founded in 19th century Iran and since then has spread worldwide. It teaches unity of all religious philosophies and accepts all of the prophets of Judaism, Christianity, and Islam as well as additional prophets including its founder Bahá'u'lláh.

- Smaller regional Abrahamic groups, including Samaritanism (primarily in Israel and the West Bank), the Rastafari movement (primarily in Jamaica), and Druze (primarily in Syria and Lebanon).

Iranian

Iranian religions are ancient religions whose roots predate the Islamization of Greater Iran. Nowadays these religions are practiced only by minorities.

- Zoroastrianism is a religion and philosophy based on the teachings of prophet Zoroaster in the 6th century BC. The Zoroastrians worship the Creator Ahura Mazda. In Zoroastrianism good and evil have distinct sources, with evil trying to destroy the creation of Mazda, and good trying to sustain it.
- Mandaeism is a monotheistic religion with a strongly dualistic worldview. Mandaeans are sometime labelled as the "Last Gnostics".
- Kurdish religions include the traditional beliefs of the Yazidi, Alevi, and Ahl-e Haqq. Sometimes these are labelled Yazdânism.

Indian

Indian religions are practiced or were founded in the Indian subcontinent. They are sometimes classified as the *dharmic religions*, as they all feature dharma, the specific law of reality and duties expected according to the religion.

- Hinduism is a synecdoche describing the similar philosophies of Vaishnavism, Shaivism, and related groups practiced or founded in the Indian subcontinent. Concepts most of them share in common include karma, caste, reincarnation, mantras, yantras, and darœana. Hinduism is the most ancient of still-active religions, with origins perhaps as far back as prehistoric times. Hinduism is not a monolithic religion but a religious category containing dozens of separate philosophies amalgamated as Sanâtana Dharma, which is the name with whom Hinduism has been known throughout history by its followers.
- Jainism, taught primarily by Parsva (9th century BCE) and Mahavira (6th century BCE), is an ancient Indian religion that prescribes a path of non-violence for all forms of living beings in this world. Jains are found mostly in India.

- Buddhism was founded by Siddhartha Gautama in the 6th century BCE. Buddhists generally agree that Gautama aimed to help sentient beings end their suffering (dukkha) by understanding the true nature of phenomena, thereby escaping the cycle of suffering and rebirth (saCsâra), that is, achieving nirvana.
  - o Theravada Buddhism, which is practiced mainly in Sri Lanka and Southeast Asia alongside folk religion, shares some characteristics of Indian religions. It is based in a large collection of texts called the Pali Canon.
  - o Mahayana Buddhism (or the "Great Vehicle") under which are a multitude of doctrines that became prominent in China and are still relevant in Vietnam, Korea, Japan and to a lesser extent in Europe and the United States. Mahayana Buddhism includes such disparate teachings as Zen, Pure Land, and Soka Gakkai.
  - o Vajrayana Buddhism first appeared in India in the 3rd century CE. It is currently most prominent in the Himalaya regions and extends across all of Asia (cf. Mikkyô).
  - o Two notable new Buddhist sects are Hòa H£o and the Dalit Buddhist movement, which were developed separately in the 20th century.
- Sikhism is a monotheistic religion founded on the teachings of Guru Nanak and ten successive Sikh gurus in 15th century Punjab. It is the fifth-largest organised religion in the world, with approximately 30 million Sikhs. Sikhs are expected to embody the qualities of a *Sant-Sipâhî*—a saint-soldier, have control over one's internal vices and be able to be constantly immersed in virtues clarified in the Guru Granth Sahib. The principal beliefs of Sikhi are faith in *Waheguru*—represented by the phrase *ik ôaEkâr*, meaning one God, who prevails in everything, along with a praxis in which the Sikh is enjoined to engage in social reform through the pursuit of justice for all human beings.

African Traditional

African traditional religion encompasses the traditional religious beliefs of people in Africa. In north Africa, these religions have included traditional Berber religion, ancient Egyptian religion, and Waaq. West African religions include Akan religion, Dahomey (Fon) mythology, Efik mythology, Odinani of the Igbo people, Serer religion, and Yoruba religion, while Bushongo mythology, Mbuti (Pygmy) mythology, Lugbara mythology, Dinka religion, and Lotuko mythology come from central Africa. Southern African traditions include Akamba mythology, Masai mythology, Malagasy mythology, San religion, Lozi mythology, Tumbuka mythology, and Zulu mythology. Bantu mythology is found throughout central, southeast, and southern Africa.

Figure: *Shango, the Orisha (god) of fire, lightning, and thunder, in the Yoruba religion, depicted on horseback*

There are also notable African diasporic religions practiced in the Americas, such as Santeria, Candomble, Vodun, Lucumi, Umbanda, and Macumba.

Indigenous and Folk

Indigenous religions or folk religions refers to a broad category of traditional religions that can be characterised by shamanism, animism and ancestor worship, where *traditional* means "indigenous, that which is aboriginal or foundational, handed down from generation to generation...". These are religions that are closely associated with a particular group of people, ethnicity or tribe; they often have no formal creeds or sacred texts. Some faiths are syncretic, fusing diverse religious beliefs and practices.

- Chinese folk religion: the indigenous religions of the Han Chinese, or, by metonymy, of all the populations of the Chinese cultural sphere. It includes Confucianism, Taoism and Wuism, as well as many new religious movements such as Falun Gong and Yiguandao.
- Other folk religions of East Asia and Southeast Asia: Korean shamanism, Japanese Shinto, Satsana Phi, Vietnamese folk religion.

- Australian Aboriginal religions.
- Folk religions of the Americas: Native American religions

Folk religions are often omitted as a category in surveys even in countries where they are widely practiced, e.g. in China.

New

New religious movements include:

- Shinshûkyô is a general category for a wide variety of religious movements founded in Japan since the 19th century. These movements share almost nothing in common except the place of their founding. The largest religious movements centred in Japan include Soka Gakkai, Tenrikyo, and Seicho-No-Ie among hundreds of smaller groups.
- Cao Đài is a syncretistic, monotheistic religion, established in Vietnam in 1926.
- Raëlism is a new religious movement founded in 1974 teaching that humans were created by aliens. It is numerically the world's largest UFO religion.
- Hindu reform movements, such as Ayyavazhi, Swaminarayan Faith and Ananda Marga, are examples of new religious movements within Indian religions.
- Unitarian Universalism is a religion characterized by support for a "free and responsible search for truth and meaning", and has no accepted creed or theology.
- Noahidism is a Biblical-Talmudic and monotheistic ideology for non-Jews based on the Seven Laws of Noah, and on their traditional interpretations within Judaism.
- Scientology teaches that people are immortal beings who have forgotten their true nature. Its method of spiritual rehabilitation is a type of counselling known as auditing, in which practitioners aim to consciously re-experience and understand painful or traumatic events and decisions in their past in order to free themselves of their limiting effects.
- Eckankar is a pantheistic religion with the purpose of making God an everyday reality in one's life.
- Wicca is a neo-pagan religion first popularised in 1954 by British civil servant Gerald Gardner, involving the worship of a God and Goddess.
- Druidry is a religion promoting harmony with nature, and drawing on the practices of the druids.

- Satanism is a broad category of religions that, for example, worship Satan as a deity (Theistic Satanism) or use "Satan" as a symbol of carnality and earthly values (LaVeyan Satanism).

Sociological classifications of religious movements suggest that within any given religious group, a community can resemble various types of structures, including "churches", "denominations", "sects", "cults", and "institutions".

Issues

Economics

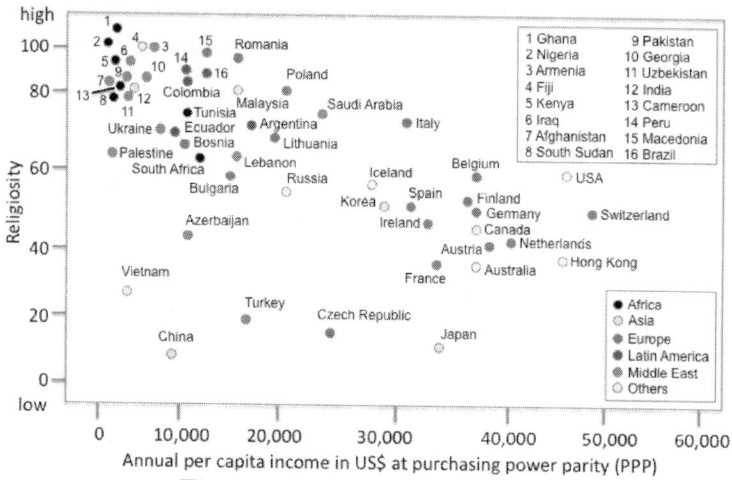

***Figure:** The national income of countries correlates negatively with their religiosity.*

While there has been much debate about how religion affects the economy of countries, in general there is a negative correlation between religiosity and the wealth of nations. In other words, the richer a nation is, the less religious it tends to be. However, sociologist and political economist Max Weber has argued that Protestant Christian countries are wealthier because of their Protestant work ethic.

Health

Mayo Clinic researchers examined the association between religious involvement and spirituality, and physical health, mental health, health-related quality of life, and other health outcomes. The authors reported that: "Most studies have shown that religious involvement and spirituality are associated with better health outcomes, including greater longevity, coping skills, and health-related quality of life (even during terminal illness) and less anxiety, depression, and suicide."

The authors of a subsequent study concluded that the influence of religion on health is "largely beneficial", based on a review of related literature. According to academic James W. Jones, several studies have discovered "positive correlations between religious belief and practice and mental and physical health and longevity."

An analysis of data from the 1998 US General Social Survey, whilst broadly confirming that religious activity was associated with better health and well-being, also suggested that the role of different dimensions of spirituality/religiosity in health is rather more complicated. The results suggested "that it may not be appropriate to generalize findings about the relationship between spirituality/religiosity and health from one form of spirituality/religiosity to another, across denominations, or to assume effects are uniform for men and women.

Violence

Charles Selengut characterizes the phrase "religion and violence" as "jarring", asserting that "religion is thought to be opposed to violence and a force for peace and reconciliation. He acknowledges, however, that "the history and scriptures of the world's religions tell stories of violence and war as they speak of peace and love."

Hector Avalos argues that, because religions claim divine favour for themselves, over and against other groups, this sense of righteousness leads to violence because conflicting claims to superiority, based on unverifiable appeals to God, cannot be adjudicated objectively.

Critics of religion Christopher Hitchens and Richard Dawkins go further and argue that religions do tremendous harm to society by using violence to promote their goals, in ways that are endorsed and exploited by their leaders.

Regina Schwartz argues that all monotheistic religions are inherently violent because of an exclusivism that inevitably fosters violence against those that are considered outsiders. Lawrence Wechsler asserts that Schwartz isn't just arguing that Abrahamic religions have a violent legacy, but that the legacy is actually genocidal in nature.

Byron Bland asserts that one of the most prominent reasons for the "rise of the secular in Western thought" was the reaction against the religious violence of the 16th and 17th centuries. He asserts that "(t)he secular was a way of living with the religious differences that had produced so much horror. Under secularity, political entities have a warrant to make decisions independent from the need to enforce particular versions of religious orthodoxy. Indeed, they may run counter to certain strongly held beliefs if made in the interest of common welfare. Thus, one of the important goals of the secular is to limit violence."

Nonetheless, believers have used similar arguments when responding to atheists in these discussions, pointing to the widespread imprisonment and mass murder of individuals under atheist states in the twentieth century:

> *And who can deny that Stalin and Mao, not to mention Pol Pot and a host of others, all committed atrocities in the name of a Communist ideology that was explicitly atheistic? Who can dispute that they did their bloody deeds by claiming to be establishing a 'new man' and a religion-free utopia? These were mass murders performed with atheism as a central part of their ideological inspiration, they were not mass murders done by people who simply happened to be atheist.* —Dinesh D'Souza

In Response to Such a Line of Argument, However, Author Sam Harris Writes:

> *The problem with fascism and communism, however, is not that they are too critical of religion; the problem is that they are too much like religions. Such regimes are dogmatic to the core and generally give rise to personality cults that are indistinguishable from cults of religious hero worship. Auschwitz, the gulag and the killing fields were not examples of what happens when human beings reject religious dogma; they are examples of political, racial and nationalistic dogma run amok. There is no society in human history that ever suffered because its people became too reasonable.* —Sam Harris

Richard Dawkins has stated that Stalin's atrocities were influenced not by atheism but by dogmatic Marxism, and concludes that while Stalin and Mao happened to be atheists, they did not do their deeds in the name of atheism. On other occasions, Dawkins has replied to the argument that Adolf Hitler and Josef Stalin were antireligious with the response that Hitler and Stalin also grew moustaches, in an effort to show the argument as fallacious. Instead, Dawkins argues in *The God Delusion* that "What matters is not whether Hitler and Stalin were atheists, but whether atheism systematically influences people to do bad things. There is not the smallest evidence that it does." Dawkins adds that Hitler in fact, repeatedly affirmed a strong belief in Christianity, but that his atrocities were no more attributable to his theism than Stalin's or Mao's were to their atheism. In all three cases, he argues, the perpetrators' level of religiosity was incidental. D'Souza responds that an individual need not explicitly invoke atheism in committing atrocities if it is already implied in his worldview, as is the case in Marxism.

Law

The study of law and religion is a relatively new field, with several thousand scholars involved in law schools, and academic departments including political science, religion, and history since 1980. Scholars in the field are not only focused on strictly legal issues about religious freedom or non-establishment, but also study religions as they are qualified through judicial discourses or legal understanding of religious phenomena. Exponents look at canon law, natural law, and state law, often in a comparative perspective. Specialists have explored themes in western history regarding Christianity and justice and mercy, rule and equity, and discipline and love. Common topics of interest include marriage and the family and human rights. Outside of Christianity, scholars have looked at law and religion links in the Muslim Middle East and pagan Rome.

Studies have focused on secularization. In particular the issue of wearing religious symbols in public, such as headscarves that are banned in French schools, have received scholarly attention in the context of human rights and feminism.

Science

Religious knowledge, according to religious practitioners, may be gained from religious leaders, sacred texts, scriptures, or personal revelation. Some religions view such knowledge as unlimited in scope and suitable to answer any question; others see religious knowledge as playing a more restricted role, often as a complement to knowledge gained through physical observation. Adherents to various religious faiths often maintain that religious knowledge obtained via sacred texts or revelation is absolute and infallible and thereby creates an accompanying religious cosmology, although the proof for such is often tautological and generally limited to the religious texts and revelations that form the foundation of their belief.

In contrast, the scientific method gains knowledge by testing hypotheses to develop theories through elucidation of facts or evaluation by experiments and thus only answers cosmological questions about the universe that can be observed and measured. It develops theories of the world which best fit physically observed evidence. All scientific knowledge is subject to later refinement, or even outright rejection, in the face of additional evidence. Scientific theories that have an overwhelming preponderance of favourable evidence are often treated as *de facto* verities in general parlance, such as the theories of general relativity and natural selection to explain respectively the mechanisms of gravity and evolution.

Regarding religion and science, Albert Einstein states (1940): "For science can only ascertain what is, but not what should be, and outside of its domain value judgments of all kinds remain necessary. Religion, on the other hand, deals only with evaluations of human thought and action; it cannot justifiably speak of facts and relationships between facts...Now, even though the realms of religion and science in themselves are clearly marked off from each other, nevertheless there exist between the two strong reciprocal relationships and dependencies. Though religion may be that which determine the goals, it has, nevertheless, learned from science, in the broadest sense, what means will contribute to the attainment of the goals it has set up."

Animal Sacrifice

Animal sacrifice is the ritual killing and offering of an animal to appease or maintain favour with a deity. Such forms of sacrifice are practised within many religions around the world and have appeared historically in almost all cultures.

Related Forms of Thought

Superstition: Superstition has been described as "the incorrect establishment of cause and effect" or a false conception of causation. Religion is more complex and includes social institutions and morality. But religions may include superstitions or make use of magical thinking. Adherents of one religion sometimes think of other religions as superstition. Some atheists, deists, and skeptics regard religious belief as superstition.

Greek and Roman pagans, who saw their relations with the gods in political and social terms, scorned the man who constantly trembled with fear at the thought of the gods (*deisidaimonia*), as a slave might fear a cruel and capricious master. The Romans called such fear of the gods *superstitio*. Early Christianity was outlawed as a *superstitio Iudaica*, a "Jewish superstition", by Domitian in the 80s AD. In AD 425, when Rome had become Christian, Theodosius II outlawed pagan traditions as superstitious.

The Roman Catholic Church considers superstition to be sinful in the sense that it denotes a lack of trust in the divine providence of God and, as such, is a violation of the first of the Ten Commandments. The

Catechism of the Catholic Church states that superstition "in some sense represents a perverse excess of religion" (para. #2110). "Superstition," it says, "is a deviation of religious feeling and of the practices this feeling imposes. It can even affect the worship we offer the true God, e.g., when one attributes an importance in some way magical to certain practices otherwise lawful or necessary. To attribute the efficacy of prayers or of sacramental signs to their mere external performance, apart from the interior dispositions that they demand is to fall into superstition. Cf. Matthew 23:16-22" (para. #2111)

Myth

The word *myth* has several meanings.

1. A traditional story of ostensibly historical events that serves to unfold part of the world view of a people or explain a practice, belief, or natural phenomenon;
2. A person or thing having only an imaginary or unverifiable existence; or
3. A metaphor for the spiritual potentiality in the human being.

Ancient polytheistic religions, such as those of Greece, Rome, and Scandinavia, are usually categorized under the heading of mythology. Religions of pre-industrial peoples, or cultures in development, are similarly called "myths" in the anthropology of religion. The term "myth" can be used pejoratively by both religious and non-religious people. By defining another person's religious stories and beliefs as mythology, one implies that they are less real or true than one's own religious stories and beliefs. Joseph Campbell remarked, "Mythology is often thought of as *other people's* religions, and religion can be defined as mis-interpreted mythology."

In sociology, however, the term *myth* has a non-pejorative meaning. There, *myth* is defined as a story that is important for the group whether or not it is objectively or provably true. Examples include the death and resurrection of Jesus, which, to Christians, explains the means by which they are freed from sin and is also ostensibly a historical event. But from a mythological outlook, whether or not the event actually occurred is unimportant. Instead, the symbolism of the death of an old "life" and the start of a new "life" is what is most significant. Religious believers may or may not accept such symbolic interpretations.

Secularism and Irreligion

The terms "atheist" (lack of belief in any gods) and "agnostic" (belief in the unknowability of the existence of gods), though specifically contrary to theistic (e.g. Christian, Jewish, and Muslim) religious teachings, do not by definition mean the opposite of "religious". There are religions (including Buddhism and Taoism), in fact, that classify some of their followers as agnostic, atheistic, or nontheistic. The true opposite of "religious" is the word "irreligious". Irreligion describes an absence of any religion; antireligion describes an active opposition or aversion toward religions in general.

As religion became a more personal matter in Western culture, discussions of society became more focused on political and scientific meaning, and religious attitudes (dominantly Christian) were increasingly seen as irrelevant for the needs of the European world. On the political side, Ludwig Feuerbach recast Christian beliefs in light of humanism, paving the way for Karl Marx's famous characterization of religion as "the opium of the people". Meanwhile, in the scientific community, T.H. Huxley in 1869 coined the term "agnostic," a term—subsequently adopted by such figures as Robert Ingersoll—that, while directly conflicting with and novel to Christian tradition, is accepted and even embraced in some other religions. Later, Bertrand Russell told the world *Why I Am Not a Christian*, which influenced several later authors to discuss their breakaway from their own religious upbringings from Islam to Hinduism.

Some atheists also construct parody religions, for example, the Church of the SubGenius or the Flying Spaghetti Monster, which parodies the equal time argument employed by intelligent design Creationism. Parody religions may also be considered a post-modern approach to religion. For instance, in Discordianism, it may be hard to tell if even these "serious" followers are not just taking part in an even bigger joke. This joke, in turn, may be part of a greater path to enlightenment, and so on *ad infinitum*.

Criticism of Religion

Religious criticism has a long history, going back at least as far as the 5th century BCE. During classical times, there were religious critics in ancient Greece, such as Diagoras "the atheist" of Melos, and in the 1st century BCE in Rome, with Titus Lucretius Carus's *De Rerum Natura.*

During the Middle Ages and continuing into the Renaissance, potential critics of religion were persecuted and largely forced to remain silent. There were notable critics like Giordano Bruno, who was burned at the stake for disagreeing with religious authority.

In the 17th and 18th century with the Enlightenment, thinkers like David Hume and Voltaire criticized religion.

In the 19th century, Charles Darwin and the theory of evolution led to increased skepticism about religion. Thomas Huxley, Jeremy Bentham, Karl Marx, Charles Bradlaugh, Robert Ingersol, and Mark Twain were noted 19th-century and early-20th-century critics. In the 20th century, Bertrand Russell, Siegmund Freud, and others continued religious criticism.

Sam Harris, Daniel Dennett, Richard Dawkins, Victor J. Stenger, and the late Christopher Hitchens were active critics during the late 20th century and early 21st century.

Critics consider religion to be outdated, harmful to the individual (e.g. brainwashing of children, faith healing, female genital mutilation, circumcision), harmful to society (e.g. holy wars, terrorism, wasteful distribution of resources), to impede the progress of science, to exert social control, and to encourage immoral acts (e.g. blood sacrifice, discrimination against homosexuals and women, and certain forms of sexual violence such as marital rape). A major criticism of many religions is that they require beliefs that are irrational, unscientific, or unreasonable, because religious beliefs and traditions lack scientific or rational foundations.

Some modern-day critics, such as Bryan Caplan, hold that religion lacks utility in human society; they may regard religion as irrational. Nobel Peace Laureate Shirin Ebadi has spoken out against undemocratic Islamic countries justifying "oppressive acts" in the name of Islam.

Chapter 4

Sociology of Religion

Sociology of religion is the study of the beliefs, practices and organisational forms of religion using the tools and methods of the discipline of sociology. This objective investigation may include the use of both quantitative methods (surveys, polls, demographic and census analysis) and qualitative approaches such as participant observation, interviewing, and analysis of archival, historical and documentary materials.

Modern academic sociology began with the analysis of religion in Émile Durkheim's 1897 study of suicide rates among Catholic and Protestant populations, a foundational work of social research which served to distinguish sociology from other disciplines, such as psychology.

The works of Karl Marx and Max Weber emphasized the relationship between religion and the economic or social structure of society. Contemporary debates have centred on issues such as secularization, civil religion, and the cohesiveness of religion in the context of globalization and multiculturalism. The contemporary sociology of religion may also encompass the sociology of irreligion (for instance, in the analysis of secular humanist belief systems).

Sociology of religion is distinguished from the philosophy of religion in that it does not set out to assess the validity of religious beliefs. The process of comparing multiple conflicting dogmas may require what Peter L. Berger has described as inherent "methodological atheism". Whereas the sociology of religion broadly differs from theology in assuming indifference to the supernatural, theorists tend to acknowledge socio-cultural reification of religious practice.

History and Relevance

Classical, seminal sociological theorists of the late 19th and early 20th century such as Durkheim, Weber, and Marx were greatly interested in religion and its effects on society. Like those of Plato and Aristotle from ancient Greece, and Enlightenment philosophers from the 17th through 19th centuries, the ideas posited by these sociologists continue to be examined today. More recent prominent sociologists of religion include Peter L. Berger, Robert N. Bellah, Thomas Luckmann, Rodney Stark, William Sims Bainbridge, Robert Wuthnow, Christian Smith, and Bryan R. Wilson.

View of Religion in Classical Sociology

Durkheim, Marx, and Weber had very complex and developed theories about the nature and effects of religion. Of these, Durkheim and Weber are often more difficult to understand, especially in light of the lack of context and examples in their primary texts. Religion was considered to be an extremely important social variable in the work of all three.

Karl Marx

"Marx was the product of the Enlightenment, embracing its call to replace faith by reason and religion by science." Despite his later influence, Karl Marx did not view his work as an ethical or ideological response to nineteenth-century capitalism (as most later commentators have). His efforts were, in his mind, based solely on what can be called applied science. Marx saw himself as doing morally neutral sociology and economic theory for the sake of human development. As Christiano states, "Marx did not believe in science for science's sake...he believed that he was also advancing a theory that would...be a useful tool...[in] effecting a revolutionary upheaval of the capitalist system in favour of socialism." (124) As such, the crux of his arguments was that humans are best guided by reason. Religion, Marx held, was a significant hindrance to reason, inherently masking the truth and misguiding followers. As we will later see, Marx viewed social alienation as the heart of social inequality. The antithesis to this alienation is freedom. Thus, to propagate freedom means to present individuals with the truth and give them a choice to accept or deny it. In this, "Marx never suggested that religion ought to be prohibited." (Christiano 126)

Central to Marx's theories was the oppressive economic situation in which he dwelt. With the rise of European industrialism, Marx and his colleague Friedrich Engels witnessed and responded to the growth of what he called "surplus value." Marx's view of capitalism saw rich capitalists getting richer and their workers getting poorer (the gap, the exploitation, was the "surplus value"). Not only were workers getting exploited, but in the process they were being further detached from the products they helped create. By simply selling their work for wages, "workers simultaneously lose connection with the object of labour and become objects themselves. Workers are devalued to the level of a commodity – a thing..." (Ibid 125) From this objectification comes alienation. The common worker is led to believe that he or she is a replaceable tool, and is alienated to the point of extreme discontent. Here, in Marx's eyes, religion enters. Capitalism utilises our tendency towards religion as a tool or ideological state apparatus to justify this alienation. Christianity teaches that those who gather up riches and power in this life will almost certainly not be rewarded in the next ("it is harder for a rich man to enter the Kingdom of Heaven than it is for a camel to pass through the eye of a needle...") while those who suffer oppression and poverty in this life, while cultivating their spiritual wealth, will be rewarded in the Kingdom of God. Thus Marx's famous line - "religion is the opium of the people", as it soothes them and dulls their senses to the pain of oppression. Some scholars have recently noted that this is a contradictory metaphor, indicating the way religion is both an 'expression' of suffering and a 'protest' against suffering.

Émile Durkheim

Émile Durkheim placed himself in the positivist tradition, meaning that he thought of his study of society as dispassionate and scientific. He was deeply interested in the problem of what held complex modern societies together. Religion, he argued, was an expression of social cohesion.

In the fieldwork that led to his famous *Elementary Forms of Religious Life,* Durkheim, a secular Frenchman, looked at anthropological data of Indigenous Australians. His underlying interest was to understand the basic forms of religious life for all societies. In *Elementary Forms,* Durkheim argues that the totems the Aborigines venerate are actually expressions of their own conceptions of society itself. This is true not only for the Aborigines, he argues, but for all societies.

Religion, for Durkheim, is not "imaginary," although he does deprive it of what many believers find essential. Religion is very real; it is an expression of society itself, and indeed, there is no society that does not have religion. We perceive as individuals a force greater than ourselves, which is our social life, and give that perception a supernatural face. We then express ourselves religiously in groups, which for Durkheim makes the symbolic power greater. Religion is an expression of our collective consciousness, which is the fusion of all of our individual consciousnesses, which then creates a reality of its own.

It follows, then, that less complex societies, such as the Australian Aborigines, have less complex religious systems, involving totems associated with particular clans. The more complex a particular society, the more complex the religious system is. As societies come in contact with other societies, there is a tendency for religious systems to emphasize universalism to a greater and greater extent. However, as the division of labour makes the individual seem more important (a subject that Durkheim treats extensively in his famous *Division of Labour in Society*), religious systems increasingly focus on individual salvation and conscience.

Durkheim's definition of religion, from *Elementary Forms,* is as follows: "A religion is a unified system of beliefs and practices relative to sacred things, that is to say, things set apart and forbidden – beliefs and practices which unite into one single moral community called a Church, all those who adhere to them." (Marx, introduction) This is a functional definition of religion, meaning that it explains what religion does in social life: essentially, it unites societies. Durkheim defined religion as a clear distinction between the sacred and the profane, in effect this can be paralleled with the distinction between God and humans.

This definition also does not stipulate what exactly may be considered sacred. Thus later sociologists of religion (notably Robert Bellah) have extended Durkheimian insights to talk about notions of civil religion, or the religion of a state. American civil religion, for example, might be said to have its own set of sacred "things": the Flag of the United States, Abraham Lincoln, Martin Luther King Jr., etc. Other sociologists have taken Durkheim's concept of what religion is in the direction of the religion of professional sports, the military, or of rock music.

Max Weber

Max Weber published four major texts on religion in a context of economic sociology and his rationalization thesis: *The Protestant Ethic and the Spirit of Capitalism* (1905), *The Religion of China: Confucianism and Taoism* (1915), *The Religion of India: The Sociology of Hinduism and Buddhism* (1915), and *Ancient Judaism* (1920).

In his sociology, Weber uses the German term "Verstehen" to describe his method of interpretation of the intention and context of human action. Weber is not a positivist – in the sense that he does not believe we can find out "facts" in sociology that can be causally linked.

Although he believes some generalized statements about social life can be made, he is not interested in hard positivist claims, but instead in linkages and sequences, in historical narratives and particular cases.

Weber argues for making sense of religious action on its own terms. A religious group or individual is influenced by all kinds of things, he says, but if they claim to be acting in the name of religion, we should attempt to understand their perspective on religious grounds first. Weber gives religion credit for shaping a person's image of the world, and this image of the world can affect their view of their interests, and ultimately how they decide to take action.

For Weber, religion is best understood as it responds to the human need for theodicy and soteriology. Human beings are troubled, he says, with the question of theodicy – the question of how the extraordinary power of a divine god may be reconciled with the imperfection of the world that he has created and rules over. People need to know, for example, why there is undeserved good fortune and suffering in the world. Religion offers people soteriological answers, or answers that provide opportunities for salvation – relief from suffering, and reassuring meaning. The pursuit of salvation, like the pursuit of wealth, becomes a part of human motivation.

Because religion helps to define motivation, Weber believed that religion (and specifically Calvinism) actually helped to give rise to modern capitalism, as he asserted in his most famous and controversial work, *The Protestant Ethic and the Spirit of Capitalism*.

In *The Protestant Ethic*, Weber argues that capitalism arose in Europe in part because of how the belief in predestination was interpreted by everyday English Puritans. Puritan theology was based on the Calvinist notion that not everyone would be saved; there was only a specific number of the elect who would avoid damnation, and this was based sheerly on God's predetermined will and not on any action you could perform in this life. Official doctrine held that one could not ever really know whether one was among the elect.

Practically, Weber noted, this was difficult psychologically: people were (understandably) anxious to know whether they would be eternally damned or not. Thus Puritan leaders began assuring members that if they began doing well financially in their businesses, this would be one unofficial sign they had God's approval and were among the saved – but only if they used the fruits of their labour well. This along with the rationalism implied by monotheism led to the development of rational bookkeeping and the calculated pursuit of financial success beyond what one needed simply to live – and this is the "spirit of capitalism." Over time, the habits associated with the spirit of capitalism lost their religious significance, and rational pursuit of profit became its own aim.

The Protestant Ethic thesis has been much critiqued, refined, and disputed, but is still a lively source of theoretical debate in sociology of religion. Weber also did considerable work in world religions, including Hinduism and Buddhism.

In his magnum opus *Economy and Society* Weber distinguished three ideal types of religious attitudes:

1. world-flying mysticism
2. world-rejecting asceticism
3. inner-worldly asceticism

He also separated magic as pre-religious activity.

Symbolic Anthropology and Phenomenology

Symbolic anthropology and some versions of phenomenology argue that all humans require reassurance that the world is safe and ordered place - that is, they have a need for ontological security. Therefore, all societies have forms of knowledge that perform this psychological task. The inability of science to offer psychological and emotional comfort explains the presence and influence of non-scientific knowledge in human lives, even in rational world.

Functionalism

Unlike Symbolic anthropology and phenomenology, functionalism points to the benefits for social organisation which non-scientific belief systems provide and which scientific knowledge fails to deliver. Belief systems are seen as encouraging social order and social stability in ways that rationally based knowledge cannot. From this perspective, the existence of non-rational accounts of reality can be explained by the benefits they offer to society.

Rationalism

Rationalists object to the phenomenological and functionalist approaches, arguing that they fail to understand why believers in systems of non-scientific knowledge do think they tell the truth and that their ideas are right, even though science has shown them to be wrong. We cannot explain forms of knowledge in terms of the beneficial psychological or societal effects that an outside observer may see them as producing. We have to look at the point of view of those who believe in them. People do not believe in God, practice magic, or think that witches cause misfortune because they think they are providing themselves with psychological reassurance, or to achieve greater cohesion for their social groups. They do so because they think their beliefs are correct - that they tell them the truth about the way the world is.

Nineteenth-century rationalist writers, reflecting the evolutionist spirits of their times, tended to explain the lack of rationality and the dominance of false beliefs in pre-modern worlds in terms of the deficient mental equipment of their inhabitants. Such people were seen as possessing pre-logical, or non-rational, mentality. Twentieth-century rationalist thinking generally rejected such a view, reasoning that pre-modern people didn't possess inferior minds, but lacked the social and cultural conditions needed to promote rationalism. Rationalists see the history of modern societies as the rise of scientific knowledge and the subsequent decline of non-rational belief. Some of these beliefs - magic, witchcraft - had disappeared, while others - such as religion - had become marginalized. This rationalist perspective has led to secularization theories of various kinds.

Typology of Religious Groups

One common typology among sociologists, religious groups are classified as ecclesias, denominations, sects, or cults (now more commonly referred to in scholarship as New Religious Movements). Note that sociologists give these words precise definitions which differ from how they are commonly used. In particular, sociologists use the words 'cult' and 'sect' without negative connotations, even though the popular use of these words is often pejorative.

Research

In prosperous democracies, higher rates of belief in and worship of a creator correlate with higher rates of homicide, juvenile and early adult mortality, STD infection rates, teen pregnancy, and abortion. As the author Stephen Law paraphrases in his book *War For the Children's Mind*, "The most theistic prosperous democracy, the U.S., is exceptional, but not in the manner Franklin predicted. The United States is almost always the most dysfunctional of the developed democracies, sometimes spectacularly so...The view of the U.S. as a "shining city on the hill" to the rest of the world is falsified when it comes to basic measures of societal health."

The study also notes that it is the more secular, pro-evolution societies that come close to "cultures of life". The authors conclude that the reasonable success of non-religious democracies like Japan, France and Scandinavia has refuted the idea that godless societies suffer disaster. They add "Contradicting these conclusions requires demonstrating a positive link between theism and societal conditions in the first world with a similarly large body of data - a doubtful possibility in view of the observable trends."

BBC news reported on a study that attempted to use mathematical modelling ('nonlinear dynamics') to predict future religious orientations of populations. The study suggests that religion is headed towards 'extinction' in various nations where it has been on the decline: Australia, Austria, Canada, the Czech Republic, Finland, Ireland, the Netherlands, New Zealand and Switzerland. The model considers, not only the changing number of people with certain beliefs, but also attempts to assign utility values of a belief as per each nation.

Secularization and Civil Religion

In relation to the processes of rationalization associated with the development of modernity, it was predicted in the works of many classical sociologists that religion would decline. Despite the claims of many classical theorists and sociologists immediately after World War II, many contemporary theorists have critiqued secularisation thesis, arguing that religion has continued to play a vital role in the lives of individuals worldwide. In the United States, in particular, church attendance has remained relatively stable in the past 40 years. In Africa, the emergence of Christianity has occurred at a high rate. While Africa could claim roughly 10 million Christians in 1900, recent estimates put that number closer to 200 million. The rise of Islam as a major world religion, especially its new-found influence in the West, is another significant development. Furthermore, arguments may be presented regarding the concept of civil religion and new world belief systems. In short, presupposed secularization as a decline in religiosity might seem to be a myth, depending on its definition and the definition of its scope. For instance, some sociologists have argued that steady church attendance and personal religious belief may coexist with a decline in the influence of religious authorities on social or political issues. Additionally, the regular attendance or affiliation do not necessarily translate into a behaviour according to their doctrinal teachings. In other words, there might be still a growing in numbers of members but it does not mean that all members are faithfully following the rules of pious behaviours expected. In that sense, religion may be seen as declining because its waning ability to influence behaviour.

Bryan Wilson

Wilson is a writer on secularization who is alarmed about the nature of life in a society dominated by scientific knowledge. His work is in the tradition of Max Weber, who saw modern societies as places in which rationality dominates life and thought. Weber saw rationality as concerned with identifying causes and working out technical efficiency, with a focus on how things work and with calculating how they can be made to work more effectively, rather than why they are as they are. According to Weber, such rational worlds are disenchanted. Existential questions about the mysteries of human existence, about who we are and why we are here, have become less and less significant.

Wilson insists that non-scientific systems - and religious ones in particular - have experienced an irreversible decline in influence. He has engaged in a long debate with those who dispute the secularization thesis, some of which argue that the traditional religions, such as church-centred ones, have become displaced by an abundance of non-traditional ones, such as cults and sects of various kinds. Others argue that religion has become an individual, rather than a collective, organised affair. Still others suggest that functional alternatives to traditional religion, such as nationalism and patriotism, have emerged to promote social solidarity. Wilson does accept the presence of a large variety of non-scientific forms of meaning and knowledge, but he argues that this is actually evidence of the decline of religion. The increase in the number and diversity of such systems is proof of the removal of religion from the central structural location that it occupied in pre-modern times.

Ernest Gellner

Unlike Wilson and Weber, Gellner (1974) acknowledges that there are drawbacks to living in a world whose main form of knowledge is confined to facts we can do nothing about and that provide us with no guidelines on how to live and how to organise ourselves. In this regard, we are worse off than pre-modern people, whose knowledge, while incorrect, at least provided them with prescriptions for living. However, Gellner insists that these disadvantages are far outweighed by the huge technological advances modern societies have experienced as a result of the application of scientific knowledge.

Gellner doesn't claim that non-scientific knowledge is in the process of dying out. For example, he accepts that religions in various forms continue to attract adherents. He also acknowledges that other forms of belief and meaning, such as those provided by art, music, literature, popular culture (a specifically modern phenomenon), drug taking, political protest, and so on are important for many people. Nevertheless, he rejects the relativist interpretation of this situation - that in modernity, scientific knowledge is just one of many accounts of existence, all of which have equal validity. This is because, for Gellner, such alternatives to science are profoundly insignificant since they are technically impotent, as opposed to science. He sees that modern preoccupations with meaning and being as a self-indulgence that is only possible because scientific knowledge has enabled our world to advance so far. Unlike those in pre-modern times, whose overriding priority is to get hold of scientific knowledge in order to begin to develop, we can afford to sit back in the luxury of our well-appointed world and ponder upon such questions because we can take for granted the kind of world science has constructed for us.

Michel Foucault

Foucault was a post-structuralist who saw human existence as being dependent on forms of knowledge - discourses- that work like languages. Languages/discourses define reality for us. In order to think at all, we are obliged to use these definitions. The knowledge we have about the world is provided for us by the languages and discourses we encounter in the times and places in which we live our lives. Thus, who we are, what we know to be true, and what we think are discursively constructed.

Foucault defined history as the rise and fall of discourses. Social change is about changes in prevailing forms of knowledge. The job of the historian is to chart these changes and identify the reasons for them. Unlike rationalists, however, Foucault saw no element of progress in this process. To Foucault, what is distinctive about modernity is the emergence of discourses concerned with the control and regulation of the body. According to Foucault, the rise of body-centred discourses necessarily involved a process of secularization. Pre-modern discourses were dominated by religion, where things were defined as good and evil, and social life was centred around these concepts. With the emergence of modern urban societies, scientific discourses took over, and medical science was a crucial element of this new knowledge. Modern life because increasingly subject to medical control - the medical gaze, as Foucault called it.

The rise to power of science, and of medicine in particular, coincided with a progressive reduction of the power of religious forms of knowledge. For example, normality and deviance became more of a matter of health and illness than of good and evil, and the physician took over from the priest the role of defining, promoting, and healing deviance.

Globalization

The sociology of religion continues to grow throughout the world, attempting to understand the relationship between religion and globalization. Two older approaches to globalization include modernisation theory, a functionalist derivative, and world systems theory, a Marxist approach. One of the differences between these theories is whether they view capitalism as positive or problematic. However, both assumed that modernisation and capitalism would diminish the hold of religion.

To the contrary, as globalization intensified many different cultures started to look into different religions and incorporate different beliefs into society. New interpretations emerged that recognise the tensions. For example, according to Paul James and Peter Mandaville:

Religion and globalization have been intertwined with each other since the early empires attempted to extend their reach across what they perceived to be world-space. Processes of globalization carried religious cosmologies – including traditional conceptions of universalism – to the corners of the world, while these cosmologies legitimated processes of globalization. This dynamic of inter-relation has continued to the present, but with changing and sometimes new and intensifying contradictions.

Types of Religious Practices

Animism

Animism (from Latin *animus, -i* "soul, life") is the worldview that non-human entities (animals, plants, and inanimate objects or phenomena) possess a spiritual essence.

Animism is used in the anthropology of religion as a term for the belief system of some indigenous tribal peoples, especially prior to the development of organised religion. Although each culture has its own different mythologies and rituals, "animism" is said to describe the most common, foundational thread of indigenous peoples' "spiritual" or "supernatural" perspectives. The animistic perspective is so fundamental, mundane, everyday and taken-for-granted that most animistic indigenous people do not even have a word in their languages that corresponds to "animism" (or even "religion"); the term is an anthropological construct rather than one designated by the people themselves.

Largely due to such ethnolinguistic and cultural discrepancies, opinion has differed on whether *animism* refers to a broad religious belief or to a full-fledged religion in its own right. The currently accepted definition of animism was only developed in the late 19th century by Sir Edward Tylor, who created it as "one of anthropology's earliest concepts, if not the first".

Animism encompasses the belief that there is no separation between the spiritual and physical (or material) world, and souls or spirits exist, not only in humans, but also in some other animals, plants, rocks, geographic features such as mountains or rivers, or other entities of the natural environment, including thunder, wind, and shadows. Animism thus rejects Cartesian dualism. Animism may further attribute souls to abstract concepts such as words, true names, or metaphors in mythology. Examples of animism can be found in forms of Shinto, Serer, Hinduism, Buddhism, Scientology, Jainism, Paganism, and Neopaganism. Some members of the non-tribal world also consider themselves animists (such as author Daniel Quinn, sculptor Lawson Oyekan, and many Neopagans).

Theories of Animism

Tylor's Definition of Animism

The term *animism* appears to have been first developed as *Animismus* by German scientist Georg Ernst Stahl, circa 1720, to refer to the "doctrine that animal life is produced by an immaterial soul." The actual English language form of *animism*, however, can only be attested to 1819. The term was taken and redefined by the anthropologist Sir Edward Tylor in his 1871 book *Primitive Culture,* in which he defined it as "the general doctrine of souls and other spiritual beings in general." According to Tylor, animism often includes "an idea of pervading life and will in nature"; i.e., a belief that natural objects other than humans have souls. This formulation was little different from that proposed by Auguste Comte as fetishism.

As a self-described "confirmed scientific rationalist", Tylor believed that animistic beliefs were "childish" and typical of "cognitive underdevelopment", and that it was therefore common in "primitive" peoples such as those living in hunter gatherer societies. In fact, Tylor based his theory of animism on his experience of modern seances thereby constructing a model of 'primitive thought' (of which he had no first hand experience) from his first-hand knowledge of spiritualism. Stringer (1999) notes that his reading of *Primitive Culture* led him to believe that Tylor was far more sympathetic in regard to "primitive" populations than many of his contemporaries, and that Tylor expressed no belief that there was any difference between the intellectual capabilities of "savage" people and westerners. To Tylor, the fundamental distinction between western and "primitive" cultures was education; and education was a social-cultural evolutionary process that produced differing levels of sophistication, or "progress," in different places.

Social Evolutionist Conceptions of Animism

Tylor's definition of animism was a part of a growing international debate on the nature of 'primitive society' by lawyers, theologians and philologists. The debate defined the field of research of a new science, Anthropology. By the end of the nineteenth century an orthodoxy on 'primitive society' had emerged although few anthropologists today would accept their definition; the 'nineteenth century armchair anthropologists' argued 'primitive society' (an evolutionary category) was ordered by kinship and was divided into exogamous descent groups related by a series of marriage exchanges. Their religion was 'animism,' the belief that natural species and objects had souls. With the development of private property, these descent groups were displaced by the emergence of the territorial state. These rituals and beliefs eventually evolved over time into the vast array of "developed" religions. According to Tylor, the more scientifically advanced a society became, the less members of that society believed in animism; however, any remnant ideologies of souls or spirits, to Tylor, represented "survivals" of the original animism of early humanity.

In 1869 (three years after Tylor proposed his definition of animism), the Edinburgh lawyer John Ferguson McLellan argued that the animistic thinking evident in fetishism gave rise to a religion he named Totemism. Primitive people believed, he argued, that they were descended of the same species as their totemic animal. Subsequent debate by the armchair anthropologists (including J. J. Bachofen, Émile Durkheim and Sigmund Freud) remained focused on totemism rather than animism, with few directly challenging Tylor's definition. Indeed, anthropologists "have commonly avoided the issue of animism and even the term itself rather than revisit this prevalent notion in light of their new and rich ethnographies." According to the anthropologist Tim Ingold, animism shares similarities to totemism but differs in its focus on individual spirit beings which help to perpetuate life, whereas totemism more typically holds that there is a primary source, such as the land itself or the ancestors, who provide the basis to life. Certain indigenous religious groups such as the Australian Aboriginals are more typically totemic, whereas others like the Inuit are more typically animistic in their worldview.

Animism as a Relational Ontology

After a lengthy period of disinterest, post-modern anthropologists are increasingly engaging with the concept of animism. Modernism is characterized by a Cartesian subject-object dualism that divides the subjective from the objective, and culture from nature; in this view, animism is the inverse of scientism, and hence inherently invalid. Drawing on the work of Bruno Latour, these anthropologists question these modernist assumptions, and theorize that all societies continue to "animate" the world around them, and not just as a Tylorian survival of primitive thought. Rather, the instrumental reason characteristic of modernity is limited to our "professional subcultures," which allows us to treat the world as a detached mechanical object in a delimited sphere of activity. We, like animists, also continue to create personal relationships with elements of the so-called objective world, whether pets, cars or teddy-bears, who we recognise as subjects. As such, these entities are "approached as communicative subjects rather than the inert objects perceived by modernists." These approaches are careful to avoid the modernist assumptions that the environment consists dichotomously of a physical world distinct from humans, and from modernist conceptions of the person as composed dualistically as body and soul.

Nurit Bird-David argues that "Positivistic ideas about the meaning of 'nature', 'life' and 'personhood' misdirected these previous attempts to understand the local concepts. Classical theoreticians (it is argued) attributed their own modernist ideas of self to 'primitive peoples' while asserting that the 'primitive peoples' read their idea of self into others!" She argues that animism is a "relational epistemology", and not a Tylorian failure of primitive reasoning. That is, self-identity among animists is based on their relationships with others, rather than some distinctive feature of the self. Instead of focusing on the essentialized, modernist self (the "individual"), persons are viewed as bundles of social relationships ("dividuals"), some of which are with "superpersons" (i.e. non-humans).

Tim Ingold, like Bird-David, argues that animists do not see themselves as separate from their environment: "Hunter-gatherers do not, as a rule, approach their environment as an external world of nature that has to be 'grasped' intellectually ... indeed the separation of mind and nature has no place in their thought and practice." Willerslev extends the argument by noting that animists reject this Cartesian dualism, and that the animist self identifies with the world, "feeling at once *within* and *apart* from it so that the two glide ceaselessly in and out of each other in a sealed circuit." The animist hunter is thus aware of himself as a human hunter, but, through mimicry is able to assume the viewpoint, senses, and sensibilities of his prey, to be one with it. Shamanism, in this view, is an everyday attempt to influence spirits of ancestors and animals by mirroring their behaviours as the hunter does his prey.

Religion and Animism

There is ongoing disagreement (and no general consensus) as to whether animism is merely a singular, broadly encompassing religious belief or a worldview in and of itself, comprising many diverse mythologies found worldwide in many diverse cultures. This also raises a controversy regarding the ethical claims animism may or may not make: whether animism ignores questions of ethics altogether or, by endowing various non-human elements of nature with spirituality or personhood, in fact promotes a complex ecological ethics. In modern usage, the term is sometimes used improperly as a catch-all classification of "other world religions" alongside major organised religions.

Characteristics

Tylor argued that animism consisted of two unformulated propositions; all parts of nature had a soul, and these souls are capable of moving without requiring a physical form. This gives rise to fetishism, the worship of visible objects as powerful, spiritual beings. The second proposition was that souls are independent of their physical forms. It gives rise to 'spiritism', the worship of the souls of the dead and the unseen spirits of the heavens. Others such as Nurit Bird-David, associate animism with various aspects of shamanism.

Fetishism/totemism

In many animistic world views, the human being is often regarded as on a roughly equal footing with other animals, plants, and natural forces. Therefore, it is morally imperative to treat these agents with respect. In this world view, humans are considered a part of nature, rather than superior to, or separate from it.

Totemism (or fetishism) includes one or more of several features, such as the mystic association of animal and plant species, natural phenomena, or created objects with unilineally related groups (lineages, clans, tribes, moieties, phratries) or with local groups and families; the hereditary transmission of the totems (patrilineal or matrilineal); group and personal names that are based either directly or indirectly on the totem; the use of totemistic emblems and symbols; taboos and prohibitions that may apply to the species itself or can be limited to parts of animals and plants (partial taboos instead of partial totems); and a connection with a large number of animals and natural objects (multiplex totems) within which a distinction can be made between principal totems and subsidiary ones (linked totems).

Ancestor Reverence

Many animistic cultures observe some form of ancestor reverence. Whether they see the ancestors as living in an other world, or embodied in the natural features of this world, animists often believe that offerings and prayers to and for the dead are an important facet of maintaining harmony with the world of the spirits.

Shamanism

A shaman is a person regarded as having access to, and influence in, the world of benevolent and malevolent spirits, who typically enters into a trance state during a ritual, and practices divination and healing. Shamanism encompasses the premise that shamans are intermediaries or messengers between the human world and the spirit worlds. Shamans are said to treat ailments/illness by mending the soul. Alleviating traumas affecting the soul/spirit restores the physical body of the individual to balance and wholeness. The shaman also enters supernatural realms or dimensions to obtain solutions to problems afflicting the community. Shamans may visit other worlds/dimensions to bring guidance to misguided souls and to ameliorate illnesses of the human soul caused by foreign elements. The shaman operates primarily within the spiritual world, which in turn affects the human world. The restoration of balance results in the elimination of the ailment.

Distinction from Pantheism

Animism is not the same as pantheism, although the two are sometimes confused. Some religions are both pantheistic and animistic. One of the main differences is that while animists believe everything to be spiritual in nature, they do not necessarily see the spiritual nature of everything in existence as being united (monism), the way pantheists do. As a result, animism puts more emphasis on the uniqueness of each individual soul. In pantheism, everything shares the same spiritual essence, rather than having distinct spirits and/or souls. Additionally, Pantheism posits a source of this "monism". This source may or may not have agency. In contrast, in Animism, the soul or essence or spirit of objects and living things are novel and separate from the whole, while still seen as irrevocably intertwined with one another in a community.

Examples of Animist Traditions

- Shinto, the traditional religion of Japan, is highly animistic. In Shinto, spirits of nature, or kami, are believed to exist everywhere, from the major (such as the goddess of the sun), which can be considered polytheistic, to the minor, which are more likely to be seen as a form of animism.

- Many traditional beliefs in the Philippines still practised to an extent today are animist and spiritist in origin in that there are rituals aimed at pacifying malevolent spirits or are apotropaic in nature.
- There are some Hindu groups which may be considered animist. The coastal Karnataka has a different tradition of praying to spirits. Likewise a popular Hindu ritual form of worship of North Malabar in Kerala, India is the Tabuh Rah blood offering to Theyyam gods, despite being forbidden in the Vedic philosophy of sattvic Hinduism, Jainism and Buddhism,

  Theyyam deities are propitiated through the cock sacrifice where the religious cockfight is a religious exercise of offering blood to the Theyyam gods.
- Mun, (also called Munism or Bongthingism) is the traditional polytheistic, animist, shamanistic, and syncretic religion of the Lepcha people.
- Many traditional Native American religions are fundamentally animistic. See, for example, the Lakota Sioux prayer Mitakuye Oyasin. The Haudenausaunee Thanksgiving Address, which can take an hour to recite, directs thanks towards every being - plant, animal and other.
- The New Age movement commonly demonstrates animistic traits in asserting the existence of nature spirits.
- Some Neopagan groups, including Eco-Pagans, describe themselves as animists, meaning that they respect the diverse community of living beings and spirits with whom humans share the world/cosmos.

Other Usages

Psychology and Animism

Animism in the broadest sense, i.e., thinking of objects as animate, and treating them as if they were animate, is near-universal. Jean Piaget applied the term in reference to an implicit understanding of the world in a child's mind which assumes that all events are the product of intention or consciousness. Piaget explains this with a cognitive inability to distinguish the external world from one's internal world.

Science and Animism

In the early 20th century, William McDougall defended a form of animism in his book *Body and Mind: A History and Defence of Animism* (1911).

The physicist Nick Herbert has argued for "quantum animism" in which mind permeates the world at every level. Werner Krieglstein wrote regarding his quantum animism:

Herbert's quantum animism differs from traditional animism in that it avoids assuming a dualistic model of mind and matter. Traditional dualism assumes that some kind of spirit inhabits a body and makes it move, a ghost in the machine. Herbert's quantum animism presents the idea that every natural system has an inner life, a conscious centre, from which it directs and observes its action.

Monism

Monism is the philosophical view that a variety of existing things can be explained in terms of a single reality or substance. The wide definition states that all existing things go back to a source which is distinct from them (e.g. in Neoplatonism everything is derived from The One). A commonly-used, restricted definition of monism asserts the presence of a unifying substance or essence.

One must distinguish "stuff monism" from "thing monism". According to stuff monism there is only one kind of stuff (e.g. matter or mind), although there may be many things made out of this stuff. According to thing-monism there exists strictly speaking only a single thing (e.g. the universe), which can only be artificially and arbitrarily divided into many things.

In contrast to monism, are metaphysical dualism and metaphysical pluralism.

The term *monism* originated from Western philosophy, and has often been applied to various religions.

History

The term Monism was introduced in the 18th century by Christian von Wolff in his work *Logic* (1728), to designate types of philosophical thought in which the attempt was made to eliminate the dichotomy of body and mind and explain all phenomena by one unifying principle, or as manifestations of a single substance.

The body-mind dichotomy in philosophy examines the relationship between mind and matter, and in particular the relationship between consciousness and the brain. The problem was addressed by René Descartes in the 17th century, resulting in Cartesian dualism, and by pre-Aristotelian philosophers, in Avicennian philosophy, and in earlier Asian and more specifically Indian traditions.

It was later also applied to the theory of absolute identity set forth by Hegel and Schelling. Thereafter the term was more broadly used, for any theory postulating a unifying principle. The opponent thesis of dualism also was broadened, to include pluralism. According to Urmson, as a result of this extended use, the term is "systematically ambiguous".

According to Jonathan Schaffer, monism lost popularity due to the emergence of Analytic philosophy in the early twentieth century, which revolted against the neo-Hegelians. Carnap and Ayer, who were strong proponents of positivism, "ridiculed the whole question as incoherent mysticism".

The mind–body problem has reemerged in social psychology and related fields, with the interest in mind–body interaction and the rejection of Cartesian mind–body dualism in the *identity thesis*, a modern form of monism. Monism is also still relevant to the philosophy of mind, where various positions are defended.

Definitions

There are two sorts of definitions for monism:

1. The wide definition: a philosophy is monistic if it postulates unity of origin of all things; all existing things go back to a source which is distinct from them.
2. The restricted definition: this requires not only unity of origin but also unity of substance and essence.

Three basic types of monism can be discerned:

1. Substantial monism, "the view that the apparent plurality of substances is due to different states or appearances of a single substance"
2. Attributive monism, "the view that whatever the number of substances, they are of a single ultimate kind"
3. Partial monism, "within a given realm of being (however many there may be) there is only one substance"

Contrasting with monism are:

- Metaphysical dualism, which asserts that there are two ultimately irreconcilable substances or realities such as Good and Evil, for example, Manichaeism,

- Metaphysical pluralism, which asserts three or more fundamental substances or realities.

Although the term "monism" originated in Western philosophy to typify positions in the mind–body problem, it has also been used to typify religious traditions. In modern Hinduism, the term "absolute monism" is being used for Advaita Vedanta.

Philosophical Monism

Types of Monism

Monism in philosophy can be divided into three broad categories:

1. Idealist, phenomenalism, or mentalistic monism which holds that only mind or spirit is real
2. Neutral monism, which holds that one sort of thing fundamentally exists, to which both the mental and the physical can be reduced
3. Material monism (also called Physicalism and materialism), which holds that only the physical is real, and that the mental or spiritual can be reduced to the physical
   a. Eliminative Materialism, according to which everything is physical and mental things do not exist
   b. Reductive physicalism, according to which mental things do exist and are a kind of physical thing

Certain positions do not fit easily into the above categories, such as functionalism, anomalous monism, and reflexive monism. Moreover, they do not define the meaning of "real".

Monistic Philosophers

Pre-Socratic

While the lack of information makes it difficult in some cases to be sure of the details, the following pre-Socratic philosophers thought in monistic terms:

- Thales: Water.
- Anaximander: Apeiron (meaning 'the undefined infinite'). Reality is some, one thing, but we cannot know what.
- Anaximenes: Air.
- Heraclitus: Change, symbolized by fire (in that everything is in constant flux).

It is clear that Parmenides was a monist since he argued that Being or Reality is an unmoving perfect sphere, unchanging, undivided.

Post-Socrates

- Neopythagorians such as Apollonius of Tyana centred their cosmologies on the Monad or One.
- Stoics taught that there is only one substance, identified as God.
- Middle Platonism under such works as Numenius taught that the Universe emanating from the Monad or One.
- Neoplatonism is Monistic. Plotinus taught that there was an ineffable transcendent god, 'The One,' of which subsequent realities were emanations. From The One emanates the Divine Mind (Nous), the Cosmic Soul (Psyche), and the World (Cosmos).

Modern

- Baruch de Spinoza
- Alexander Bogdanov
- Hegel
- Ernst Haeckel

Religious Monism

Philosophy is a part of religion, but religion also entails religious practices, ethical guidelines, and social rules and behaviour to direct one's life and experience. According to Momen, religious experience is a central aspect of religion. Critics have pointed out that the centrality of religious experience is of recent origin.

Pantheism, Panentheism and Pandeism

There are pantheists, panentheists and pandeists in:

- Zoroastrianism
- Hinduism (particularly in Advaita and Vishistadvaita)
- Judaism (panentheism is especially found in Kabbalah and Hasidic philosophy)
- Islam (among the Sufis, especially the Bektashi)

Pantheism

Pantheism is the belief that everything composes an all-encompassing, immanent God, or that the universe (or nature) is identical with divinity. Pantheists thus do not believe in a personal or anthropomorphic god, but believe that interpretations of the term differ.

Pantheism was popularized in the modern era as both a theology and philosophy based on the work of the 17th century philosopher

Baruch Spinoza, whose *Ethics* was an answer to Descartes' famous dualist theory that the body and spirit are separate. Spinoza held that the two are the same, and this monism is a fundamental quality of his philosophy. He was described as a "God-intoxicated man," and used the word God to describe the unity of all substance. Although the term pantheism was not coined until after his death, Spinoza is regarded as its most celebrated advocate.

Following a long and still current tradition H.P. Owen (1971: 65) claimed that:

- Pantheists are 'monists'...they believe that there is only one Being, and that all other forms of reality are either modes (or appearances) of it or identical with it.
- Pantheism is closely related to monism, as pantheists too believe all of reality is one substance, called Universe, God or Nature. Panentheism, a slightly different concept (explained below), however is dualistic. Some of the most famous pantheists are the Stoics, Giordano Bruno and Spinoza.

Panentheism

Panentheism is a belief system which posits that the divine (be it a monotheistic God, polytheistic gods, or an eternal cosmic animating force), interpenetrates every part of nature, but is not one with nature. Panentheism differentiates itself from pantheism, which holds that the divine is synonymous with the universe.

In panentheism, there are two types of substance, "pan" the universe and God. The universe and the divine are not ontologically equivalent. God is viewed as the eternal animating force within the universe. In some forms of panentheism, the cosmos exists within God, who in turn "transcends", "pervades" or is "in" the cosmos.

While pantheism asserts that 'All is God', panentheism claims that God animates all of the universe, and also transcends the universe. In addition, some forms indicate that the universe is contained within God, like in the concept of Tzimtzum. Much Hindu thought is highly characterized by panentheism and pantheism. Hasidic Judaism merges the elite ideal of nullification to paradoxical transcendent Divine Panentheism, through intellectual articulation of inner dimensions of Kabbalah, with the populist emphasis on the panentheistic Divine immanence in everything and deeds of kindness.

Such a concept is more compatible with God as personal while not barring a bridge between God and creation. Paul Tillich has argued for such a concept within Christian theology, as has liberal biblical scholar Marcus Borg and mystical theologian Matthew Fox, an Episcopal priest.

Pandeism

Pandeism or pan-deism (from Ancient Greek: ð¶v *pan* "all" and Latin: *deus* meaning "god" in the sense of deism), is a term describing beliefs coherently incorporating or mixing logically reconcilable elements of pantheism (that "God", or a metaphysically equivalent creator deity, is identical to Nature) and deism (that the creator-god who designed the universe no longer exists in a status where it can be reached, and can instead be confirmed only by reason). It is therefore most particularly the belief that the creator of the universe actually became the universe, and so ceased to exist as a separate entity.

Through this synergy pandeism claims to answer primary objections to deism (why would God create and then not interact with the universe?) and to pantheism (how did the universe originate and what is its purpose?).

Asian Traditions

Characteristics

The central problem in Asian (religious) philosophy is not the body-mind problem, but the search for an unchanging Real or Absolute beyond the world of appearances and changing phenomena, and the search for liberation from dukkha and the liberation from the cycle of rebirth. In Hinduism, substance-ontology prevails, seeing Brahman as the unchanging real beyond the world of appearances. In Buddhism process ontology is prevalent, seeing reality as empty of an unchanging essence.

Characteristic for various Asian religions is the discernment of levels of truth, an emphasis on intuitive-experiential understanding of the Absolute such as jnana, bodhi and kensho, and an emphasis on the integration of these levels of truth and its understanding.

Hinduism

Hinduism has a rich diversity of religious traditions and philosophies.

Purucârtha — Chief Aims of Human Life

Indian philosophy emphasizes that "every acceptable philosophy should aid man in realising the Purucârthas, the chief aims of human life:

- Dharma: the right way to life, the "duties and obligations of the individual toward himself and the society as well as those of the society toward the individual";

- Artha: the means to support and sustain one's life;
- Kâma: pleasure and enjoyment;
- Mokca: liberation, release.

According to Puligandla: Any philosophy worthy of its title should not be a mere intellectual exercise but should have practical application in enabling man to live an enlightened life. A philosophy which makes no difference to the quality and style of our life is no philosophy, but an empty intellectual construction.

Vedas

The Vedas are a large body of texts originating in ancient India. The texts constitute the oldest layer of Sanskrit literature and the oldest scriptures of Hinduism.

The Vedic texts or œruti are organised around four canonical collections of metrical material known as *SaChitâs*, of which the first three are related to the performance of yajna (sacrifice) in Vedic Hinduism:

1. The Rigveda, containing hymns to be recited by the hot[;
2. The Yajurveda, containing formulas to be recited by the adhvaryu or officiating priest;
3. The Samaveda, containing formulas to be sung by the udgât[.
4. The fourth is the Atharvaveda, a collection of spells and incantations, apotropaic charms and speculative hymns.

The various Indian philosophies and sects have taken differing positions on the Vedas. Schools of Indian philosophy which cite the Vedas as their scriptural authority are classified as "orthodox" (âstika). Other traditions, notably Buddhism and Jainism, which did not regard the Vedas as authorities are referred to by traditional Hindu texts as "heterodox" or "non-orthodox" (nâstika) schools.

According to Sehgal, "the Vedas and the Upanishads preach and propagate neither pantheism nor polytheism but monotheism and monism". There are many Gods, but they represent different aspect of the same Reality. Monism and monotheism are found intertwined. In many passages ultimate Reality is represented as immanent, while in other passaged ultimate Reality is represented as transcendent. Monism sees Brahman as the ultimate Reality, while monotheism represents the personal form of Brahman.

Jeaneane D. Fowler too discerns a "metaphysical monotheism" in the Vedas. The Vedas contain sparse monism. The Nasadiya Sukta of the Rigveda speaks of the One being-non-being that 'breathed without breath'. The manifest cosmos cannot be equated with it, "for "That" is a limitless, indescribable, absolute principle that can exist independently of it - otherwise it cannot be the Source of it." It is the closest the Vedas come to monism, but Fowler argues that this cannot be called a "superpersonal monism", nor "the quintessence of monistic thought", because it is "more expressive of a panentheistic, totally transcendent entity that can become manifest by its own power. It exists in itself, unmanifest, but with the potential for all manifestations of the cosmos".

Vedanta

Vedanta is the inquiry into and systematisation of the Vedas and Upanishds, to harmonise the various and contrasting ideas which can be found in those texts. Within Vedanta, different schools exist:

- Advaita Vedanta, of which Adi Shankara is the best-known representative;
- Vishishtadvaita, attributive monism, is from the school of Ramanuja;
- Shuddhadvaita, in-essence monism, is the school of Vallabha;
- Dvaitadvaita, differential monism, is a school founded by Nimbarka;
- Dvaita, dualism, is a school founded by Madhvacharya is probably the only Vedantic System which is opposed to all types of monism. It believes that God is eternally different from souls and matter in both form and essence.

Advaita Vedanta

Monism is most clearly identified in Advaita Vedanta, though Renard points out that this may be a western interpretation, bypassing the intuitive understanding of a nondual reality.

In Advaita Vedanta, Brahman is the eternal, unchanging, infinite, immanent, and transcendent reality which is the Divine Ground of all matter, energy, time, space, being, and everything beyond in this Universe. The nature of Brahman is described as transpersonal, personal and impersonal by different philosophical schools.

Advaita Vedanta gives an elaborate path to attain moksha. It entails more than self-inquiry or bare insight into one's real nature. Practice, especially Jnana Yoga, is needed to "destroy one's tendencies (vAasanA-s)" before real insight can be attained.

Advaita took over from the Madhyamika the idea of levels of reality. Usually two levels are being mentioned, but Shankara uses sublation as the criterion to postulate an ontological hierarchy of three levels:

- Pâramârthika (paramartha, absolute), the absolute level, "which is absolutely real and into which both other reality levels can be resolved". This experience can't be sublated by any other experience.
- Vyâvahârika (vyavahara), or samvriti-saya (empirical or pragmatical), "our world of experience, the phenomenal world that we handle every day when we are awake". It is the level in which both *jiva* (living creatures or individual souls) and *Iswara* are true; here, the material world is also true.
- Prâthibhâsika (pratibhasika, apparent reality, unreality), "reality based on imagination alone". It is the level in which appearances are actually false, like the illusion of a snake over a rope, or a dream.

Vaishnava

Vaishnavism is one of the major branches of Hinduism along with Shaivism, Smartism, and Shaktism. It is focused on the veneration of Vishnu. Vaishnavites, or the followers of the Supreme Lord Vishnu, lead a way of life promoting differentiated monotheism, which gives importance to Lord Vishnu and His ten incarnations.

All Vaishnava schools are panentheistic and view the universe as part of Krishna or Narayana, but see a plurality of souls and substances within Brahman. Monistic theism, which includes the concept of a personal god as a universal, omnipotent Supreme Being who is both immanent and transcendent, is prevalent within many other schools of Hinduism as well.

Tantra

Tantra sees the Divine as both immanent and transcendent. The Divine can be found in the concrete world. Practices are aimed at transforming the passions, instead of transcending them.

Tantra has been very influential in both Hinduism and Buddhism, where it is known as Vajrayana, but is relatively unknown in the west, apart from the popular interest in Tantric sexuality.

Modern Hinduism

The colonisation of India by the British had a major impact on Hindu society. In response, leading Hindu intellectuals started to study western culture and philosophy, integrating several western notions into Hinduism. This modernised Hinduism, at its turn, has gained popularity in the west.A major role was played in the 19th century by Swami Vivekananda in the revival of Hinduism, and the spread of

Advaita Vedanta to the west via the Ramakrishna Mission. His interpretation of Advaita Vedanta has been called "Neo-Vedanta".

Vivekananda emphasized samadhi as a means to attain liberation. Yet this emphasis is not to befound in the Upanishads nor with Shankara. For Shankara, meditation and Nirvikalpa Samadhi are means to gain knowledge of the already existing unity of Brahman and Atman, not the highest goal itself:

Yoga is a meditative exercise of withdrawal from the particular and identification with the universal, leading to contemplation of oneself as the most universal, namely, Consciousness. This approach is different from the classical Yoga of complete thought suppression.

Vivekananda's Modernisation has been Criticized: Without calling into question the right of any philosopher to interpret Advaita according to his own understanding of it, [...] the process of Westernization has obscured the core of this school of thought. The basic correlation of renunciation and Bliss has been lost sight of in the attempts to underscore the cognitive structure and the realistic structure which according to Sankaracharya should both belong to, and indeed constitute the realm of mâyâ.

Buddhism

Monism in Buddhism: According to the Pâli Canon, both pluralism (*nânatta*) and monism (*çkatta*) are speculative views. A Theravada commentary notes that the former is similar to or associated with nihilism (*ucchçdavâda*), and the latter is similar to or associated with eternalism (sassatavada).

In the Madhyamaka school of Mahayana Buddhism, the ultimate nature of the world is described as Úûnyatâ or "emptiness", which is inseparable from sensorial objects or anything else. That appears to be a monist position, but the Madhyamaka views - including variations like rangtong and shentong - will refrain from asserting any ultimately existent entity. They instead deconstruct any detailed or conceptual assertions about ultimate existence as resulting in absurd consequences. The Yogacara view, a minority school now only found among the Mahayana, also rejects monism.

Levels of Truth

Within Buddhism, a rich variety of philosophical and pedagogical models can be found. Various schools of Buddhism discern levels of truth:

- The Two truths doctrine of the Madhyamaka
- The Three Natures of the Yogacara

- Essence-Function, or Absolute-relative in Chinese and Korean Buddhism
- The Trikaya-formule, consisting of
  - o The *Dharmakâya* or *Truth body* which embodies the very principle of enlightenment and knows no limits or boundaries;
  - o The *Sambhogakâya* or *body of mutual enjoyment* which is a body of bliss or clear light manifestation;
  - o The *NirmâGakâya* or *created body* which manifests in time and space.

The Prajnaparamita-sutras and Madhyamaka emphasize the non-duality of form and emptiness: "form is emptiness, emptiness is form", as the heart sutra says. In Chinese Buddhism this was understood to mean that ultimate reality is not a transcendental realm, but equal to the daily world of relative reality. This idea fitted into the Chinese culture, which emphasized the mundane world and society. But this does not tell how the absolute is present in the relative world:

To deny the duality of samsara and nirvana, as the Perfection of Wisdom does, or to demonstrate logically the error of dichotomizing conceptualization, as Nagarjuna does, is not to address the question of the relationship between samsara and nirvana -or, in more philosophical terms, between phenomenal and ultimate reality [...] What, then, is the relationship between these two realms?

This question is answered in such schemata as the Five Ranks of Tozan, the Oxherding Pictures, and Hakuin's Four ways of knowing.

Abrahamic Faiths

Judaism

Jewish thought considers God as separate from all physical, created things (transcendent) and as existing outside of time (eternal).

According to Chasidic Thought (particularly as propounded by the 18th century, early 19th century founder of Chabad, Shneur Zalman of Liadi), God is held to be immanent within creation for two interrelated reasons:

1. A very strong Jewish belief is that "[t]he Divine life-force which brings [the universe] into existence must constantly be present... were this life-force to forsake [the universe] for even one brief moment, it would revert to a state of utter nothingness, as before the creation..."

2. Simultaneously, Judaism holds as axiomatic that God is an absolute unity, and that he is Perfectly Simple - thus if his sustaining power is within nature, then his essence is also within nature.

The Vilna Gaon was very much against this philosophy, for he felt that it would lead to pantheism and heresy. According to some this is the main reason for the Gaon's ban on Chasidism.

According to Maimonides, God is an incorporeal being that caused all other existence. In fact, God is defined as the necessary existent that caused all other existence. According to Maimonides, to admit corporeality to God is tantamount to admitting complexity to God, which is a contradiction to God as the First Cause and constitutes heresy. While Hasidic mystics considered the existence of the physical world a contradiction to God's simpleness, Maimonides saw no contradiction.

Christianity

Creator-creature Distinction: Much of Christianity strongly maintains the Creator-creature distinction as fundamental. Many Christians maintain that God created the universe ex nihilo and not from His own substance, so that the creator is not to be confused with creation, but rather transcends it (metaphysical dualism) (cf. Genesis). It is, however, within Him, as Saint Paul says in Acts 17:28, "in him we live and move and are." Even the more immanent concepts and theologies are to be defined together with God's omnipotence, omnipresence and omniscience, due to God's desire for intimate contact with his own creation (cf. Acts 17:27). Another use of the term "monism" is in Christian anthropology to refer to the innate nature of humankind as being holistic, as usually opposed to bipartite and tripartite views.

Rejection of Radical Dualism

While some might say the Christian metaphysics are dualistic in that they describe the Creator's transcendence of creation, they reject radical dualism such as the idea that God is eternally struggling with other equal powers such as Satan (cf. Gospel of John 14:30). In *On Free Choice of the Will*, Augustine argued, in the context of the problem of evil, that evil is not the opposite of good, but rather merely the absence of good, something that does not have existence in itself. Likewise, C. S. Lewis described evil as a "parasite" in *Mere Christianity*, as he viewed evil as something that cannot exist without good to provide it with existence. Lewis went on to argue against dualism from the basis of moral absolutism, and rejected the dualistic notion that God and Satan are opposites, arguing instead that God has no equal, hence no opposite.

Lewis rather viewed Satan as the opposite of Michael the archangel. Due to this, Lewis instead argued for a more limited type of dualism. Other theologians, such as Greg Boyd, have argued in more depth that the Biblical authors held a "limited dualism", meaning that God and Satan do engage in real battle, but only due to free will given by God, for the duration God allows.

Theosis

In Catholic and Orthodox Christianity, while human beings are not ontologically identical with the Creator, they are nonetheless capable with uniting with his Divine Nature via theosis, and especially, through the devout reception of the Holy Eucharist. This is a supernatural union, over and above that natural union, of which St. John of the Cross says, "it must be known that God dwells and is present substantially in every soul, even in that of the greatest sinner in the world, and this union is natural." Julian of Norwich, while maintaining the orthodox duality of Creator and creature, nonetheless speaks of God as "the true Father and true Mother" of all natures; thus, he indwells them substantially and thus preserves them from annihilation, as without this sustaining indwelling everything would cease to exist.

Christian Monism

Some Christian theologians are avowed monists, such as Paul Tillich. Since God is he "in whom we live and move and have our being" (Book of Acts 17.28), it follows that everything that has being partakes in God. Dualism with regard to God and creation also barred the possibility of a mystical union with God, as John Calvin rejected, according to Max Weber in *The Protestant Ethic and the Spirit of Capitalism*. Such a dualism also leads to the problematic position of positing God as a particular being the existence of which can be argued for or against, failing to recognise God as the ground and origin of being itself, as in Acts 17, or in Hashem, YHWH, meaning "He causes to come into being." Such a view was called by Tillich pantheism: God is in all things, neither identical to, nor totally separate from, all things.

Islam

Quran: According to Vincent J. Cornell, the Qur'an also provides a monist image of God by describing the reality as a unified whole, with God being a single concept that would describe or ascribe all existing things:

He is the First and the Last, the Outward and the Inward; He is the Knower of everything. (Sura 57:3)

Another Verse in the Quran is: To God belongs the East and the West, Wheresoever you look is the presence of Allah. (Sura 2:115)

Sufism

Many followers of Sufism advocated monism. Most notably the 13th-century Persian poet Jalal ad-Din Muhammad Balkhi-Rumi (1207–73) in his didactic poem Masnavi espoused monism. Rumi says in the Masnavi. In the shop for Unity (wahdat); anything that you see there except the One is an idol.

Bahá'í

Although the Bahá'v teachings have a strong emphasis on social and ethical issues, there exist a number of foundational texts that have been described as mystical. Some of these include statements of a monist nature (e.g. the *Seven Valleys* and the *Hidden Words*). The differences between dualist and monist views are reconciled by the teaching that these opposing viewpoints are caused by differences in the observers themselves, not in that what is observed. This is not a 'higher truth/ lower truth' position. God is unknowable. For man it is impossible to get any knowledge of God or the Absolute, because any knowledge that one has, is relative.

Non-dualism

"Nondualism" is a modern, western New religious movement, with a reflexive-monist understanding of reality. It is typified by a syncretistic understanding of various religious traditions. According to nondualism, many forms of religion are based on an experiential or intuitive understanding of "the Real". Nondualism, a modern reinterpretation of these religions, prefers the term "nondualism", instead of monism, because this understanding is "nonconceptual", "not graspapable in an idea".

To these nondual traditions belong Hinduism (including Vedanta, some forms of Yoga, and certain schools of Shaivism), Taoism, Pantheism, Rastafari and similar systems of thought. With increasing awareness of these systems of thought, the western spiritual and philosophical climate has seen a growing understanding of monism. Moreover, the New Thought and New Age movements embraced many monistic concepts during the twentieth century and continue up to the present day.

Religious Pluralism

Religious pluralism is an attitude or policy regarding the diversity of religious belief systems co-existing in society. It can indicate one or more of the following:

- As the name of the worldview according to which one's religion is not the sole and exclusive source of truth, and thus the acknowledgement that at least some truths and true values exist in other religions.
- As acceptance of the concept that two or more religions with mutually exclusive truth claims are equally valid. This may be considered a form of either toleration (a concept that arose as a result of the European wars of religion) or moral relativism.
- The understanding that the exclusive claims of different religions turn out, upon closer examination, to be variations of universal truths that have been taught since time immemorial. This is called *Perennialism* (based on the concept of *philosophia perennis*) or Traditionalism.
- Sometimes as a synonym for ecumenism, i.e., the promotion of some level of unity, co-operation, and improved understanding between different religions or different denominations within a single religion.
- As term for the condition of harmonious co-existence between adherents of different religions or religious denominations.
- As a social norm and not merely a synonym for religious diversity.

Definition and Scope

Religious pluralism, to paraphrase the title of a recent academic work, goes beyond mere toleration. Chris Beneke, in *Beyond Toleration: The Religious Origins of American Pluralism*, explains the difference between religious tolerance and religious pluralism by pointing to the situation in the late 18th century United States. By the 1730s, in most colonies religious minorities had obtained what contemporaries called religious toleration: "The policy of toleration relieved religious minorities of some physical punishments and some financial burdens, but it did not make them free from the indignities of prejudice and exclusion. Nor did it make them equal. Those 'tolerated' could still be barred from civil offices, military positions, and university posts." In short, religious toleration is only the absence of religious persecution, and does not necessarily preclude religious discrimination. However, in the following decades something extraordinary happened in the Thirteen Colonies, at least if one views the events from "a late eighteenth-century perspective". Gradually the colonial governments expanded the policy of religious toleration, but then, between the 1760s and the 1780s, they replaced it with "something that is usually called religious liberty". Mark Silka, in "Defining Religious Pluralism in America: A Regional Analysis", states that Religious pluralism "enables a country made up of people of different faiths to exist without sectarian warfare or the persecution of religious minorities. Understood differently in different times and places, it is a cultural construct that embodies some shared conception of how a country's various religious communities relate to each other and to the larger nation whole."

Religious pluralism can be defined as "respecting the otherness of others". Freedom of religion encompasses all religions acting within the law in a particular region. Exclusivist religions teach that theirs is the only way to salvation and to religious truth, and some of them would even argue that it is necessary to suppress the falsehoods taught by other religions. Some Protestant sects argue fiercely against Roman Catholicism, and fundamentalist Christians of all kinds teach that religious practices like those of paganism and witchcraft are pernicious. This was a common historical attitude prior to the Enlightenment, and has appeared as governmental policy into the present day under systems like Afghanistan's Taliban regime, which destroyed the ancient Buddhas of Bamyan.

Giving one religion or denomination special rights that are denied to others can weaken religious pluralism. This situation was observed in Europe through the Lateran Treaty and Church of England. In modern era, many Islamic countries have laws that criminalize the act of leaving Islam to someone born in Muslim family, forbid entry to non-Muslims into Mosques, and forbit construction of Church, Synagogue or Temples inside their countries.

Relativism, the belief that all religions are equal in their value and that none of the religions gives access to absolute truth, is an extreme form of inclusivism. Likewise, syncretism, the attempt to take over creeds of practices from other religions or even to blend practices or creeds from different religions into one new faith is an extreme form of inter-religious dialogue. Syncretism must not be confused with ecumenism, the attempt to bring closer and eventually reunite different denominations of one religion that have a common origin but were separated by a schism.

History

Cultural and religious pluralism has a long history and development that reaches from antiquity to contemporary trends in post-modernity. Fuerbauch and Ernst Troeltsch concluded that Asian religious traditions, in particular Hinduism and Buddhism were earliest proponents of religious pluralism and granting of freedom to the individual to choose the faith and develop a personal religious construct within it. Jainism, another ancient Indian religion, as well as Daoism have also always been inclusively flexible and have long favoured religious pluralism for those who disagree with their religious viewpoints. The Age of Enlightenment in Europe triggered a sweeping transformation about religion, segregation of state and religion, with rising acceptance of religious pluralism. These pluralist trends in Western thought, particularly since the 18th century, brought mainstream Christianity and Judaism closer to the Asian traditions of philosophical pluralism, states Chad Meister.

Discussion

Buddhism: The earliest reference to Buddhist views on religious pluralism in a political sense is found in the Edicts of Emperor Ashoka:

All religions should reside everywhere, for all of them desire self-control and purity of heart. Rock Edict Nb7 (S. Dhammika)

Contact (between religions) is good. One should listen to and respect the doctrines professed by others. Beloved-of-the-Gods, King Piyadasi, desires that all should be well-learned in the good doctrines of other religions. Rock Edict Nb12 (S. Dhammika)

When asked, "Don't all religions teach the same thing? Is it possible to unify them?" the Dalai Lama said:

People from different traditions should keep their own, rather than change. However, some Tibetan may prefer Islam, so he can follow it. Some Spanish prefer Buddhism; so follow it. But think about it carefully. Don't do it for fashion. Some people start Christian, follow Islam, then Buddhism, then nothing.

In the United States I have seen people who embrace Buddhism and change their clothes! Like the New Age. They take something Hindu, something Buddhist, something, something... That is not healthy.

For individual practitioners, having one truth, one religion, is very important. Several truths, several religions, is contradictory.

I am Buddhist. Therefore, Buddhism is the only truth for me, the only religion. To my Christian friend, Christianity is the only truth, the only religion. To my Muslim friend, [Islam] is the only truth, the only religion. In the meantime, I respect and admire my Christian friend and my Muslim friend. If by unifying you mean mixing, that is impossible, useless.

Classical Greek and Roman Paganism

Ancient Greeks employed *Interpretatio Graeca* whereby the gods of other religions were equated with those of their own pantheon. The Romans easily accomplished this task by subsuming the entire set of gods from other faiths into their own religion. This was done on rare occasion by adding a new god to their own pantheon; on most occasions they identified another religion's gods with their own.

Because divinity was the basis for the mandate of the state, atheism was considered a capital crime in both ancient Greece and Rome. This was further solidified as the *status quo* following the installation of the Roman imperial cult of deification of sitting emperors, and Roman pluralism was not officially extended to Christianity until the Edict of Milan in 313 CE.

Christianity

Some Christians have argued that religious pluralism is an invalid or self-contradictory concept. Maximal forms of religious pluralism claim that all religions are equally true, or that one religion can be true for some and another for others. Some Christians hold this idea to be logically impossible from the Principle of contradiction.

Other Christians have held that there can be truth value and salvific value in other faith traditions. John Macquarrie, described in the *Handbook of Anglican Theologians* (1998) as "unquestionably Anglicanism's most distinguished systematic theologian in the second half of the twentieth century", wrote that "there should be an end to proselytizing but that equally there should be no syncretism of the kind typified by the Baha'i movement" (p. 2). In discussing 9 founders of major faith traditions (Moses, Zoroaster, Lao-zu, Buddha, Confucius, Socrates, Krishna, Jesus, and Muhammad), which he called "mediators between the human and the divine", Macquarrie wrote that:

I do not deny for a moment that the truth of God has reached others through other channels - indeed, I hope and pray that it has. So while I have a special attachment to one mediator, I have respect for them all. (p. 12)

The Church of Jesus Christ of Latter-day Saints also teaches a form of religious pluralism, that there is at least some truth in almost all religions and philosophies.

Classical Christian Views

Before the Great Schism, mainstream Christianity confessed "one holy catholic and apostolic church", in the words of the Nicene Creed.

Roman Catholics, Orthodox Christians, Episcopalians and most Protestant Christian denominations still maintain this belief.

Church unity was something very visible and tangible, and schism was just as serious an offence as heresy. Following the Great Schism, Roman Catholicism sees and recognises the Orthodox Sacraments as valid. Eastern Orthodoxy does not have the concept of "validity" when applied to Sacraments, but it considers the *form* of Roman Catholic Sacraments to be acceptable, if still devoid of actual spiritual content. Both generally regard each other as "heterodox" and "schismatic", while continuing to recognise each other as Christian.

Modern Christian Views

Some Protestants hold that only believers which believe in certain fundamental doctrines know the true pathway to salvation. The core of this doctrine is that Jesus Christ was a perfect man, is the Son of God and that he died and rose again for the wrongdoing of those who will accept the gift of salvation. They continue to believe in "one" church, believing in fundamental issues there is unity and non-fundamental issues there is liberty. Some evangelicals are doubtful if the Roman Catholicism or Eastern Orthodoxy are still valid manifestations of the Church and usually reject religious (typically restorationist) movements rooted in 19th century American Christianity, such as Mormonism, Christian Science, or Jehovah's Witnesses as not distinctly Christian.

Hinduism

Hinduism is naturally pluralistic. A well-known *Rig Vedic* hymn says: "Truth is One, though the sages know it variously" (*Ékam sat vipra bahudâ vadanti*). Similarly, in the *Bhagavad Gîtâ* (4:11), God, manifesting as an incarnation, states: "As people approach me, so I receive them. All paths lead to me" (*ye yathâ mâC prapadyante tâCs tathâiva bhajâmyaham mama vartmânuvartante manucyâ% pârtha sarvaúa%*). The Hindu religion has no theological difficulties in accepting degrees of truth in other religions. Hinduism emphasizes that everyone actually worships the same God, whether one knows it or not. Just as Hindus worshipping Ganesh is seen as valid by those worshipping Vishnu, so someone worshipping Jesus or Allah is accepted. Many *foreign* deities become assimilated into Hinduism, and some Hindus may sometimes offer prayers to Jesus along with their traditional forms of God.

Islam

Religious pluralism is a controversial subject in Islam. The primary sources that guide Islam, namely Quran and Hadiths, offer contradictory positions on religious pluralism. Some verses support religious pluralism, while others discourage it. The acceptability of religious pluralism within Islam remains a topic of active debate.

Acceptability of Religious Pluralism in Islam

In several Surah, Quran asks Muslims to remain steadfast with Islam, and not yield to the vain desires of other religions and unbelievers. These verses have been interpreted to imply pluralism in religions. For example, Surah Al-Ma'idah verses 47 through 49 state:

Let the people of the Gospel judge by what Allah hath revealed therein. If any do fail to judge by the light of what Allah hath revealed, they are no better than those who rebel. To thee We sent the Scripture in truth, confirming the scripture that came before it, and guarding it in safety: so judge between them by what Allah hath revealed, and follow not their vain desires, diverging from the Truth that hath come to thee. To each among you have we prescribed a law and an open way. If Allah had so willed, He would have made you a single people, but His plan is to test you in what He hath given you: so strive as in a race in all virtues. The goal of you all is to Allah; it is He that will show you the truth of the matters in which ye dispute; And this (He commands): Judge thou between them by what Allah hath revealed, and follow not their vain desires, but beware of them lest they beguile thee from any of that (teaching) which Allah hath sent down to thee. And if they turn away, be assured that for some of their crime it is Allah's purpose to punish them. And truly most men are rebellious. (Quran 5:47–49)

Surah Al-Ankabut verse 45 Through 47 State: Recite what is sent of the Book by inspiration to thee, and establish regular Prayer: for Prayer restrains from shameful and unjust deeds; and remembrance of Allah is the greatest thing in life without doubt. And Allah knows the deeds that ye do. And dispute ye not with the People of the Book, except with means better than mere disputation, unless it be with those of them who inflict wrong (and injury): but say, "We believe in the revelation which has come down to us and in that which came down to you; Our Allah and your Allah is one; and it is to Him we bow in Islam." And thus it is that We have sent down the Book to thee. So the People of the Book believe therein, as also do some of these pagan Arabs: and none but Unbelievers reject our signs. (Quran 29:45–47)

Surah Al-E-Imran Verses 62 Through 66 State: This is the true account: There is no god except Allah; and Allah-He is indeed the Exalted in Power, the Wise. But if they turn back, Allah hath full knowledge of those who do mischief. Say: "O People of the Book! come to common terms as between us and you: That we worship none but Allah; that we associate no partners with him; that we erect not, from among ourselves, Lords and patrons other than Allah." If then they turn back, say ye: "Bear witness that we at least are Muslims bowing to Allah's Will. Ye People of the Book! Why dispute ye about Abraham, when the Law and the Gospel Were not revealed Till after him? Have ye no understanding? Ah! Ye are those who fell to disputing even in matters of which ye had some knowledge! but why dispute ye in matters of which ye have no knowledge? It is Allah Who knows, and ye who know not! (Quran 3:62–66)

Surah Al-Kafiroon Verse 1 Through 6 State

Say : O ye that reject Faith! I worship not that which ye worship, nor will ye worship that which I worship. And I will not worship that which ye have been wont to worship, nor will ye worship that which I worship. To you be your Way, and to me mine. (Quran 109:1–6)

Unacceptability of Religious Pluralism in Islam

In several Surah, Quran asks Muslims to persecute the unbelievers, Christians, Jews, pagan (idol worshippers, polytheists), apostates or those who reject Islam. These verses have been interpreted to imply rejection of religious pluralism by Islam. For example, Surah Al-Tawba verse 1 through 5 asks the Muslim to slay the pagans (with verse 9.5 called the 'sword verse' in scholarly literature,):

A (declaration) of immunity from Allah and His Messenger, to those of the Pagans with whom ye have contracted mutual alliances:- Go ye, then, for four months, backwards and forwards, (as ye will), throughout the land, but know ye that ye cannot frustrate Allah (by your falsehood) but that Allah will cover with shame those who reject Him. And an announcement from Allah and His Messenger, to the people (assembled) on the day of the Great Pilgrimage,- that Allah and His Messenger dissolve (treaty) obligations with the Pagans. If then, ye repent, it were best for you; but if ye turn away, know ye that ye cannot frustrate Allah. And proclaim a grievous penalty to those who reject Faith. But when the forbidden months are past, then fight and slay the Pagans wherever ye find them, seize them, beleaguer them, and lie in wait for them in every stratagem of war; but if they repent, and establish regular prayers and practise regular charity, then open the way for them: for Allah is Oft-forgiving, Most Merciful. (Quran 9:1–5)

In Surah Al-Tawba, verse 29 demands Muslims to fight all who do not believe in Islam, including Christians and Jews (People of the Book), until they pay the Jizya with willing submission.

Fight those who believe not in Allah nor the Last Day, nor hold that forbidden which hath been forbidden by Allah and His Messenger, nor acknowledge the religion of Truth, even if they are of the People of the Book, until they pay the Jizya with willing submission, and feel themselves subdued. (Quran 9:29)

In Surah Al-Nisa, verse 89 Demands Muslims to slay the Apostates.

They but wish that ye should reject Faith, as they do, and thus be on the same footing as they: But take not friends from their ranks until they flee in the way of Allah from what is forbidden. But if they turn renegades, seize them and slay them wherever ye find them; and (in any case) take no friends or helpers from their ranks. (Quran 4:89)

In Surah Al-Bayyina verses 6 through 7 calls People of the Book and Polytheists who reject truth revealed by Islam as worst of creatures:

Those who reject Truth [Islam], among the People of the Book and among the Polytheists, will be in Hell-Fire, to dwell therein for aye. They are the worst of creatures. Those who have faith and do righteous deeds - they are the best of creatures. (Quran 98:6–7)

In Modern Practice

Religious pluralism is a contested issue in modern Islamic countries. Twenty three (23) Islamic countries have laws, as of 2014, which make it a crime, punishable with death penalty or prison, for a Muslim, by birth or conversion, to leave Islam or convert to another religion. In Muslim countries such as Algeria, it is illegal to preach, persuade or attempt to covert a Muslim to another religion. Saudi Arabia and several Islamic nations have strict laws against the construction of Christian Church, Jewish Synagogue, Hindu Temple and Buddhist Stupa anywhere inside the country, by anyone including minorities working there. Brunei in southeast Asia adopted Sharia law in 2013 that prescribes a death penalty for any Muslim who coverts from Islam to another religion. Other Islamic scholars state Sharia does not allow non-Muslim minorities to enjoy religious freedoms in a Muslim-majority nation.

Sufism

The Sufis were practitioners of the esoteric mystic traditions within an Islam at a certain point. Sufism is defined by the Sufi master or Pir (Sufism) or fakeer or Wali in the language of the people by dancing and singing and incorporating various philosophies, theologies, ideologies and religions together (e.g., Christianity, Judaism, Paganism, Platonism, Zoroastrianism, Buddhism, Hinduism, Sikhism and so forth with time). Famous Sufi masters are Rumi, Shadhili, Sheikh Farid, Bulleh Shah, Shah Hussain, Shams Tabrizi, Waris Shah, Ghazali, Mian Mir, Attar of Nishapur, Amir Khusrow, Salim Chishti. See many more famous Sufis at the List of Sufis. The Sufis were considered by many to have divine revelations with messages of peace, tolerance, equality, pluralism, love for all and hate for no one, humanitarians, philosophers, psychologists and much more. Many had the teaching if you want to change the world, change yourself and you will change the whole world. The views of the Sufi poets, philosophers and theologians have inspired multiple forms of modern day academia as well as philosophers of other religions.

Persian Poet Rumi Says: I looked for God. I went to a temple, and I didn't find him there. Then I went to a church, and I didn't find him there. And then I went to a mosque, and I didn't find him there. And then finally I looked in my heart, and there he was.

Rumi also Says: How many paths are there to God? There are as many paths to God as there are souls on the Earth.

Rumi also Says: A true Lover doesn't follow any one religion, be sure of that. Since in the religion of Love, there is no irreverence or faith. When in Love, body, mind, heart and soul don't even exist. Become this, fall in Love, and you will not be separated again.

The Sufi platform was considered by exoteric dogmatic Muslims as a trojan horse ideology executing doctrine of deception to convert others while others considered it outright heresy, blasphemy, innovation (biddah), kuffar, apostasy, haram. Many Sufis have gone under persecutions and executions for apostasy and treason charges at which point many tended to have supernatural events taking place similar to Jesus crucifixion. For example, many Sufis throughout their lives display religious healing, miracles and supernatural events which seem as if God has connected with the Sufis similar to the Vedic and Buddhist enlightenment.

Ahmadiyya

Ahmadis recognise many founders of world religions to be from God, who all brought teaching and guidance from God to all peoples. According to the Ahmadiyya understanding of the Quran, every nation in the history of mankind has been sent a prophet, as the Quran states: *And there is a guide for every people.* Though the Quran mentions only 24 prophets, the founder of Islam, Muhammad states that the world has seen 124,000 prophets. Thus other than the prophets mentioned in the Quran, Ahmadis, with support from theological study also recognise Buddha, Krishna, founders of Chinese religions to be divinely appointed individuals.

The Second Khalifatul Maish of the Ahmadiyya Muslim Community writes: "According to this teaching there has not been a single people at any time in history or anywhere in the world who have not had a warner from God, a teacher, a prophet. According to the Quran there have been prophets at all times and in all countries. India, China, Russia, Afghanistan, parts of Africa, Europe, America—all had prophets according to the theory of divine guidance taught by the Quran. When, therefore, Muslims hear about prophets of other peoples or other countries, they do not deny them. They do not brand them as liars. Muslims believe that other peoples have had their teachers. If other peoples have had prophets, books, and laws, these constitute no difficulty for Islam."

Mirza Ghulam Ahmad, founder of the Ahmadiyya Muslim Community wrote in his book *A Message of Peace*: "Our God has never discriminated between one people and another. This is illustrated by the fact that all the potentials and capabilities (Prophets) which have been granted to the Aryans (Hindus) have also been granted to the races inhabiting Arabia, Persia, Syria, China, Japan, Europe and America."

Bahá'í Faith

Bahá'u'lláh, founder of Bahá'í Faith, a religion with roots in Islam but currently not a sect of Islam, urged the elimination of religious intolerance. He taught that God is one, and has manifested himself to humanity through several historic messengers. Bahá'u'lláh taught that Bahá'ís must associate with peoples of all religions, showing the love of God in relations with them, whether this is reciprocated or not.

Bahá'í's refer to the concept of Progressive revelation, which means that God's will is revealed to mankind progressively as mankind matures and is better able to comprehend the purpose of God in creating humanity. In this view, God's word is revealed through a series of messengers: Abraham, Krishna, Moses, Buddha, Jesus, Mohammed, and Bahá'u'lláh (the founder of the Bahá'í Faith) among them. In the *Kitáb-i-Íqán* (*Book of Certitude*), Bahá'u'lláh explains that messengers of God have a twofold station, one of divinity and one of an individual. According to Bahá'í writings, there will not be another messenger for many hundreds of years. There is also a respect for the religious traditions of the native peoples of the planet who may have little other than oral traditions as a record of their religious figures.

Jainism

Anekântavâda, the principle of relative pluralism, is one of the basic principles of Jainism. In this view, the truth or the reality is perceived differently from different points of view, and no single point of view is the complete truth. Jain doctrine states that an object has infinite modes of existence and qualities and they cannot be completely perceived in all its aspects and manifestations, due to inherent limitations of the humans. Only the Kevalins—the omniscient beings—can comprehend the object in all its aspects and manifestations, and all others are capable of knowing only a part of it. Consequently, no one view can claim to represent the absolute truth. Jains compare all attempts to proclaim absolute truth with *andhgajnyaya* or the "maxim of the blind men and elephant", wherein all the blind men claimed to explain the true appearance of the elephant, but could only partly succeed due to their narrow perspective.

Judaism

The Mosaic law categorically warns the Jews to refrain from polytheism. First and the second commandment, you shall not have another God except me, worship your God with all your heart and with all your soul. Throughout the Hebrew Bible the sovereignty of Yahweh as the only God is the key pillar of a chosen community of Israel.

Sikhism

The Sikh Gurus (religious leaders) have propagated the message of "many paths" leading to the one God and ultimate salvation for all souls who treading on the path of righteousness. They have supported the view that proponents of all faiths, by doing good and virtuous deeds and by remembering the Lord, can certainly achieve salvation. Sikhs are told to accept all leading faiths as possible vehicles for attaining spiritual enlightenment, provided the faithful study, ponder and practice the teachings of their prophets and leaders. Sikhism had many interactions with Sufism as well as Hinduism, influenced them and was influenced by them.

The Holy Book of the Sikhs (the Sri Guru Granth Sahib) Says: Do not say that the Vedas and the Koran (semitic books i.e. Bible, Torah and Q'uran) are false. Those who do not contemplate them are false. (Guru Granth Sahib page 1350)

As Well as: Some call the Lord "Ram, Ram", and some "Khuda". Some serve Him as "Gusain", others as "Allah". He is the Cause of causes, and Generous. He showers His Grace and Mercy upon us. Some pilgrims bathe at sacred shrines, others go on Hajj to Mecca. Some do devotional worship, whilst others bow their heads in prayer. Some read the Vedas, and some the Koran. Some wear blue robes, and some wear white. Some call themselves Muslim, and some call themselves Hindu. Some yearn for paradise, and others long for heaven. Says Nanak, one who realises the Hukam of God's Will, knows the secrets of his Lord Master. (Sri Guru Granth Sahib Page:885)

One who recognises that all spiritual paths lead to the One shall be emancipated. One who speaks lies shall fall into hell and burn. In all the world, the most blessed and sanctified are those who remain absorbed in Truth. (SGGS Ang 142) The seconds, minutes, and hours, days, weeks and months and various seasons originate from One Sun; O nanak, in just the same way, the many forms originate from the Creator. (Guru Granth Sahib page 12,13)

The Guru Granth Sahib also says that Bhagat Namdev and Bhagat Kabir, who were both believed to be Hindus, both attained salvation though they were born before Sikhism took root and were clearly not Sikhs. This highlights and reinforces the Guru's saying that "peoples of other faiths" can join with God as true and also at the same time signify that Sikhism is not the exclusive path for liberation.

Additionally the Guru Granth Sahib Says: First, Allah (God) created the Light; then, by His Creative Power, He made all mortal beings. From the One Light, the entire universe welled up. So who is good, and who is bad? | |1| |

Again, the Guru Granth Sahib Provides this Verse: Naam Dayv the printer, and Kabeer the weaver, obtained salvation through the Perfect Guru. Those who know God and recognise His Shabad ("word") lose their ego and class consciousness. (Guru Granth Sahib page 67) Most of the 15 Sikh Bhagats who are mentioned in their holy book were non-Sikhs and belonged to Hindu and Muslim faiths, which were the most prevalent religions of this region.

The pluralistic dialogue of Sikhism began with the founder of Sikhism Guru Nanak after becoming enlightened saying the words *Na koi hindu na koi musalman* - "There is no Hindu, there is no Muslim". He recognised that religious labels held no value and it is the deeds of human that will be judged in the hereafter what we call ourselves religiously holds no value.

Sikhs have always being eager exponents of interfaith dialogue and will not only accept the right of other to practise their faith but have in the past fought and laid down their lives to protect this right for others. The sacrifice of the ninth Sikh Guru, Guru Tegh Bahadar who on the final desperate and heart-rending pleas of the Kashmiri

Pandit, agreed to put up a fight for their right to practise their religion in which he was executed so another religion besides his own could have the freedom to practice their religion against the tyrant moghul empire who were forcing people to accept Islam.

Religious Pluralism and Human Service Professions

The concept of religious pluralism is also relevant to human service professions, such as psychology and social work, as well as medicine and nursing, in which trained professionals may interact with clients from diverse faith traditions. For example, psychologist Kenneth Pargament has described four possible stances toward client religious and spiritual beliefs, which he called *rejectionist*, *exclusivist*, *constructivist*, and *pluralist*. Unlike the constructivist stance, the pluralist stance:

> *...recognises the existence of a religious or spiritual absolute reality but allows for multiple interpretations and paths toward it. In contrast to the exclusivist who maintains that there is a single path "up the mountain of God," the pluralist recognises many paths as valid. Although both the exclusivist and the pluralist may agree on the existence of religious or spiritual reality, the pluralist recognises that this reality is expressed in different cultures and by different people in different ways. Because humans are mortal and limited, a single human religious system cannot encompass all of the religious or spiritual absolute reality.... (p. 167)*

Importantly, "the pluralistic therapist can hold personal religious beliefs while appreciating those of a client with different religious beliefs. The pluralist recognises that religious value differences can and will exist between counsellors and clients without adversely affecting therapy" (p. 168). The stances implied by these four helping orientations on several key issues, such as "should religious issues be discussed in counselling?", have also been presented in tabular form.

The profession of chaplaincy, a religious profession, must also deal with issues of pluralism and the relevance of a pluralistic stance. For example, Friberg (2001) argues: "With growing populations of immigrants and adherents of religions not previously seen in significant numbers in North America, spiritual care must take religion and diversity seriously. Utmost respect for the residents' spiritual and religious histories and orientations is imperative" (p. 182).

Chapter 5

Religion and Science

The Nature of Science and the Nature of Religion

Science

The first thing to say, here, is that it is exceedingly difficult to characterize these phenomena. First, consider science: what exactly is science? How can we characterize it? What are the necessary and sufficient conditions for a given inquiry or theory or claim to be scientific, a part of science? This is far from easy to say. Many conditions have been proposed as essential to science. According to Jacques Monod, "The cornerstone of the scientific method is the postulate that nature is objective.... In other words, the *systematic* denial that 'true' knowledge can be got by interpreting nature in terms of final causes ..." (Monod 1971, 21, Monod's emphasis). In the 1930s, the eminent German Chemist Walther Nernst claimed that science, by definition, requires an infinite universe; hence Big Bang theory, he said, isn't science (von Weizsäcker 1964, 151). Another proposed constraint: science can't involve moral judgments, or value judgments more generally.

Clearly there is an intimate connection between the nature of science and its aim, the conditions under which something is *successful* science. Some say the aim of science is explanation (whether or not this is put in the service of truth). Some (realists) say the aim of science is to produce *true* theories; others say the aim of science is to produce *empirically adequate* theories, whether or not they are true (van Fraassen 1980). Some say science can't deal with the subjective, but only with what is public and sharable (and thus reports of consciousness are a better subject for scientific study than consciousness itself). Some say that science can deal only with what is repeatable; others deny this. In the furor, over the teaching of "Intelligent Design" (ID) in public schools, some have said that scientific theories must be *falsifiable*, and, since the proposition that living things (rabbits, say) have been designed by one or more intelligent designers isn't falsifiable, ID isn't science. Others point out that many eminently scientific claims—for example, *there are electrons*—aren't falsifiable in isolation: what is falsifiable are whole *theories* about electrons. And while the proposition *living things have been designed by an intelligent being* is not falsifiable in isolation, the proposition *an intelligent being has designed and created 800 lb. rabbits that live in Cleveland* is clearly falsifiable (and false). The first group may reply that this proposition about 800 lb. rabbits is really just equivalent to its empirical implications, i.e., to the proposition that there are 800 lb. rabbits that live in Cleveland, so that the bit about the designer really drops out. The second group may then retort that if so, the same must hold for theories about electrons; but then theories about electrons are really just equivalent to their empirical implications, so that electrons drop out.

Still others claim that science is constrained by 'methodological naturalism' (MN)—the idea that neither the data for a scientific investigation nor a scientific theory can properly refer to supernatural beings (God, angels, demons); thus one couldn't properly propose (as part of science) a theory according to which the recent outbreak of weird and irrational behaviour in Washington D.C. is to be accounted for in terms of increased demonic behaviour in that neighbourhood. How do we know that MN really is an essential constraint on science? Some claim that it is simply a matter of definition; thus Nancey Murphy: "... there is what we might call *methodological atheism,* which is by definition common to all natural science" (Murphy 2001, 464). She continues: "This is simply the principle that scientific explanations are to be in terms of natural (not supernatural) entities and processes". Similarly for Michael Ruse: "The Creationists believe that the world started miraculously. But miracles lie outside of science, which by definition deals only with the natural, the repeatable, that which is governed by law" (Ruse 1982, 322).

By definition of what? By definition of the term 'science' one supposes. But others then ask: what about the Big Bang: if it turns out to be unrepeatable, must we conclude that it can't be studied scientifically? And consider the claim that science, by definition, deals only with that which is governed by law—natural law, one supposes. Some empiricists (in particular, Bas van Fraassen) argue that there *aren't* any natural laws (but only regularities): if they are right, would it follow that there is nothing at all for science to study? Still further, while some people argue that MN is an essential constraint on science, others dispute this: but can a serious dispute be settled just by citing a definition?

Giving plausible necessary and sufficient conditions for science, therefore, is far from trivial; and many philosophers of science have given up on the "demarcation problem," the problem of proposing such conditions (Laudan 1988). Perhaps the best we can do is point to paradigmatic examples of science and paradigmatic examples of non-science. Of course it may be a mistake to suppose that there is just *one* activity here, and just one aim. The sciences are enormously varied; there is the sort of activity that goes on in highly theoretical branches of physics (for example, investigating what happened during the first 10^{-43}seconds, or trying to figure out how to subject string theory to empirical check). But there is also the sort of project exemplified by an attempt to learn how the population of touconderos has responded to the decimation of the Amazon jungle over the last 25 years. In the first kind of account it may make sense to think what is desired is an empirically adequate theory, with the question of the truth of the theory at least temporarily bracketed. Not so in cases of the second kind; here nothing but the sober truth will do.

Similarly with methodological naturalism. Some scientific projects are clearly constrained by MN; a condition for theoretical adequacy, for them, will certainly be that the account in question is naturalistic. But is MN just part of the very nature of science as such? According to Isaac Newton, often said to be the greatest scientist of all time, the orbits of the planets would decay into chaos without outside intervention; he therefore proposed that God periodically adjusted their orbits. While that hypothesis is one of which we no longer have need, is it clear that its addition to Newton's account of the motions of the planets resulted in something that wasn't science at all? That seems unduly harsh.

Perhaps we should think of the concept of science as one of those cluster concepts called to our attention by Thomas Aquinas and Ludwig Wittgenstein. Perhaps there are several quite different activities that go under the name 'science'; these activities are related to each other by similarity and analogy, but there is no one single activity which is just science as such. There are projects for which the criterion of success involves producing *true* theories; there are others where the criterion of success involves producing theories that are empirically adequate, whether or not they are also true. There are projects constrained by

MN; there are other projects that are not so constrained. These projects or activities all fall under the meaning of the term 'science'; but there is no single activity of which all are examples. (In the same way, chess, basketball and poker are all games; but there is no single game of which they are all versions.) Perhaps the best we can do, with respect to characterizing science, is to say that the term 'science' applies to any activity that is (1) a systematic and disciplined enterprise aimed at finding out truth about our world, and (2) has significant empirical involvement. This is of course vague (How systematic? How disciplined? How much empirical involvement?) and perhaps unduly permissive. (Does astrology count as science, even if only bad science?) Still, we do have many excellent examples of science, and excellent examples of non-science.

Religion

If it is difficult to give an account of the nature of science, it is not much easier to say just what a religion is. Of course there are multifarious examples: Christianity, Islam, Judaism, Hinduism, Buddhism and many others. What characteristics are necessary and sufficient for something's being a religion? How does one distinguish a religion from a way of life, such as Confucianism? That's not easy to say. Not all religions involve belief in something like the almighty and all-knowing, morally perfect God of the theistic religions, or even in any supernatural beings at all. (Of course a substantial majority of them do.) With respect to our present inquiry, what is of special importance is the notion of a religious *belief*: what does a belief have to be like to be religious?

Once more, that's not easy to say. To cite the furor over intelligent design again, some say the proposition that there is an intelligent designer of the living world is religion, not science. But not just any belief involving an intelligent designer, indeed, not just any belief involving God, is automatically religious. According to the New Testament book of James, "the devils believe [that God exists] and tremble"; the devils' beliefs, presumably, aren't religious. Someone might propose theories about an omnipotent, omniscient and wholly good being as a key part of a metaphysical system: belief in such theories need not be religious. And what about a system of beliefs that answers the same great human questions answered by the clear examples of religion: questions about the fundamental nature of the universe and what is most real and basic in it, about the place of human beings in that universe, about whether there is such a thing as sin or an analogue, and if there is, what there is to be done about it, where we must look to improve the human condition, whether human beings survive their deaths and how a rational person should act? Will any system of beliefs that provides answers to those questions count as a religion? Again, not easy to say; probably not. The truth here, perhaps, is that a belief isn't religious *just in itself*. The property of being religious isn't intrinsic to a belief; it is rather one a belief acquires when it functions in a certain way in the life of a given person or community. To be a religious belief, the belief in question would have to be appropriately connected with characteristically religious attitudes on the part of the believer, such attitudes as worship, love, commitment, awe, and the like. Consider someone who believes that there is such a person as God, all right, because the existence of God helps with several metaphysical problems (for example, the nature of causation, the nature of propositions, properties and sets, and the nature of proper function in creatures that are not human artifacts). However, this person has no inclination to worship or love God, no commitment to try to further God's projects in our world; perhaps, like the devils, he hates God and intentionally does whatever he can to frustrate God's purposes in the world. For such a person, belief that there is such a person as God need not be a religious belief. In this way it's possible that a pair of people share a given belief which functions as a religious belief in the life of only one of them.

It is therefore extremely difficult to give (informative) necessary and sufficient conditions for either science or religion. Perhaps for present purposes that is not a really serious problem; we do have many excellent examples of each, and perhaps that will suffice for our inquiry.

Epistemology and Science and Religion

There are many interesting epistemological questions about science. A central topic has been the under determination of theory by evidence: evidence for a theory seldom entails the theory, in which case there will be several empirically equivalent theories—theories with the same consequences with respect to experience. Can empirically equivalent theories differ in epistemic status or value? If so, what makes the difference? Here it is common to appeal to the so-called theoretical virtues, such as simplicity, fecundity, beauty and the like. What shall we think of the "pessimistic induction" according to which nearly all past scientific theories have been later rejected; should that reduce our confidence in present scientific theories? How much, if any, of current scientific lore constitutes knowledge? And how far does the scientific method reach? Are there subjects science isn't competent to deal with? Is science more competent to deal with some subjects than others? Scientific modes of procedure seem to have been most successful in the hard sciences; the human sciences seem to lag. Are there differences in epistemic well-foundedness between different sciences, or perhaps between the hard sciences and the softer sciences? Questions of this sort, while of great intrinsic interest, aren't directly relevant to our present inquiry. What is most important to see is that the epistemology of science is really the epistemology of the main human cognitive faculties: memory, perception, rational intuition (logic and mathematics), testimony, perhaps Reid's sympathy, induction, and the like. What is characteristic of science is that these faculties are employed in a particularly disciplined and systematic way, and that there is particular emphasis upon perceptual experience.

With respect to religious belief, there are also several sorts of epistemological questions. Are there good arguments for the existence of God? If there aren't, does it matter? Is the existence of evil, in all the horrifying forms it displays, *evidence against* theistic belief? Does it constitute a *defeater* for theistic belief? What about the question of pluralism: religion comes in so many kinds—Christianity, Islam, Judaism, Hinduism, Buddhism (with sub versions of each kind), but also a host of less widely practiced varieties. According to Jean Bodin, "each is refuted by all" (Bodin 1975, 256); does this variety constitute a defeater for each particular variety of religious belief? Some religious doctrines—Trinity, Incarnation, Atonement—are not easy to understand; does that mean they cannot be known or even rationally believed? If religious belief is based on faith rather than on reason, does that mean that it is at best seriously insecure, so that talk of a 'leap of faith', or 'blind faith' is appropriate? These questions have been most fully investigated with respect to Christian belief; hence what follows will concentrate on some questions about the epistemology of Christian belief.

For present purposes, perhaps the main epistemological question is this: what is the source of rationality, or warrant, or positive epistemic status, if any, enjoyed by religious belief? Is it of the same sort as that enjoyed by belief in the teachings of current science? Is the evidence, if any, for religious belief of the same sort as that for scientific beliefs? Or is there some special source of positive epistemic status for religious belief? This is really a contemporary version of a question that goes back a long way: the question about the relation between faith and reason. It is connected with the question whether there are cogent arguments (rational arguments, arguments drawn from the deliverances of reason) for theistic belief, and whether the existence of cogent argument is required for rational acceptance of religious belief.

Here there are fundamentally two views. According to 'evidentialism', the source of positive epistemic status for religious belief, if indeed it has such status, is just reason—the ensemble of rational faculties including, preeminently, perception, memory, rational intuition, testimony, and the like. The source of positive epistemic status for religious belief, therefore, is the same as that for scientific belief. This view goes back at least to John Locke (1689) and has prominent contemporary representatives. On this view, the existence of cogent arguments for a religious belief is required for rational acceptance of that belief, or at any rate is intimately related to rational acceptance. Some who endorse this view believe there aren't any such cogent arguments; accordingly they reject religious belief as unfounded and rationally unacceptable (Mackie 1982); others hold that in fact there are excellent arguments for theism and even for specifically Christian belief. Here the most prominent contemporary spokesperson would be Richard Swinburne, whose work over the last 30 years or so has resulted in the most powerful, complete and sophisticated development of natural theology the world has so far seen (see, e.g., Swinburne (1979, 2004), (1981, 2005)).

The other main view, one adopted by, for example, both Thomas Aquinas (*Summa Theologiae*) and John Calvin (1559), is that belief in God in the first place, and in the distinctive teachings of Christianity in the second, can be rationally accepted even if there are no cogent arguments for them from the deliverances of reason; they have a source of warrant or positive epistemic status independent of the deliverances of reason. This view also has prominent contemporary representation (Alston 1991; Plantinga and Wolterstorff 1984; Plantinga 2000). To use Calvin's terminology, there is the *Sensus Divinitatis*, which is a source of belief in God, and the Internal Testimony of the Holy Spirit, which is the source of belief in the distinctive doctrines of Christianity. Beliefs produced by these sources go beyond reason in the sense that the source of their warrant is not the deliverances of reason; of course it does not follow that such beliefs are irrational, or contrary to reason; nor does it follow that there is something especially dicey or insecure, or chancy about them, as if faith were necessarily blind or a leap in the dark. Indeed, John Calvin defines faith as "a firm and certain *knowledge* of God's benevolence towards us, ..." (Calvin, 1559, p. 551 (emphasis added)). On this view, religion and faith have a source of properly rational belief independent of reason and science; it would therefore be possible for religion and faith to correct as well as be corrected by science and reason.

There is some reason to think that if theism is indeed true, if indeed there is an all-powerful, all-knowing perfectly good person who has created the world and created human beings in his image, then religious belief would be independent of arguments from reason; it would not require such argument for rationality or positive epistemic status. For if theism is true, God would presumably want human beings to know of his presence (and in fact the vast majority of the human population believe in God or something very much like him); he would therefore arrange for human beings to be able to come to knowledge of him. But if knowledge of God depended on the theistic arguments, or other arguments from the deliverances of reason, then, as Aquinas says, only a few human beings would ever come to a knowledge of this truth, and they only after a long time, and with a substantial admixture of error.

Conflict and Concord

Concord

Let's begin with concord. The early pioneers and heroes of modern Western science—Copernicus, Galileo, Kepler, Newton, Boyle, and so on—were all serious Christians, if occasionally, as with Newton, Christologically unorthodox. Furthermore, many (Foster 1934, 1935, 1936; Ratzsch 2009) have pointed out that theistic belief and empirical science display a deep concord, fit together neatly. This is in part a result of the doctrines of creation embraced by theistic religions—in particular two aspects of those doctrines. First, there is the thought that God has created the world, and has of course therefore also created human beings. Furthermore, he has created human beings in his own image. Now God, according to theistic belief, is a person: a being who has knowledge, affection (likes and dislikes), and executive will, and who can act on his beliefs in order to achieve his ends. One of the chief features of the divine image in human beings, then, is the ability to form beliefs and to acquire knowledge. As Thomas Aquinas puts it, "Since human beings are said to be in the image of God in virtue of their having a nature that includes an intellect, such a nature is most in the image of God in virtue of being most able to imitate God" (ST Ia q. 93 a. 4). God has therefore created both us and the world, and arranged for the former to know the latter. Thinking of science at the most basic level as the project of acquiring knowledge of ourselves and our world, it is clear, from this perspective, that the doctrine of *imago dei* underwrites this project. Indeed, the pursuit of science is a clear example of the development and enhancement of the image of God in human beings, both individually and collectively.

Second, there is the thought that divine creation is *contingent*. According to theism, many of God's properties—his omniscience and omnipotence, his goodness and love—are essential to him: he has them in every possible world in which he exists. (And since, according to most theistic thought, he is a necessary being, one that exists in every possible world, he has those properties in every possible world.) Not so, however, with his property of creating. He isn't obliged, by his nature or anything else, to create the world; it is rather a free action on his part. Furthermore, given that he does create, he isn't obliged to do so in any particular way, or to create any particular kinds of things; that he has created the kinds of things we actually find is again contingent, a free action on his part.

It is this doctrine of the contingency of divine creation that underwrites the empirical character of modern Western science (Ratzsch, 2009). For the realm of the necessary is (for the most part) the realm of *a priori* knowledge; here we have mathematics and logic and much philosophy. What is contingent, on the other hand, is the domain or realm of *a posteriori* knowledge, the sort of knowledge produced by perception, memory, and the empirical methods of science. This relationship between the contingency of creation and the importance of the empirical was recognised very early. Thus Roger Cotes, from the preface he wrote to Newton's *Principia Mathematica*:

Without all doubt this world, so diversified with that variety of forms and motions we find in it, could arise from nothing but the perfect free will of God directing and presiding over it.

From this fountain it is that those laws, which we call the laws of Nature, have flowed, in which there appear many traces of the most wise contrivance, but not the least shadow of necessity. These *therefore* we must not seek from uncertain conjectures, *but learn them from observations and experiments* (Cotes 1953, 132–33) [emphasis added].

What we've just seen is that in a certain way theistic belief supports modern science by licensing or endorsing the whole project of empirical investigation; it is also sometimes claimed that science supports theistic belief. Here there are several arguments, arguments that have historically fallen into two basic types: biological and cosmological. An example of the first type is the argument proposed by Michael Behe (Behe, 1996), according to which some structures at the molecular level exhibit "irreducible complexity." These systems display several finely matched interacting parts all of which must be present and working properly in order for the system to do what it does; the removal of any part would preclude the thing's functioning. Among the phenomena Behe cites are the bacterial flagellum, the cilia employed by several kinds of cells for locomotion and other functions, blood clotting, the immune system, the transport of materials within cells, and the incredibly complex cascade of biochemical reactions and events that occur in vision. Such irreducibly complex structures and phenomena, he argues, can't have come to be by gradual, step-by-step Darwinian evolution (unguided by the hand of God or any other person); at any rate the probability that they should do so is vanishingly small. They therefore present what he calls a Lilliputian challenge to unguided Darwinism; if he is right, they present it with a Gargantuan challenge as well. Not only do they challenge Darwinism; they are also, he says, obviously *designed*: their design is about as obvious as an elephant in a living room: "to a person who does not feel obliged to restrict his search to unintelligent causes, the straightforward conclusion is that many biochemical systems were designed" (Behe, p. 193). Others, for example Paul Draper (2002) and Kenneth R. Miller (1999, 130–64), argue that Behe has not proved his case.

A second type of argument for theism starts from the apparent fine-tuning of several of the physical parameters. Starting in the late sixties and early seventies, astrophysicists and others noted that several of the basic physical constants must fall within very narrow limits if there is to be the development of intelligent life—at any rate in a way anything like the way in which we think it actually happened. Thus B. J. Carr and M. J. Rees:

The basic features of galaxies, stars, planets and the everyday world are essentially determined by a few microphysical constants and by the effects of gravitation... . several aspects of our Universe—some of which seem to be prerequisites for the evolution of any form of life—depend rather delicately on apparent 'coincidences' among the physical constants (Carr and Rees, 1979, 605).

For example, if the force of gravity were even slightly stronger, all stars would be blue giants; if even slightly weaker, all would be red dwarfs; in neither case could life have developed (Carter 1979, 72). The same goes for the weak and strong nuclear forces; if either had been even slightly different, life, at any rate life of the sort we have, could probably not have developed.

Apparently life is possible only because the universe is expanding at just the rate required to avoid recollapse. At an earlier time, the fine-tuning had to be even more remarkable:

> *... we know that there has to have been a very close balance between the competing effect of explosive expansion and gravitational contraction which, at the very earliest epoch about which we can even pretend to*

speak (called the Planck time, 10–43 sec. after the big bang), would have corresponded to the incredible degree of accuracy represented by a deviation in their ratio from unity by only one part in 10 to the sixtieth (Polkinghorne 1989, 22).

Other examples: the value of cosmological constant, of the vacuum expectation value of the Higgs field, and the ratio of the mass of the proton to the electron must all be fine-tuned to an incredible degree for the universe to be life-permitting (Barr 2003, 123-130). A particularly informed and technically detailed account of some of these fine-tunings is to be found in Robin Collins's "Evidence for Fine-Tuning" (Collins 2003). Many see these apparent enormous coincidences as substantiating the theistic claim that the universe has been created by a personal God who intends that there be life and indeed intelligent life; they take fine-tuning as offering the material for a properly restrained theistic argument. These arguments take several versions; perhaps the most successful versions argue that the epistemic probability of these fine-tuning phenomena on theism is much greater than their epistemic probability on the atheistic chance hypothesis. Here the conclusion is not (as such) that probably theism is true, but rather that theism is much better supported by these phenomena than the chance hypothesis is (Swinburne 2003; Collins 1999).

Objections come in many varieties. Some who offer these arguments, in particular those associated with the so-called 'Intelligent Design' movement, take them to be contributions to *science* rather than philosophy or theology; the most common objection is that they don't meet the conditions for being science, in particular because their conclusion, that the universe has been designed by an intelligent being, isn't *falsifiable*. Others (as we saw above) reply that falsifiability is ordinarily not a property of individual propositions, but of entire theories, and that theories involving intelligent design can perfectly well be falsifiable.

A more interesting objection to fine-tuning arguments is the "many universe" suggestion: perhaps there are very many, even infinitely many different universes or worlds; the cosmological constants take on different values in different worlds, so that very many (perhaps all possible) different sets of such values get exemplified in one world or another. Couldn't there be an eternal cycle of 'big bangs', with subsequent expansion to a certain limit and then subsequent contraction to a 'big crunch' at which the cosmological values are arbitrarily reset? (Dennett 1995, 179) Alternatively, couldn't it have been that at the Big Bang, there was enormous initial inflation, resulting in many cosmoi with many different settings for the physical constants? In either case it isn't at all surprising that in one or another of the resulting universes, the values of the cosmological constants are such as to be life-permitting. Nor is it at all surprising that the universe in which we find ourselves has life-permitting values; we couldn't exist elsewhere. If so, then the fine-tuning argument is ineffective: the probability of fine-tuning on the many worlds suggestion together with atheism is at least as large as the probability of fine-tuning on theism. There are responses (for example, that on this account there would have to be a universe generator which was itself fine-tuned (Collins 1999), or that even if it is likely that *some* universe be fine-tuned, nevertheless the likelihood that *this* universe be fine-tuned is unaffected by the pluriverse suggestion (White 2003)) and responses to the responses, and so on; not surprisingly, there is no consensus as to whether these fine-tuning arguments are successful.

Conflict?

The Christian doctrine of creation supports a deep concord between Christian belief and science; yet it is of course compatible with this sort of concord that there also be conflict. Many have claimed that there is conflict, indeed warfare, between religion and science (Draper 1875) (White 1895). This is certainly too strong; but obviously the relation between the two has not always been smooth and irenic. There is the famous Galileo incident, often portrayed as a contest between the Catholic hierarchy, representing the forces of repression and tradition, the voice of the old world, the dead hand of the past, and, on the other hand, the forces of progress and the dulcet voice of reason and science. This way of looking at the matter is simplistic (Brooke 1991, 8–9); much more was involved. The dominant Aristotelian thought of the day was heavily *a prioristic*; hence part of what was involved was a dispute about the relative importance of observation and *a priori* thought in astronomy. Also involved were questions about what the Christian (and Jewish) Bible teaches in this area: does a passage like *Joshua* 10:12–15 (in which Joshua commanded the sun to stand still) favour the Ptolemaic system over the Copernican? And of course the usual questions of power and authority were also present.

More recently, a central locus of alleged conflict has been the theory of evolution. This particular flap is of course still very much with us. Many Christian fundamentalists accept a literal interpretation of the creation account in the first two chapters of Genesis; they therefore find incompatibility between the contemporary Darwinian evolutionary accounts of our origins and the Christian faith, at least as they understand it. Many Darwinian fundamentalists (as the late Stephen J. Gould called them) second that motion: they too claim there is conflict between Darwinian evolution and classical Christian or theistic belief. Contemporaries who champion this conflict view would include, for example, Richard Dawkins (1986, 2003), and Daniel Dennett (1995). An important part of the alleged conflict turns on the Christian belief that human beings and other creatures have been *designed*—designed by God; according to evolution, however, (so say Dawkins and Dennett), human beings have not been designed, but are a product of the unguided blind process of natural selection operating on some such source of genetic variation as random genetic mutation. Thus Dawkins:

> All appearances to the contrary, the only watchmaker in nature is the blind forces of physics, albeit deployed in a very special way. A true watchmaker has foresight: he designs his cogs and springs, and plans their interconnections, with a future purpose in his mind's eye. Natural selection, the blind, unconscious automatic process which Darwin discovered, and which we now know is the explanation for the existence and apparently purposeful form of all life, has no purpose in mind. It has no mind and no mind's eye. It does not plan for the future. It has no vision, no foresight, no sight at all. If it can be said to play the role of watchmaker in nature, it is the *blind* watchmaker. (Dawkins 1986, 5)

Others point out that this proposed conflict is far from obvious. The central feature of the modern doctrine of evolution is that the main driving force of the process is natural selection, winnowing some form of genetic variation, the most popular version being random genetic mutation. It is no part of the theory to say that these mutations occur just by chance in a sense of that term that implies that they are uncaused; they are random only in the sense that they do not arise from the design plan of the creatures to which they accrue, and do not occur because they enhance the organism's reproductive fitness. Thus Ernst Mayr, the dean of post-World War II biology: "When it is said that mutation or variation is random, the statement simply means that there is no correlation between the production of new genotypes and the adaptational needs of an organism in the given environment" (Mayr 1998, 98). If so, evolution, as currently stated and currently understood, is perfectly compatible with God's orchestrating and overseeing the whole process; indeed, it is perfectly compatible with that theory that God *causes* the random genetic mutations that are winnowed by natural selection. Those who claim that evolution shows that humankind and other living things have not been designed, so say their opponents, confuse a naturalistic gloss on the scientific theory with the theory itself. The claim that evolution demonstrates that human beings and other living creatures have not, contrary to appearances, been designed, is not part of or a consequence of the scientific theory, but a metaphysical or theological add-on (van Inwagen 2003).

A second area of alleged conflict has to do with divine action in the world. According to classical theistic religion, God has created the world; he also upholds and conserves it, preserves it in being. Apart from his conserving activity, the world would disappear like a candle flame in a high wind. So there is creation and conservation; but, so say the classical theistic religions, there is also *special* divine action, action going beyond creation and conservation. There are the miracles reported in both the Jewish and Christian Bibles: the parting of the Red Sea, for example, as well as Jesus's walking on water, feeding the 5,000, and rising from the dead. Miracles are also reported in the Koran. Many believers don't think of these special divine actions as restricted to Bible times: God still, at present, responds to prayers and accomplishes miraculous healings. Further, according to Christian ways of thought, God works in the hearts and minds of his children in such a way as to produce faith; Thomas Aquinas called this divine activity 'the internal instigation of the Holy Spirit' and John Calvin called it 'the internal witness (or testimony) of the Holy Spirit.' All of these would be examples of special divine action.

Now many see here conflict with modern science. Among them are a large number of theologians; thus according to Langdon Gilkey,

> ... contemporary theology does not expect, nor does it speak of, wondrous divine events on the surface of natural and historical life. The causal nexus in space and time which the Enlightenment science and philosophy introduced into the Western mind ... is also assumed by modern theologians and scholars; since they participate in the modern world of science both intellectually and existentially, they can scarcely do anything else. Now this assumption of a causal order among phenomenal events, and therefore of the authority of the scientific interpretation of observable events, makes a great difference to the validity one assigns to biblical narratives and so to the way one understands their meaning. Suddenly a vast panoply of divine deeds and events recorded in scripture are no longer regarded as having actually happened... Whatever the Hebrews believed, we believe that the biblical people lived in the same causal continuum of space and time in which we live, and so one in which no divine wonders transpired and no divine voices were heard. (Gilkey 1983,31)

Of course many philosophers and scientists would agree. The problem is alleged to be with God's *special* action in the world; there is no particular problem with creation and conservation, but divine action going beyond that is widely thought to be incompatible with modern science. Where exactly is this incompatibility thought to arise? The thought seems to be that special divine activity would be incompatible with *the laws of nature* as disclosed by science. Thus the distinguished biologist H. Allen Orr:

It is not that some sects of one religion invoke miracles but that many sects of many religions do. (Moses, after all, parted the waters and Krishna healed the sick.) I agree of course that no sensible scientists can tolerate such exceptionalism with respect to the laws of nature (Orr, 2004).

Now Gilkey and the others are apparently thinking in terms of a *Newtonian* world-picture, according to which the universe is like a great machine proceeding according to the laws disclosed in science. This isn't sufficient for the hands-off, anti-interventionist theology of these theologians. After all, Newton himself, one hopes, accepted the Newtonian world-picture, and Newton proposed that God periodically adjusted the planetary orbits, which according to his calculations would otherwise gradually go awry. What Gilkey and his friends add, here, apparently, is *determinism*: the thought that the laws of nature together with the state of the universe at any time, entail the state of the universe at any other time. Here the classical source is Pierre Laplace:

We ought then to regard the present state of the universe as the effect of its previous state and as the cause of the one which is to follow. Given for one instant a mind which could comprehend all the forces by which nature is animated and the respective situation of the beings that compose it—a mind sufficiently vast to subject these data to analysis—it would embrace in the same formula the movements of the greatest bodies of the universe and those of the lightest atom; for it, nothing would be uncertain and the future, as the past, would be present to its eyes. (Laplace 1796)

It is the Laplacian world-picture that apparently animates Gilkey, et al. It is worth noting, however, that determinism and the Laplacian world-picture don't follow from classical science. That is because the great conservation laws deduced from Newton's Laws are stated for *closed* or *isolated* systems. Thus Sears and Zemansky (1963):

The principle of conservation of energy states that the internal energy of an isolated system remains constant. This is the most general statement of the principle of conservation of energy. (p. 415)

Newton's laws (as well as Maxwell's later physics of electricity and magnetism) apply to *isolated* or *closed* systems; they describe how the world works *provided that the world is a closed (isolated) system, subject to no outside causal influence.* But it is no part of Newtonian mechanics or classical science generally to declare that the material universe is indeed a closed system. (How could a thing like that be experimentally verified?) Hence there is nothing in classical science (at least in this area) incompatible with God's changing the velocity or direction of a particle, or a whole system of particles (or, for that matter, creating *ex nihilo* a full-grown horse). Energy, momentum and the like are conserved in a closed system; but the claim that the material universe is in fact a closed system is not part of classical physics; it is another metaphysical or theological add-on. So here there is no conflict between classical physics and special divine action in the world.

This classical, Laplacian picture has of course been superseded by the development of quantum mechanics, beginning in the first couple of decades of the 20 century. According to quantum mechanics, associated with any physical system, a system of particles, for example, there is a wave function whose evolution through time is governed by the Schrödinger equation for that system. Now the interesting thing about quantum mechanics is that, unlike classical mechanics, it doesn't specify or predict a single configuration for this system of particles at a future time *t*. The wave function assigns a value at *t* to each of the configurations possibly resulting from the initial conditions; by applying Born's Rule to those values we get an assignment of probabilities to each of those possible configurations at *t*. Accordingly, we aren't told which configuration will in fact result (given the initial conditions) when the system is measured at *t*; instead we are given a distribution of probabilities for the many possible outcomes. Clearly miracles (parting the waters, rising from the dead, etc.) are not incompatible with these assignments. (No doubt such events would be assigned very low probabilities; but of course we don't need quantum mechanics to know that such events are improbable.) Further, on collapse interpretations such as those of Ghirardi, Rimini, and Weber, there is plenty of room for divine activity. Indeed, God could actually be the cause of the collapses, and of the way in which they occur (i.e., where *P* is the possibility that gets actualized at t, it could be that God causes *P* to be actualized then). (This could perhaps be seen as a halfway house between occasionalism and secondary causation.) With the advent of quantum mechanics, therefore, there seems to be even less reason to see special divine action in the world as somehow incompatible with science.

Nevertheless, many who are entirely aware of the quantum mechanical revolution still find a problem with special divine action. For example, there is the "Divine Action Project" (Wildman 1988–2003, 31–75), a 15-year series of conferences and publications that began in 1988. So far these conferences have resulted in some 6 books of essays involving at least 50 or more authors from various fields of science together with philosophers and theologians, including many of the most prominent writers in the field. Most of these authors find a problem with special divine action. That is because they believe that a satisfactory account of God's action in the world would have to be *noninterventionist*, as Wildman says. Thus Arthur Peacocke, commenting on a certain proposal for divine action:

God would have to be conceived of as actually manipulating micro-events (at the atomic, molecular, and according to some, quantum levels) in these initiating fluctuations on the natural world in order to produce the results at the macroscopic level which God wills. But such a conception of God's action ... would then be no different in principle from that of God *intervening* in the order of nature with all the problems that evokes for a rationally coherent belief in God as the creator of that order. (Peacocke 2004)

Apparently, then, the project is to develop a conception of special divine action (action beyond creation and conservation) that doesn't involve intervention. But what would intervention *be* in the quantum mechanical picture? That's not easy to say. Indeed, it's not easy to see how intervention could be distinct from divine action beyond creation and conservation. If they aren't distinct, however, special divine action would just be intervention, in which case the project of developing a conception of special divine action that doesn't involve intervention is unhopeful.

Still a third area of alleged conflict between religious belief and science has to do with the different epistemic attitudes associated with each. Thus, for example, John Worrall:

Science, or rather a scientific attitude, is incompatible with religious belief. Science and religion are in irreconcilable conflict ... There is no way in which you can be *both* properly scientifically minded *and* a true religious believer (Worrall 2004, p. 60).

In science, the dominant epistemic attitude (so the claim goes) is one of critical empirical investigation, issuing in theories which are held tentatively and provisionally; one is always prepared to give up a theory in favour of a more satisfactory successor. In religious (e.g., Christian) belief, the epistemic attitude of *faith* plays an important role, an attitude which differs both in the source of the belief in question, and in the readiness to give it up.

Others (Ratzsch, 2004), however, point out that there isn't obviously a conflict here. Clearly those two attitudes are indeed *different*, and perhaps they can't be taken simultaneously with respect to the same proposition. Does that show a *conflict* between science and religious belief? Perhaps some ways of forming belief are appropriate in one area and others in other areas. To get a conflict, we must add that the scientific epistemic attitude is the only one appropriate to *any* area of cognitive endeavour. *That* claim, however, is not itself part of the scientific attitude; it is an epistemological declaration for which substantial argument is required (but not so far in evidence). Furthermore, scientists themselves don't seem to take the scientific epistemic attitude (as characterized above) to *all* of what they believe, or even all of what they believe as scientists. Thus it is common for scientists to believe that there has been a past, and indeed they sometimes tell us how long ago the earth, or our galaxy, or even the entire universe, was formed. Scientists seldom hold this belief—that there has been a past—as a result of empirical investigation; nor do they ordinarily hold it in that tentative, critical way, always looking for a better alternative.

In these areas, therefore, it is hard to find conflict between theistic religious belief and contemporary science.

Where There is Conflict?

Other areas of science, however, do appear to produce conflict. First, there is the relatively new but rapidly growing discipline of evolutionary psychology. The heart and soul of this project is the effort to explain distinctive human traits—our art, humor, play, love, poetry, sense of adventure, love of stories, our music, our morality, and our religion—the heart and soul of this project is to explain all of these traits in terms of our evolutionary origin and history. And here we do find theories incompatible with religious belief. One important topic in this area has been *altruistic behaviour*—behaviour that promotes the reproductive fitness of someone else at the expense of the altruist's own reproductive fitness. How is it that there are people like missionaries and Mother Teresa, people who devote their entire lives to the service of others, paying little attention to their own reproductive prospects? Herbert Simon attempts to explain altruism from an evolutionary perspective in terms of two mechanisms, docility and limited rationality:

Docile persons tend to learn and believe what they perceive others in the society want them to learn and believe. Thus the content of what is learned will not be fully screened for its contribution to personal fitness. Because of bounded rationality, the docile individual will often be unable to distinguish socially prescribed behaviour that contributes to fitness from altruistic behaviour [i.e., socially prescribed behaviour that does not contribute to fitness]. In fact, docility will reduce the inclination to evaluate independently the contributions of behaviour to fitness. … . By virtue of bounded rationality, the docile person cannot acquire the personally advantageous learning that provides the increment, *d*, of fitness without acquiring also the altruistic behaviours that cost the decrement (Simon 1990, 3, 4).

Simon's theory is carefully worked out, well developed, and of considerable interest; it is also incompatible with theistic religious belief. According to his theory, the explanation of the altruist's behaviour is failure to see that the behaviour in question compromises evolutionary fitness. Hence, according to Simon's theory, the answer to the question 'Why did Mother Teresa behave in such a way as to compromise her evolutionary fitness?' is 'Due to bounded rationality, she was unable to see that her mode of behaviour would compromise her fitness.' From a Christian perspective, that's not at all the right answer, which would rather be something like 'She wanted to follow the example of Jesus and do what she could do to help the poor and sick.'

Another example from this area is provided by the many theories of religion and religious belief. According to some of these theories, religious belief is false but adaptive; according to others it is false and maladaptive. An example of the first group would be the theory proposed by David Sloan Wilson, who says that religion is a group adaptation: "Many features of religion, such as the nature of supernatural agents and their relationships with humans can be explained as adaptations designed to enable human groups to function as adaptive units" (Wilson 2002, p. 51). Religious belief, he says, is fictitious, but adaptive at the group level: it promotes cooperation, mutual respect, and solidarity, thus enabling the group to do well in competition with other groups.

That religious belief can function as a group adaptation is of course consistent with theistic belief; what about the bit about religious belief's—theistic belief, for example—being fictitious? How could the claim that there is no such person as God be part of empirical science? And even if it could be, Wilson's theory, one thinks, would be on more solid ground if that easily detachable theological add-on were detached. What is not so easily detachable is the claim that religious belief (unlike memory, perceptual beliefs, rational intuition) is produced by cognitive faculties or processes that are not aimed at the production of true belief. According to Wilson, these processes or faculties have a function conferred on them by evolution; but it is not that of producing true beliefs. It is rather the function of producing beliefs that promote cooperation and solidarity; ultimately their function is to produce beliefs that are adaptive, i.e., promote reproductive fitness.

Here a comparison with Sigmund Freud's views of theistic belief may be illuminating. Freud claims that theistic belief is *illusion*. This doesn't mean that theistic belief is false (although Freud thinks it *is* false); what it means is that theistic belief is produced by a cognitive process (wishful thinking) that is not 'reality oriented'; its purpose is not the production of true belief, but (in this case) a belief that enables the believer to avoid the depression and apathy that would set in if she saw clearly the miserably appalling condition in which we human beings actually find ourselves. Wilson's view is like Freud's, then, in that he too proposes that theistic belief is produced by cognitive faculties that are not reality oriented. Whereas Freud takes a dim view of theistic belief, Wilson is much more appreciative:

In the first place, much religious belief is not detached from reality .... Rather, it is intimately connected to reality by motivating behaviours that are adaptive in the real world—an awesome achievement when we appreciate the complexity that is required to become connected in this practical sense. ... Adaptation is the gold standard against which rationality must be judged, along with all other forms of thought. Evolutionary biologists should be especially quick to grasp this point because they appreciate that the well-adapted mind is ultimately an organ of survival and reproduction (Wilson 2002, p. 228).

Although Wilson has kind words for religion, his claim that religious belief is not aimed at the truth is incompatible with theistic religious belief. According to Christianity, for example, faith, including belief in the essentials of the Christian faith, is a divine gift; and the process producing it in the believer (the internal instigation of the Holy Spirit, according to Thomas Aquinas, the internal witness or testimony of the Holy Spirit, according to John Calvin) is indeed aimed at the truth and has as its function the production of true belief.

So here there is conflict between science and religion. What accounts for this conflict? Several things, no doubt; but part of the explanation is to be found in *methodological naturalism*, a widely accepted constraint on science. According to methodological naturalism (MN), in doing science one must proceed "as if God is not given", to use the words of Hugo Grotius. Exactly what does that mean? There are various suggestions; here is one. According to MN, (1) the *data set* (data model) for a proper scientific theory can't refer to God or other supernatural agents (angels, demons), or employ what one knows or thinks one knows by way of (divine) revelation. Thus the data for a theory wouldn't include, for example, the proposition that there has recently been an outbreak of demon possession in Washington, D. C. (2) A proper scientific *theory* can't refer to God or any other supernatural agents, or employ what one knows or thinks one knows by way of revelation. So if the data model contained the proposition that there has been an outbreak of weird and irrational behaviour in Washington, one couldn't properly propose a theory involving demon possession to explain it. (3) Note first that the probability or plausibility of theory candidates and their capacity to explain the data, as well as their empirical implications, is always relative to an array of *background information* or an *epistemic base.*

The third constraint, then, is that the epistemic base of a proper scientific theory can't include propositions obviously entailing the existence of God or other supernatural agents, or propositions one knows or thinks one knows by way of revelation. So consider someone who in fact accepts the main lines of one of the theistic religions, and works in the area of evolutionary psychology. No doubt she will honor MN as a constraint on her scientific activity. If so, for scientific purposes she will eliminate from her evidence base propositions obviously entailing the existence of God or other supernatural beings, as well as what she knows or thinks she knows by way of faith or revelation. But then she might very well come up with theories of the kind we've been pointing to, theories incompatible with theistic religion.

A rather different area with the same dialectic: historical biblical criticism (HBC). HBC is to be contrasted with traditional biblical commentary. The practitioner of the latter assumes that the bible is the word of God, and tries to lay bare the meaning of what is taught in various parts of the bible. The practitioner of HBC, on the other hand, specifically brackets the belief that the bible is divine revelation, and intends instead to study it *scientifically*. Thus the late Raymond Brown, a highly respected Catholic scripture scholar, believes that HBC is "scientific biblical criticism" (Brown 1973, p. 6); it yields "factual results" (p. 9); he intends his own contributions to be "scientifically respectable" (p. 11): and practitioners of HBC investigate the scriptures with "scientific exactitude". To study the bible scientifically, therefore, is to study it in a way constrained by MN.

Naturally enough, there has been considerable tension between HBC, so construed, and traditional Christians, going back as least as far as David Strauss in 1835: "Nay, if we would be candid with ourselves, that which was once sacred history for the Christian believer is, for the enlightened portion of our contemporaries, only fable." As for contemporary tensions, according to Luke Timothy Johnson:

The Historical Jesus researchers insist that the 'real Jesus' must be found in the facts of his life before his death. The resurrection is, when considered at all, seen in terms of visionary experience, or as a continuation of an 'empowerment' that began before Jesus's death. Whether made explicit or not, the operative premise is that there is no 'real Jesus' after his death (Johnson 1997, p. 144).

And according to Van Harvey "So far as the biblical historian is concerned, ... there is scarcely a popularly held traditional belief about Jesus that is not regarded with considerable skepticism" (Harvey 1986, p. 193)

An absolutely central characteristic of HBC is this effort to be scientific. Of course we might ask whether HBC, or any historical study, is really science; its advocates say that it is, but are they right? In view of the difficulty of the demarcation problem however, it is probably unwise to transform this question into an objection. (Further, even if historical studies of this kind are not precisely science, they are certainly very much *like* science.) And insofar as HBC requires conformity to MN, one who practices it brackets or suspends or sets aside any theological views, or what is known by revelation. Just as with evolutionary psychology, therefore, one who works at HBC might in fact accept theistic religion of one sort or another, but in his work as a practitioner of HBC, come to conclusions incompatible with his religious belief. So far, therefore, there is the same dialectic here as with evolutionary psychology: theories incompatible with theistic religion arising (at least in part) out of MN.

In at least these two areas, therefore, there is conflict between scientific theories and religious belief. In a certain very important respect, however, this conflict is superficial. That is because the theories and claims of evolutionary psychology and HBC need not constitute defeaters, even partial defeaters, for those elements of religious belief with which they are incompatible—even though theism is committed to taking science with great seriousness and even if it is conceded that the theories in question constitute good science. And *that* is precisely because MN is taken as constraining scientific activity. We can see this as follows. As already suggested, scientific investigation or inquiry is always conducted against the background of an evidence base, a body of background knowledge or belief. An important part of MN, furthermore, is that this evidence base must not contain propositions obviously entailing the existence of supernatural beings, or propositions that are accepted by way of faith. It follows that the evidence base of an adherent of a theistic religion will contain the scientific evidence base as a *proper part*; it will include all the propositions to be found in the scientific evidence base, plus more—perhaps those specific to Christian belief. Now suppose a given theory—Simon's theory on altruism, or Wilson's on religion, or some minimalist account of Jesus's life and activity—is in fact proper science, and is indeed the most plausible, scientifically most satisfactory theoretical response to the evidence, given EB_S, the scientific evidence base. This means that from the point of view of EB_S together with current evidence, that theory is the scientifically best or most plausible result. Still, that doesn't automatically give a believer a defeater for those of her beliefs with which the theory are incompatible. That is because EB_S is only part of her evidence base. And it can easily happen that a proposition *P* is the plausible response, given a *part* of my evidence base (together with the current evidence), that *P* is incompatible with one of my beliefs, and that *P* fails to provide me with a defeater for that belief.

For example, suppose I tell you that I saw you at the mall yesterday afternoon. Then with respect to part of your total evidence base—a part that includes your knowledge that I told you I saw you there, together with your knowledge that I have decent vision and am ordinarily reliable, and the like—the right thing to think is that you were at the mall. Nevertheless, we may suppose, you know perfectly well that you *weren't* there; you remember that you were home all afternoon thinking about methodological naturalism. Here the right thing to think from the perspective of a proper part of your evidence base is that you were at the mall; but this does not give you a defeater for your belief that you were not there. Another example: we can imagine a renegade group of whimsical physicists proposing to reconstruct physics, refusing to use *memory* beliefs, or if that is too fantastic, memories of anything more than 1 minute ago. Perhaps something could be done along these lines, but it would be a poor, paltry, truncated, trifling thing. And now suppose that the best theory, from this limited evidence base, is inconsistent with general relativity. Should that give pause to the more traditional physicists who employ what they know by way of memory as well as what the renegade physicists use? I should think not. This truncated physics could hardly call into question physics of the fuller variety, and the fact that from a proper part of the scientific evidence base, something inconsistent with general relativity is the best theory—that fact would hardly give more traditional physicists a defeater for general relativity.

Similarly for the case under question. The traditional Christian thinks she knows *by faith* that Jesus was divine and that he rose from the dead. But then she need not be moved by the fact that these propositions are not especially probable on the evidence base to which HBC limits itself—i.e., one constrained by MN and therefore one that deletes any knowledge or belief dependent upon faith. The findings of HBC, if findings they are, need not give her a defeater for those of her beliefs with which they are incompatible. The point is not that HBC, evolutionary psychology and other scientific theorizing couldn't in principle produce defeaters for Christian belief; the point is only that its coming up with theories incompatible with Christian belief doesn't automatically produce such a defeater. Everything depends on the particular evidence adduced in the case in question, and the bearing of that evidence given the believer's total evidence base. In the case in question, for example, it may be that given EB_S and the relevant data base, it is unlikely that Jesus arose from the dead. But given an evidence base including not only EB_S but also belief in God together with the specifically Christian beliefs that Jesus is the second person of the trinity incarnate, and that the New Testament is a reliable source of information on these matters—given these things, the proposition that he rose from the dead may not be at all improbable. Similar considerations would hold, of course, for the other theistic religions and proposed scientific defeaters.

Someone might complain that this looks like a recipe for intellectual irresponsibility, for hanging on to beliefs in the teeth of the evidence. Can't a believer always say something like this, no matter what proposed defeater presents itself? "Perhaps *B* (the proposed defeatee) is improbable or unlikely with respect to part of what I believe," she says, "but it is certainly not improbable with respect to the totality of what I believe, that totality including, of course, *B* itself." Obviously that can't be right; if it were, every putative defeater could be turned aside in this way and defeat would be impossible. But defeat is not impossible; it sometimes happens that one *does* acquire a defeater for a belief *B*, by learning that *B* is improbable with respect to some proper subset of one's evidence base. According to the book of *Isaiah* (41:9), God says "I took you from the ends of the earth, from its farthest corners I called you. I said, 'You are my servant'; I have chosen you and have not rejected you." Someone might believe *R*, the proposition that the earth is a rectangular solid with ends and corners, on the basis of this text; she will have a defeater for this belief when confronted with the scientific evidence—photographs of the earth from space, for example—against it. At any rate she will have a defeater for *R* if the rest of her noetic structure is at all like ours. The same goes for someone who holds pre-Copernican beliefs on the basis of such a text as "The earth stands fast; it shall not be moved" (Psalm 104:5). Why is there a defeater in some cases, but not in others? What makes the difference?

Here is a suggestion. Consider some religious belief *B* incompatible with a deliverance of some current scientific theory: *B* might be, for example, the belief that Mother Teresa was perfectly rational in behaving in that altruistic fashion. Let the scientific theory in question be Herbert Simon's account of altruism, and let EB_S be the believer's evidence base. Our question is whether *A*, the belief that Simon's theory is proper science (and that it entails the denial of *B*), is a defeater for *B*. Add *A* to *S*'s evidence base; and now the right question, perhaps, is this: is *B* epistemically improbable or unlikely with respect to the conjunction of *A* with EB_S? Of course *B* itself might initially be a member of EB_S, in which case it will certainly not be improbable with respect to it. If that were sufficient for *A*'s not being a defeater of *B*, however, no member of the evidence base could ever be defeated by a new discovery; and that can't be right. So let's delete *B* from EB_S. Call the result of deleting *B* from *S*'s evidence base 'EB_S reduced with respect to *B*' — 'EB_S"*B*' for short. And now the suggestion — call it 'the reduction test for defeat' — is that *A* is a defeater for *B* just if *B* is appropriately improbable with respect to the conjunction of *A* with EB_S"*B*.

Suppose we apply this test to the belief *B* that Mother Teresa was rational in behaving altruistically, with *A* being the belief that Simon's theory of altruism is good science and is incompatible with *B;* and let's suppose that *S* is a Christian believer. To apply the reduction test, we must ask whether *B* is improbable with respect to the conjunction of *A* with EB_S"*B*. The answer, I should think, is that *B* is not improbable with respect to that conjunction. For EB_S"*B* includes the empirical evidence, whatever exactly it is, appealed to by Simon, but also the proposition that we human beings have been created by God and created in his image, along with the rest of the main lines of the Christian story. With respect to the conjunction of *A* with *that* body of propositions, it is not likely that if Mother Teresa had been more rational, smarter, she would have acted so as to increase her reproductive fitness rather than live altruistically. Hence, on the proposed reduction test, the fact that Simon's theory is good science and is more likely than not with respect to the scientific evidence base—that fact does not give *S* a defeater for what she thinks about Mother Teresa.

Consider, on the other hand, the belief *B** that the earth has corners and edges and the photographic evidence against that belief: here, plausibly, the reduction test gives the result that the latter is a defeater for *B**. (True: a Christian might think that the Bible is infallible, since God is its ultimate author; but of course that leaves open the question what God intends to teach in the passage in question.) So the reduction test gives sensible results in these two cases. It can't be right in general, however—more exactly, it is right in general only on a certain very important assumption the believer is likely to reject. For it might be, clearly enough, that *B* has a lot of warrant on its own, warrant it doesn't get from the other members of EB_S or indeed any other propositions. *B* may be *basic* with respect to warrant; *B* might get warrant from a source different from any involved in the scientific theory with which it is incompatible. If so, the fact that *B* is unlikely with respect to EB_S"*B* doesn't show that *S* has a defeater for *B* in the fact that *B* is unlikely with respect to EB_S"*B* together with the relevant *A*.

By way of illustrative example: you are on trial for some crime; the evidence against you is strong, and you are convicted. Nevertheless, you remember very clearly that at the time the crime occurred, you were on a solitary walk in the woods. Your belief that you were walking in the woods isn't based on argument or inference from other propositions (You don't note, e.g., that you feel a little tired and that your walking shoes are muddy, and that there is a map of the area in your parka pocket, concluding that the best explanation of these phenomena is that you were walking there.) So consider EB_{you}"*P*, your evidence base diminished with respect to *P*, the proposition that you didn't commit the crime and were walking in the woods when it was committed. With respect to EB_{you}"*P*, *P* is epistemically improbable; after all, you have the same evidence as the jury for $\neg P$, and the jury is quite properly (if mistakenly) convinced that you did the crime. Still, you certainly don't have a defeater, here, for your belief that you are innocent. The reason, of course, is that *P* has for you a source of warrant independent of the rest of your beliefs: you *remember* it. In a case like this, whether you have a defeater for the belief *P* in question will depend, on the one hand, upon the strength of the intrinsic warrant enjoyed by *P*, and, on the other, the strength of the evidence against *P* from EB_{you}"*P*. Very often the intrinsic warrant will be the stronger.

The same will go for religious beliefs, if they do in fact have intrinsic warrant. If *S* holds a religious belief *B* and if *B* has warrant in the basic way, then even if the probability of B on EB_S"B together with the relevant A is low, it won't follow that A is a defeater of B for S. Perhaps the reduction test offers a necessary condition of A's being a defeater for B for S; it is also sufficient only if religious beliefs don't have warrant or positive epistemic status in the basic way, and only if they don't acquire warrant or positive epistemic status from a source other than those that confer that status on scientific beliefs. This is part of the importance of the question noted above in section 2.

Naturalism and Science

So far we've examined alleged conflict between theistic religious belief and science with respect to several areas: evolution, divine action in the world, the difference between the scientific attitude and the religious attitude, evolutionary psychology, and HBC. But some have suggested a science/religion (or science/quasi-religion) conflict of a wholly different sort: one between *naturalism* and science. (Otte 2002; Plantinga 1993, 2002a; Rea 2002; Taylor 1963); there are also hints of this effect in Nietzsche (2003) and in Darwin himself (1887).

Now naturalism comes in several different colours and flavours. First, there is the view that nature is all there is; there are no supernatural beings. Of course this is a bit slim as an explanation of naturalism; we need to know what nature is, and what allegedly supernatural beings might be like. Perhaps a way to proceed would be to say that naturalism, so conceived, is the view that there is no such person as the God of theism, or anything like God (see, e.g., Beilby 2002). Call this 'naturalism$_1$'. Another variety of naturalism, 'scientific naturalism', we might call it, would be the claim that there are no entities in addition to those endorsed by contemporary science (Kornblith 1994). Given that current science endorses no supernatural beings, scientific naturalism implies naturalism$_1$. There is also what we might call 'epistemological naturalism', according to which, roughly speaking, the methods of science are the only proper epistemic methods (Krikorian 1944). With the help of a couple of fairly obvious premises, epistemological naturalism also implies naturalism$_1$, and I'll use 'naturalism' to refer to the disjunction of the three versions of naturalism sketched. Advocates of naturalism thus conceived would be (for example) Bertrand Russell (1957), Daniel Dennett (1995), Richard Dawkins (1986), David Armstrong (1978), and the many others that are sometimes said to endorse "The Scientific World-View."

Naturalism is presumably not a religion. In one very important respect, however, it resembles religion: it can be said to perform the cognitive function of a religion. There is that range of deep human questions to which a religion typically provides an answer (above, Section I): what is the fundamental nature of the universe: for example, is it mind first, or matter (non-mind) first? What is most real and basic in it, and what kinds of entities does it display? What is the place of human beings in the universe, and what is their relation to the rest of the world? Are there prospects for life after death? Is there such a thing as sin, or some analogue of sin? If so, what are the prospects of combating or overcoming it? Where must we look to improve the human condition? Is there such a thing as a *summum bonum*, a highest good for human beings, and if so what is it? Like a typical religion, naturalism gives a set of answers to these and similar questions. We may therefore say that naturalism performs the cognitive function of a religion, and hence can sensibly be thought of as a quasi-religion.

Next, note many thinkers going back at least to Nietzsche (Nietzsche 2003) and possibly William Whewell (Curtis 1986) have pointed to a potentially worrisome implication of evolutionary theory. The worry can be put as follows. According to orthodox Darwinism, the process of evolution is driven mainly by two mechanisms: random genetic mutation and natural selection. The former is the chief source of genetic variability; by virtue of the latter, a mutation resulting in a heritable, fitness-enhancing trait is likely to spread through that population and be preserved as part of the genome. It is fitness-enhancing behaviour and traits that get rewarded by natural selection; what get penalized are maladaptive traits and behaviours. In crafting our cognitive faculties, natural selection will favour cognitive faculties and processes that result in adaptive behaviour; it cares not a whit about true belief (as such) or about cognitive faculties that reliably give rise to true belief. As evolutionary psychologist Donald Sloan Wilson puts it, "the well-adapted mind is ultimately an organ of survival and reproduction" (Wilson 2002, 228). What our minds are *for* (if anything) is not the production of true beliefs, but the production of adaptive behaviour: that our species has survived and evolved at most guarantees that our behaviour is adaptive; it does not guarantee or even make it likely that our belief-producing processes are for the most part reliable, or that our beliefs are for the most part true. That is because our behaviour could perfectly well be adaptive, but our beliefs false as often as true. Darwin himself apparently worried about this question: "With me," says Darwin, the horrid doubt always arises whether the convictions of man's mind, which has been developed from the mind of the lower animals, are of any value or at all trustworthy. Would any one trust in the convictions of a monkey's mind, if there are any convictions in such a mind? (Darwin 1887)

We can briefly state Darwin's doubt as follows. Let *R* be the proposition that our cognitive faculties are reliable, *N* the proposition that naturalism is true and *E* the proposition that we and our cognitive faculties have come to be by way of the processes to which contemporary evolutionary theory points us: what is the conditional probability of *R* on *N&E*? I.e., what is *P*(*R* | *N&E*)? Darwin fears it may be rather low.

Of course it is only *unguided* natural selection that prompts the worry. If natural selection were guided and orchestrated by the God of theism, for example, the worry would disappear; God would presumably use the whole process to create creatures of the sort he wanted, creatures in his own image, creatures with reliable cognitive faculties. So it is unguided evolution, and metaphysical beliefs that entail unguided evolution, that prompt this worry about the reliability of our cognitive faculties. Now naturalism entails that evolution, if it occurs, is indeed unguided. But then, so the suggestion goes, it is unlikely that our cognitive faculties are reliable, given the conjunction of naturalism with the proposition that we and our cognitive faculties have come to be by way of natural selection winnowing random genetic variation. If so, one who believes that conjunction will have a defeater for the proposition that our faculties are reliable—but if that's true, she will also have a defeater for any belief produced by her cognitive faculties—including, of course, the conjunction of naturalism with evolution. That conjunction is thus seen to be self-refuting. If so, however, this conjunction cannot rationally be accepted, in which case there is conflict between naturalism and evolution, and hence between naturalism and science.

We Can State the Argument Schematically as Follows:

1. *P*(*R* | *N&E*) is low.
2. Anyone who accepts *N&E* and sees that (1) is true has a defeater for *R*.
3. Anyone who has a defeater for *R* has a defeater for any other belief she holds, including *N&E* itself. Therefore
4. Anyone who accepts *N&E* and sees that (1) is true has a defeater for *N&E*; hence *N&E* can't be rationally accepted.

Of course this is brief and merely a schematic version of the argument; there is no space here for the requisite qualifications. Support for (1) could go as follows. First, in order to avoid influence from our natural assumption that our cognitive faculties are reliable, think not about us, but about hypothetical creatures a lot like us, perhaps existing in some other part of the universe; and suppose *N* and *E* are true with respect to them. Next, note that naturalism apparently implies materialism (about human beings); current science does not endorse the existence of immaterial souls or minds or selves. So take naturalism to include materialism. What would a belief *be*, from this point of view? Presumably something like a long-term event or structure in the nervous system—perhaps a structured group of neurons connected and related in certain ways. Such a neural structure will have *neurophysiological* properties ('NP properties'): properties specifying the number of neurons involved, the way in which those neurons are connected with each other and with other structures (with muscles, glands, sense organs, other neuronal events, etc.), the average rate and intensity of neuronal firing in various parts of this event, and the ways in which these rates of fire change over time and in response to input from other areas. If this event is really a *belief*, however, then it will also have *content*; it will be the belief that *p*, for some proposition *p*—perhaps the proposition *naturalism is all the rage these days.*

What is the relation between NP properties, on the one hand, and content properties—such properties as *having the proposition that naturalism is all the rage these days as content*—on the other? Perhaps the most popular position here is "nonreductive materialism" (NRM): content properties are distinct from but *supervene on* NP properties. Supervenience can be either broadly logical or nomic. In the latter case, there would be psychophysical laws relating NP properties to content properties: laws of the sort *any structure with such and such NP properties will have such and such content.* These laws presumably will be contingent (in the broadly logical or metaphysical sense). In the former case, there will also be such laws, but they will be necessary rather than contingent.

Now take any belief *B* you like on the part of a member of that hypothetical population: what is the (epistemic) probability that *B* is true, given *N&E* and nonreductive materialism—what is *P*(*B* | *N&E*&NRM)? What we know is that *B* has a certain content (call it '*C*'), and (we may assume or concede) having *B* is adaptive in the circumstances in which that creature finds itself. What, then, is the probability that *C*, the content of *B*, is *true*? Well, what is the probability that the relevant psychophysical law *L* connecting NP properties and content properties yields a *true* proposition as content in this instance? Having *B* is adaptive, in the circumstances in which the creature finds itself; its displaying the NP properties on which *C* supervenes causes adaptive behaviour. But why think the content connected with those NP properties by *L* will be true in this creature's circumstances? What counts for adaptivity are the NP properties and the behaviour they cause; it doesn't matter whether the supervening content is true. The NP properties are indeed adaptive; but that provides no reason, so far, for thinking the supervening content is true. Having *B* is adaptive by virtue of its causing adaptive behaviour, not by virtue of having true content. Of course if theism is true, then human beings (as opposed to those hypothetical creatures, for whom naturalism is true) are made in the divine image, which includes the capacity for knowledge; so God would presumably have chosen the psychophysical laws in such a way that in the relevant circumstances, the neurophysiology yields true content. But nothing like that is true given naturalism; to suppose that the content properties that are adaptive, for the most part also lead to true content, would be wholly unjustified optimism.

So what is *P*(*B* | *N*&*E*&NRM)? Well, since the truth of *B* doesn't make a difference to the adaptivity of *B*, *B* could indeed be true, but is equally likely to be false; we'd have to estimate the probability that it is true as about the same as the probability that it is false. But that means that it is improbable that the believer in question has reliable cognitive faculties, i.e., faculties that produce a sufficient preponderance of true over false beliefs. For example, if so, if the believer in question has 1000 independent beliefs, each as likely to be false as true, the probability that, say, 3/4 of them are true (and this would be a modest requirement for reliability) will be very low—less than 10^{-58}. So *P*(*B* | *N*&*E*&NRM) specified to these creatures will be low. But of course the same would hold for us, if naturalism is true: *P*(*B* | *N*&*E*&NRM) specified to us is equally low.

That's the argument for the first premise. According to the second premise, one who sees this and also accepts *N*&*E* has a *defeater* for *R*, a reason to give it up, to cease believing it. The support offered for this premise is by way of analogy from clear cases. Suppose I believe there is a drug—call it XX—that destroys cognitive reliability; I believe 95% of those who ingest XX become cognitively unreliable. Suppose further that I now believe both that I've ingested XX and that *P*(*R* | I've ingested XX) is low; taken together, these two beliefs give me a defeater for my initial belief or assumption that my cognitive faculties are reliable. Furthermore, I can't appeal to any of my *other* beliefs to show or argue that my cognitive faculties are still reliable; any such other belief is also now suspect or compromised, just as *R* is. Any such other belief *B* is a product of my cognitive faculties: but then in recognising this and having a defeater for *R*, I also have a defeater for *B*. Of course there will be many other examples: I'll get the same result if I believe that I am a brain in a vat and that *P*(*R* | I'm a brain in a vat) is low; the same goes for the classic Cartesian version of the same idea (namely that I've been created by a being who delights in deception) and for other more homely scenarios, for example, the belief that I've gone insane (perhaps by way of contracting mad cow disease). In all of these cases I get a defeater for *R*.

Now according to the third premise, one who has a defeater for *R* has a defeater for any belief she takes to be a product of her cognitive faculties—which is, of course, *all* of her beliefs. She therefore has a defeater for *N&E* itself; so one who *accepts* *N&E* (and sees that *P*(*R* | *N&E*) is low) has a *defeater* for *N&E*, a reason to doubt or reject or be agnostic with respect to it. Nor could she get independent evidence for *R*; the process of doing so would of course *presuppose* that her faculties are reliable. She'd be relying on the accuracy of her faculties in believing that the alleged evidence is in fact present and that it is in fact evidence for *R*. Thomas Reid (1785, 276) put it like this:

If a man's honesty were called into question, it would be ridiculous to refer to the man's own word, whether he be honest or not. The same absurdity there is in attempting to prove, by any kind of reasoning, probable or demonstrative, that our reason is not fallacious, since the very point in question is, whether reasoning may be trusted.

The argument concludes that the conjunction of naturalism with the theory of evolution cannot rationally be accepted—at any rate by someone who is apprised of this argument and sees the connection between *N&E* and *R*.

As one might expect, this argument has been controversial; a number of objections have been raised against it. (Beilby 1997; Ginet 1995, 403; O'Connor 1994, 527; Ross 1997; Fitelson and Sober 1998; Robbins 1994; Fales 1996; Lehrer 1996; Nathan 1997; Levin 1997; Fodor 1998) There have been responses to the objections (Plantinga 2002a; 2003), responses to those responses (Talbott, forthcoming), and so on; there is nothing like consensus regarding the argument. If the argument is correct, however, and *N&E* can't rationally be accepted, then there is a conflict between naturalism and evolution; one can't rationally accept them both.

Hence there is conflict between naturalism and one of the chief pillars of contemporary science. Insofar as naturalism is a quasi-religion by virtue of performing the cognitive function of a religion, there is a sort of religion/science conflict—not between theistic religion and science, but between naturalism and science.

Secularization

Secularization or secularisation is the transformation of a society from close identification with religious values and institutions toward nonreligious (or irreligious) values and secular institutions. The *secularization thesis* refers to the belief that as societies progress, particularly through modernisation and rationalization, religion loses its authority in all aspects of social life and governance. The term secularization is also used in the context of the lifting of the monastic restrictions from a member of the clergy.

Secularization refers to the historical process in which religion loses social and cultural significance. As a result of secularization the role of religion in modern societies becomes restricted. In secularized societies faith lacks cultural authority, religious organisations have little social power.

Secularization has many levels of meaning, both as a theory and a historical process. Social theorists such as Karl Marx, Sigmund Freud, Max Weber, and Émile Durkheim, postulated that the modernisation of society would include a decline in levels of religiosity. Study of this process seeks to determine the manner in which, or extent to which religious creeds, practices and institutions are losing social significance. Some theorists argue that the secularization of modern civilization partly results from our inability to adapt broad ethical and spiritual needs of mankind to the increasingly fast advance of the physical sciences.

The term also has additional meanings, primarily historical and religious. Applied to church property, historically it refers to the seizure of monastic lands and buildings, such as Henry VIII's Dissolution of the Monasteries in England and the later acts during the French Revolution as well as by various anti-clerical European governments during the 18th and 19th centuries, which resulted in the expulsion and suppression of the religious communities which occupied them. Otherwise, secularization involves the abandonment of goods by the Church where it is sold to purchasers after the government seizes the property, which most commonly happens after reasonable negotiations and arrangements are made.

Still another form of Secularization refers to the act of Prince-Bishops or holders of a position in a Monastic or Military Order - holding a combined religious and secular authority under the Catholic Church - who broke away and made themselves into completely secular (typically, Protestant) hereditary rulers.

For example, Gotthard von Kettler, the last Master of the Livonian Order, converted to Lutheranism, secularised (and took to himself) the lands of Semigallia and Courland which he had held on behalf of the order - which enabled him to marry and leave to his descendants the Duchy of Courland and Semigallia.

In Catholic canon law, the term can also denote the permission or authorization given for a member of a religious order to live outside his or her religious community or monastery, either for a fixed or permanent period.

Background

Secularization is sometimes credited both to the cultural shifts in society following the emergence of rationality and the development of science as a substitute for superstition—Max Weber called this process the "disenchantment of the world"—and to the changes made by religious institutions to compensate. At the most basic stages, this begins with a slow transition from oral traditions to a writing culture that diffuses knowledge. This first reduces the authority of clerics as the custodians of revealed knowledge. As the responsibility for education has moved from the family and community to the state, two consequences have arisen:

- *Collective conscience* as defined by Durkheim is diminished
- Fragmentation of communal activities leads to religion becoming more a matter of individual choice rather than an observed social obligation.

A major issue in the study of secularization is the extent to which certain trends such as decreased attendance at places of worship indicate a decrease in religiosity or simply a privatization of religious belief, where religious beliefs no longer play a dominant role in public life or in other aspects of decision making.

The issue of secularization is discussed in various religious traditions. The government of Turkey is an often cited example, following the abolition of the Ottoman Caliphate and foundation of the Turkish republic in 1923. This established popular sovereignty in a secular republican framework, in opposition to a system whose authority is based on religion. As one of many examples of state modernisation, this shows secularization and democratization as mutually reinforcing processes, relying on a separation of religion and state. In expressly secular states like India, it has been argued that the need was to legislate for toleration and respect between quite different religions, and likewise, the secularization of the West was a response to drastically violent intra-Christian feuds between Catholicism and Protestantism. Some have therefore argued that Western and Indian secularization is radically different in that it deals with autonomy from religious regulation and control. Considerations of both tolerance and autonomy are relevant to any secular state.

Definitions

John Somerville (1998) outlined six uses of the term secularization in the scientific literature. The first five are more along the lines of 'definitions' while the sixth is more of a 'clarification of use':

1. When discussing macro social structures, secularization can refer to *differentiation*: a process in which the various aspects of society, economic, political, legal, and moral, become increasingly specialised and distinct from one another.
2. When discussing individual institutions, secularization can denote the transformation of a religious into a secular institution. Examples would be the evolution of institutions such as Harvard University from a predominantly religious institution into a secular institution (with a divinity school now housing the religious element illustrating differentiation).
3. When discussing activities, secularization refers to the transfer of activities from religious to secular institutions, such as a shift in provision of social services from churches to the government.
4. When discussing mentalities, secularization refers to the transition from *ultimate* concerns to *proximate* concerns. E.g., individuals in the West are now more likely to moderate their behaviour in response to more immediately applicable consequences rather than out of concern for *post-mortem* consequences. This is a personal religious decline or movement toward a secular lifestyle.
5. When discussing populations, secularization refers to broad patterns of societal decline in levels of religiosity as opposed to the individual-level secularization of (4) above. This understanding of secularization is also distinct from (1) above in that it refers specifically to religious decline rather than societal differentiation.
6. When discussing religion, secularization can only be used unambiguously to refer to religion in a generic sense. For example, a reference to Christianity is not clear unless one specifies exactly which denominations of Christianity are being discussed.

Abdel Wahab Elmessiri (2002) Outlined two Meanings of the Secularization Term

1. Partial Secularization: which is the common meaning of the word, and expresses "The separation between religion and state".
2. Complete Secularization: this definition is not limited to the partial definition, but exceeds it to "The separation between all (religion, moral, and human) values, and (not just the state) but also to (the human nature in its public and private sides), so that the holiness is removed from the world, and this world is transformed into a usable matter that can be employed for the sake of the strong".

Sociological use and Differentiation

As studied by sociologists, one of the major themes of secularization is that of "differentiation"—i.e., the tendency for areas of life to become more distinct and specialised as a society becomes modernised. European sociology, influenced by anthropology, was interested in the process of change from the so-called primitive societies to increasingly advanced societies.

In the United States, the emphasis was initially on change as an aspect of progress, but Talcott Parsons refocused on society as a system immersed in a constant process of increased differentiation, which he saw as a process in which new institutions take over the tasks necessary in a society to guarantee its survival as the original monolithic institutions break up. This is a devolution from single, less differentiated institutions to an increasingly differentiated subset of institutions.

Following Parsons, this concept of differentiation has been widely applied. As phrased by Jose Casanova, this "core and the central thesis of the theory of secularization is the conceptualization of the process of societal modernisation as a process of functional differentiation and emancipation of the secular spheres—primarily the state, the economy, and science—from the religious sphere and the concomitant differentiation and specialisation of religion within its own newly found religious sphere".

Casanova also describes this as the theory of "privatization" of religion, which he partially criticizes. While criticizing certain aspects of the traditional sociological theory of secularization, however, David Martin argues that the concept of social differentiation has been its "most useful element".

Institutional Secularization

In most Western countries, government, nonprofits, and the private sector have taken over the provision of social welfare but in Germany, secularization has not occurred to the same degree. There are still about 100,000 church-based charitable foundations providing services from preschool education to health care for the elderly, making the two major churches the second largest employers after government. This is funded partly by the churches out of their own revenues, with the balance coming from general tax revenue.

Critics argue that by allowing the churches to play such a major role, the state is breaching its duty of neutrality under Article 4 of the *Grundgesetz*, and they consider it inappropriate for heavy subsidies to be given to the churches. On their part, the churches see this work as a natural part of their Christian mission.

Current Issues in Secularization

At present, secularization as understood in the West is being debated in the sociology of religion. In his works *Legitimacy of the Modern Age* (1966) and *The Genesis of the Copernican World* (1975), Hans Blumenberg has rejected the idea of a historical continuity - fundamental the so-called 'theorem of secularization'; the Modern age in his view represents an independent epoch opposed to Antiquity and the Middle Ages by a rehabilitation of human curiosity in reaction to theological absolutism. "Blumenberg targets Löwith's argument that progress is the secularization of Hebrew and Christian beliefs and argues to the contrary that the modern age, including its belief in progress, grew out of a new secular self-affirmation of culture against the Christian tradition." Wolfhart Pannenberg, a student of Löwith, has continued the debate against Blumenberg.

Charles Taylor in "A Secular Age" challenges what he calls 'the subtraction thesis' - that science lead to religion being subtracted from more and more areas of life.

Proponents of "secularization theory" demonstrate widespread declines in the prevalence of religious belief throughout the West, particularly in Europe. Some scholars (e.g., Rodney Stark, Peter Berger) have argued that levels of religiosity are not declining, while other scholars (e.g., Mark Chaves, N. J. Demerath) have countered by introducing the idea of neo-secularization, which broadens the definition of secularization to include the decline of religious authority and its ability to influence society.

In other words, rather than using the proportion of irreligious apostates as the sole measure of secularity, neo-secularization argues that individuals increasingly look outside of religion for authoritative positions. Neo-secularizationists would argue that religion has diminishing authority on issues such as birth control, and argue that religion's authority is declining and secularization is taking place even if religious affiliation may not be declining in the United States (a debate still taking place).

Finally, some claim that demographic forces offset the process of secularization, and may do so to such an extent that individuals can consistently drift away from religion even as society becomes more religious. This is especially the case in societies like Israel (with the ultra-Orthodox and religious Zionists) where committed religious groups have several times the birth rate of seculars. The religious fertility effect operates to a greater or lesser extent in all countries, and is amplified in the West by religious immigration. For instance, even as native whites became more secular, London, England, has become more religious in the past 25 years as religious immigrants and their descendants have increased their share of the population.

Religious Revivalism

Religious revivalism is term applied to mass movements which are based upon intense religious upheaval. Periodic religious revivals which seek to restore commitment and attachment to the group are a regular sociological feature of religious traditions. Revivalism happened in 18th century in western world among methodists. In India Arya Samaj is one of the most important revivalist movements which were based on shudhi movement. It aimed at converting Hindus back to the fold who had converted to other religions. This had profound impact on Hindu especially lower caste Hindus. They sought to other religions to improve their social status. They also gave equality to women especially in education.

Fundamentalism

Fundamentalism has been defined by its leading historian as the demand for a strict adherence to certain theological doctrines, in reaction against Modernist theology. The term was originally coined by its supporters to describe what they claimed were five specific classic theological beliefs of Christianity, and that developed into a Christian fundamentalist movement within the Protestant community of the United States in the early part of the 20th century.

The term usually has a religious connotation indicating unwavering attachment to a set of irreducible beliefs, but fundamentalism has come to be applied to a broad tendency among certain groups, mainly, although not exclusively, in religion. This tendency is most often characterized by a markedly strict literalism as applied to certain specific scriptures, dogmas, or ideologies, and a strong sense of the importance of maintaining ingroup and outgroup distinctions, which can lead to an emphasis on purity and the desire to return to a previous ideal from which it is believed that members have begun to stray. Rejection of diversity of opinion as applied to these established "fundamentals" and their accepted interpretation within the group is often the result of this tendency.

Fundamentalism is sometimes used as a pejorative term, particularly when combined with other epithets (as in the phrase "right-wing fundamentalists").

Christian

Fundamentalism as a movement arose in the United States, starting among conservative Presbyterian theologians at Princeton Theological Seminary in the late 19th century. It soon spread to conservatives among the Baptists and other denominations around 1910 to 1920. The movement's purpose was to reaffirm key theological tenets and defend them against the challenges of liberal theology and higher criticism.

The term "fundamentalism" has its roots in the Niagara Bible Conference (1878–1897), which defined those tenets it considered *fundamental* to Christian belief. The term was popularized by the *The Fundamentals*, a collection of twelve books on five subjects published in 1910 and funded by the brothers Milton and Lyman Stewart. This series of essays came to be representative of the "Fundamentalist-Modernist Controversy", which appeared late in the 19th century within some Protestant denominations in the United States, and continued in earnest through the 1920s. The first formulation of American fundamentalist beliefs can be traced to the Niagara Bible Conference and, in 1910, to the General Assembly of the Presbyterian Church, which distilled these into what became known as the "five fundamentals":

- Biblical inspiration and the inerrancy of scripture as a result of this
- Virgin birth of Jesus
- Belief that Christ's death was the atonement for sin

- Bodily resurrection of Jesus
- Historical reality of the miracles of Jesus

By the late 1910s, theological conservatives rallying around the Five Fundamentals came to be known as "fundamentalists". In practice, the first point regarding the Bible was the focus of most of the controversy. Fundamentalist groups generally decline to participate in events with any group that does not share its essential doctrines. They reject the existence of commonalities with theologically related religious traditions. For instance, fundamentalist Christians are less likely to group Christianity, Islam, and Judaism as being in one Abrahamic family of religions. In contrast, Evangelical groups, while they typically agree on the theology "fundamentals" as expressed in *The Fundamentals*, often are willing to participate in events with religious groups who do not hold to the essential doctrines.

Jewish

The term Jewish fundamentalism may refer to militant religious Zionism or Ashkenazi or Sephardic Haredi Judaism.

Ian S Lustik has stated that Jewish fundamentalism is aptly characterised as "an ultranationalist, eschatologically based, irredentist ideology", and Gush Emunim as the "dynamism that underlay the shift toward fundamentalism"

Islamic

The Shia and Sunni religious conflicts since the 7th century created an opening for radical ideologists, such as Ali Shariati (1933–77), to merge social revolution with Islamic fundamentalism, as exemplified by Iran in the 1970s. Islamic fundamentalism has appeared in many countries; the Wahhabi version is promoted worldwide and financed by Saudi Arabia, Qatar and Pakistan.

The Iran hostage crisis of 1979–80 marked a major turning point in the use of the term "fundamentalism". The media, in an attempt to explain the ideology of Ayatollah Khomeini and the Iranian Revolution to a Western audience described it as a "fundamentalist version of Islam" by way of analogy to the Christian fundamentalist movement in the U.S. Thus was born the term "Islamic fundamentalist", which would come to be one of the most common usages of the term in the following years.

Hindu

Hinduism is a conglomeration of distinct intellectual or philosophical points of view, rather than a rigid common set of beliefs, thus the basic definition of fundamentalism cannot apply to Hinduism as a whole considering that it does not contain any fundamentals binding upon all Hindus. However scholars identify several politically active Hindu movements (including the RSS, BJP and VHP) as part of the "Hindu fundamentalist family."

A recent phenomenon in India has been the rise of Hindu fundamentalism that has led to political mobilization against Muslims.

Buddhist

In the most recent instances, Buddhist fundamentalism has also targeted other religious and ethnic groups, such as that in Burma. As a Buddhist dominated nation, Burma has seen recent tensions between Muslim minorities and the Buddhist majority, especially during the 2013 Burma anti-Muslim riots, allegedly instigated by hardliner groups such as the 969 Movement.

There are historic and contemporary examples of Buddhist fundamentalism in each of the three main branches of Buddhism: Theravada, Mahayana and Vajrayana. In Japan, a prominent example has been the practice of shakubuku among some members of the Nichiren sect — a method of proselytizing involving strident condemnation other sects as deficient or evil. Similarly, some members of the New Kadampa Tradition of Tibetan Buddhism and the Western Shugden Society have appropriated the controversial and fiercely sectarian protector deity Dorje Shugden as a symbol of maintaining the purity of the Gelugpa sect from contamination by teachings from other sects, condemning the Dalai Lama's eclectic approach.

Non-religious

Some pejoratively refer to any philosophy which they see as literal-minded or they believe carries a pretense of being the sole source of objective truth as *fundamentalist*, regardless of whether it is usually called a religion. For instance, the Archbishop of Wales has criticized "atheistic fundamentalism" broadly and said "Any kind of fundamentalism, be it Biblical, atheistic or Islamic, is dangerous". He also said, "the new fundamentalism of our age ... leads to the language of expulsion and exclusivity, of extremism and polarisation, and the claim that, because God is on our side, he is not on yours."

In *The New Inquisition*, Robert Anton Wilson lampoons the members of skeptical organisations like the Committee for the Scientific Investigation of Claims of the Paranormal as fundamentalist materialists, alleging that they dogmatically dismiss any evidence that conflicts with materialism as hallucination or fraud.

In France, the imposition of restrictions on some displays of religion in state-run schools has been labelled by some as "secular fundamentalism". In the United States, private or cultural intolerance of women wearing the hijab (Islamic headcovering) and political activism by Muslims also has been labelled "secular fundamentalism" by some Muslims in the U.S.

The term "fundamentalism" is sometimes applied to signify a counter-cultural fidelity to a principle or set of principles, as in the pejorative term "market fundamentalism" applied to an exaggerated religious-like faith in the ability of unfettered *laissez-faire* or free market economic views or policies to solve economic and social problems. According to economist John Quiggin, the standard features of "economic fundamentalist rhetoric" are "dogmatic" assertions and the claim that anyone who holds contrary views is not a real economist. Retired professor in religious studies Roderick Hindery first lists positive qualities attributed to political, economic, or other forms of cultural fundamentalism. They include "vitality, enthusiasm, willingness to back up words with actions, and the avoidance of facile compromise." Then, negative aspects are analyzed, such as psychological attitudes, occasionally elitist and pessimistic perspectives, and in some cases literalism.

Atheist

In December 2007, the Archbishop of Wales Barry Morgan criticized what he referred to as "atheistic fundamentalism", claiming that it advocated that religion has no substance and "that faith has no value and is superstitious nonsense." He claimed it led to situations such as councils calling Christmas "Winterval", schools refusing to put on nativity plays and crosses removed from chapels. Others have countered that some of these attacks on Christmas are urban myths, not all schools do nativity plays because they choose to perform other traditional plays like A Christmas Carol or the The Snow Queen and, because of rising tensions between various religions, opening up public spaces to alternate displays than the Nativity scene is an attempt to keep government religion neutral.

Criticism

Many criticisms of fundamentalist positions have been offered. One of the most common is that some claims made by a fundamentalist group cannot be proven, and are irrational, demonstrably false, or contrary to scientific evidence. For example, some of these criticisms were famously asserted by Clarence Darrow in the Scopes Monkey Trial.

Sociologist of religion Tex Sample asserts that it is a mistake to refer to a Muslim, Jewish, or Christian Fundamentalist. Rather, a fundamentalist's fundamentalism is their primary concern, over and above other denominational or faith considerations.

A criticism by Elliot N. Dorff:

> *In order to carry out the fundamentalist program in practice, one would need a perfect understanding of the ancient language of the original text, if indeed the true text can be discerned from among variants. Furthermore, human beings are the ones who transmit this understanding between generations. Even if one wanted to follow the literal word of God, the need for people first to understand that word necessitates human interpretation. Through that process human fallibility is inextricably mixed into the very meaning of the divine word. As a result, it is impossible to follow the indisputable word of God; one can only achieve a human understanding of God's will.*

Howard Thurman was interviewed in the late 1970s for a BBC feature on religion. He told the interviewer: I say that creeds, dogmas, and theologies are inventions of the mind. It is the nature of the mind to make sense out of experience, to reduce the conglomerates of experience to units of comprehension which we call principles, or ideologies, or concepts. Religious experience is dynamic, fluid, effervescent, yeasty. But the mind can't handle these so it has to imprison religious experience in some way, get it bottled up. Then, when the experience quiets down, the mind draws a bead on it and extracts concepts, notions, dogmas, so that religious experience can make sense to the mind. Meanwhile religious experience goes on experiencing, so that by the time I get my dogma stated so that I can think about it, the religious experience becomes an object of thought.

Albert Camus opposed both Nazi fascism and Stalinist communism, leading to a split with Jean-Paul Sartre. In the *Myth of Sisyphus* he developed the concept of philosophical suicide. This is any ideological system or belief that claims to bridge the gap between man's yearning for absolute unity versus what he saw as the inherent irrational nature of the universe.

Influential criticisms of Fundamentalism include James Barr's books on Christian Fundamentalism and Bassam Tibi's analysis of Islamic Fundamentalism.

There are also some criticisms against the political usage of the term "fundamentalism". "Fundamentalism" has been often used by a political group to attack their political enemies. The term would be used flexibly depending on the political interests and context of the time. According to Judith Nagata, a professor of Asia Research Institute in the National University of Singapore, The Afghan *mujahiddin*, locked in combat with the Soviet enemy in the 1980s, could be praised as "freedom fighters" by their American backers at the time, while the present Taliban, viewed, among other things, as protectors of American enemy Osama bin Laden, are unequivocally "fundamentalist".""

A study at the University of Edinburgh has found that of its six measured dimensions of religiousity "lower intelligence is most associated with higher levels of fundamentalism."

Controversy

The Associated Press' *AP Stylebook* recommends that the term fundamentalist not be used for any group that does not apply the term to itself. A great many scholars have adopted a similar position. A good many scholars, however, use the term in the broader descriptive sense to refer to various groups in various religious traditions including those groups that would object to being classified as fundamentalists. That is the way that the term is used in *The Fundamentalism Project* by Martin Marty, et al., from the University of Chicago.

Christian fundamentalists, who generally consider the term to be pejorative when used to refer to themselves, often object to the placement of themselves and Islamist groups into a single category given that the fundamentals of Christianity are different from the fundamentals of Islam. They feel that characteristics based on the new definition are wrongly projected back onto Christian fundamentalists by their critics.

Many Muslims object to the use of the term when referring to Islamist groups, and oppose being placed in the same category as Christian fundamentalists, whom they see as theologically incomplete. Unlike Christian fundamentalist groups, Islamist groups do not use the term fundamentalist to refer to themselves. Shia groups which are often considered fundamentalist in the western world generally are not described that way in the Islamic world.

Chapter 6

Kinship

In anthropology, kinship is the web of social relationships that form an important part of the lives of most humans in most societies, although its exact meanings even within this discipline are often debated. Anthropologist Robin Fox states that "the study of kinship is the study of what man does with these basic facts of life - mating, gestation, parenthood, socialization, siblingship etc." Human society is unique, he argues, in that we "are working with the same raw material as exists in the animal world, but [we] can conceptualize and categorize it to serve social ends." These social ends include the socialization of children, and the formation of basic economic, political, and religious groups.

Kinship can refer both to the patterns of social relationships themselves, or it can refer to the study of the patterns of social relationships in one or more human cultures (i.e. kinship studies). Over its history, anthropology has developed a number of related concepts and terms in the study of kinship, such as descent, descent group, lineage, affine, cognate and fictive kinship. Further, even within these two broad usages of the term, there are different theoretical approaches.

Broadly, kinship patterns may be considered to include people related by both descent (one's social relations during development), and by marriage. Human kinship relations through marriage are commonly called "affinity" in contrast to the relationships that arise in one's group of origin, which may be called one's descent group. In some cultures, kinship relationships may be considered to extend out to people an individual has economic or political relationships with, or other forms of social connections. Within a culture, some descent groups may be considered to lead back to gods or animal ancestors (totems). This may be conceived of on a more or less literal basis.

Kinship can also refer to a principle by which individuals or groups of individuals are organised into social groups, roles, categories, and genealogy by means of kinship terminologies. Family relations can be represented concretely (mother, brother, grandfather) or abstractly by degrees of relationship (or kinship distance). A relationship may be relative (e.g., one is a father in relation to a child), or reflect an absolute (e.g., status difference between a mother and a childless woman). Degrees of relationship are not identical to heirship or legal succession. Many codes of ethics consider the bond of kinship as creating obligations between the related persons stronger than those between strangers, as in Confucian filial piety.

In a more general sense, kinship may refer to a similarity or affinity between entities on the basis of some or all of their characteristics that are under focus. This may be due to a shared ontological origin, a shared historical or cultural connection, or some other perceived shared features that connect the two entities. For example, a person studying the ontological roots of human languages (etymology) might ask whether there is kinship between the English word *seven* and the German word *sieben*. It can be used in a more diffuse sense as in, for example, the news headline "Madonna feels kinship with vilified Wallis Simpson", to imply a felt similarity or empathy between two or more entities.

In biology, it typically refers to the degree of genetic relatedness or coefficient of relationship between individual members of a species (e.g. kin selection theory). It may also be used in this specific sense when applied to human relationships, in which case its meaning is closer to consanguinity or genealogy.

Family

In human context, a family (from Latin: *familia*) is a group of people affiliated by consanguinity (by recognised birth), affinity (by marriage), or co-residence/shared consumption. Members of the immediate family may include a spouse, parent, brother and sister, and son and daughter. Members of the extended family may include grandparent, aunt, uncle, cousin, nephew and niece, or sibling-in-law. In most societies the family is the principal institution for the socialization of children. As the basic unit for raising children, anthropologists most generally classify family organisation as matrifocal (a mother and her children); conjugal (a husband, his wife, and children; also called nuclear family); avuncular (for example, a grandparent, a brother, his sister, and her children); or extended family in which parents and children co-reside with other members of one parent's family. As a unit of socialization, the family is the object of analysis for anthropologists and sociologists of the family. Sexual relations among the members are regulated by rules concerning incest such as the incest taboo. Family also spend time together to know each other. "Family" is used metaphorically to create more inclusive categories such as community, nationhood, global village and humanism. Genealogy is a field which aims to trace family lineages through history. Family is also an important economic unit studied in family economics.

Social Reproduction

One of the primary functions of the family involves providing a framework for the production and reproduction of persons, biologically and/or socially. This can occur through the sharing of material substances (such as food); the giving and receiving of care and nurture (nurture kinship); jural rights and obligations; and moral and sentimental ties. Thus, one's experience of one's family shifts over time. From the perspective of children, the family is a "family of orientation": the family serves to locate children socially and plays a major role in their enculturation and socialization. From the point of view of the parent(s), the family is a "family of procreation," the goal of which is to produce and enculturate and socialize children. However, producing children is not the only function of the family; in societies with a sexual division of labour, marriage, and the resulting relationship between two people, it is necessary for the formation of an economically productive household.

Christopher Harris notes that the western conception of family is ambiguous, and confused with the household, as revealed in the different contexts in which the word is used:

> *"We have seen that people can refer to their relatives as 'the family.' 'All the family turned up for the funeral.... But of course, my brother didn't bring his family along - they're much too young.' Here the reference is to the offspring (as distinct from 'all' the family). The neighbours were very good, too. 'The Jones came, and their two children. It was nice, the whole family turning up like that.' Here the usage is more restricted than 'relatives' or 'his relatives,' but includes just both parents and offspring. 'Of course, the children will be leaving home soon. It's always sad to see the family break up like that.' Here the reference is not only to parents and children but to their co-residence, that is, to the household."*

Olivia Harris states this confusion is not accidental, but indicative of the familial ideology of capitalist, western countries that pass social legislation that insists members of a nuclear family should live together, and that those not so related should not live together; despite the ideological and legal pressures, a large percentage of families do not conform to the ideal nuclear family type.

Types

The diverse data coming from ethnography, history, law and social statistics, establish that the human family is an institution and not a biological fact found on the natural relationship of consanguinity. The different types of families occur in a wide variety of settings, and their specific functions and meanings depend largely on their relationship to other social institutions. Although the concept of consanguinity originally referred to relations by "blood," cultural anthropologists have argued that one must understand the idea of "blood" metaphorically and that many societies understand family through other concepts rather than through genetic distance. Sociologists have a special interest in the function and status of these forms in stratified (especially capitalist) societies.

According to the work of scholars Max Weber, Alan Macfarlane, Steven Ozment, Jack Goody and Peter Laslett, the huge transformation that led to modern marriage in Western democracies was "fuelled by the religio-cultural value system provided by elements of Judaism, early Christianity, Roman Catholic canon law and the Protestant Reformation".

Much sociological, historical and anthropological research dedicates itself to the understanding of this variation, and of changes in the family that form over time. "Times have changed; it is more acceptable and encouraged for mothers to work and fathers to spend more time at home with the children. The way roles are balanced between the parents will help children grow and learn valuable life lessons. There is great importance of communication and equality in families, in order to avoid role strain."

Extended Family

An extended family is a family that extends beyond the immediate family, consisting of grandparents, aunts, uncles, and cousins all living nearby or in the same household. An example is a married couple that lives with either the husband or the wife's parents. The family changes from immediate household to extended household. In some circumstances, the extended family comes to live either with or in place of a member of the immediate family. These families include, in one household, near relatives in addition to an immediate family. An example would be an elderly parent who moves in with his or her children due to old age. This places large demands on the caregivers, particularly on the female relatives who choose to perform these duties for their extended family. In modern Western cultures dominated by immediate family constructs, the term has come to be used generically to refer to grandparents, uncles, aunts, and cousins, whether they live together within the same household or not. However, it may also refer to a family unit in which several generations live together within a single household. In some cultures, the term is used synonymously with consanguineous family.

In a stem family, a type of extended family, first presented by Frédéric Le Play, parents will live with one child and his or her spouse, as well as the children of both, while other children will leave the house or remain in it unmarried. The stem family is sometimes associated with inegalitarian inheritance practices, as in Japan and Korea, but the term has also been used in some contexts to describe a family type where parents live with a married child and his or her spouse and children, but the transfer of land and moveable property is more or less egalitarian, as in the case of traditional Romania, northeastern Thailand or Mesoamerican indigenous peoples. In these cases, the child who cares for the parents usually receives the house in addition to his or her own share of land and moveable property.

In an extended family, parents and their children's families may often live under a single roof. This type of joint family often includes multiple generations in the family. From culture to culture, the variance of the term may have different meanings. For instance, in India, the family is a patriarchal society, with the sons' families often staying in the same house.

In the joint family set-up, the workload is shared among the members, often unequally. The roles of women are often restricted to housewives and this usually involves cooking, cleaning, and organising for the entire family. The patriarch of the family (often the oldest male member) lays down the rules and arbitrates disputes. Other senior members of the household babysit infants in case their mother is working. They are also responsible in teaching the younger children their mother tongue, manners, and etiquette. Grandparents often take the leading roles due to the fact that they have the most experience with parenting and maintaining a household.

Amy Goyer, AARP multigenerational issues expert, said the most common multigenerational household is one with a grandparent as head of household and his adult children having moved in with their children, an arrangement usually spurred by the needs of one or both to combine resources and save money. The second most popular is a grandparent moving in with an adult child's family, usually for care-giving reasons. She noted that 2.5 million grandparents say they are responsible for the basic needs of the grandchild living with them.

The house often has a large reception area and a common kitchen. Each family has their own bedroom. The members of the household also look after each other when a member is ill.

Sociology

It has often been presumed that extended family groups sharing a single household enjoy certain advantages, such as a greater sense of security and belonging due to sharing a wider pool of members to serve as resources during a crisis, and more role models to help perpetuate desired behaviour and cultural values. However, even in cultures where adults are expected to leave home after marriage to begin their own nuclear-based households, the extended family often forms an important support network offering similar advantages. Particularly in working-class communities, grown children tend to establish their own households within the same general area as their parents, aunts, uncles, and grandparents. These extended family members tend to gather often for family events and to feel responsible for helping and supporting one another, both emotionally and financially.

While contemporary families may be considered more mobile in general than in the past, sociologists find that this has not necessarily resulted in the disintegration of extended family networks. Rather, technological aids such as the Internet and social networking sites such as Facebook are now commonly used to retain contact and maintain these family ties.

Particularly in the case of single-parent households, it can be helpful for extended family members to share a single household in order to share the burden of meeting expenses. On the other hand, sharing a household can present a disadvantage depending on the sizes and number of families involved, particularly when only a few members shoulder most of the responsibility to meet expenses for the family's basic needs.

An estimated 49 million Americans (16.1% of the total population) live in homes comprising three or more generations, up from 42 million in 2000. This situation is similar in Western Europe. Another 34 percent live within a kilometre of their children.

Around the World

In many cultures, such as in those of many of the Asians, Middle Easterners, Africans, Eastern Europeans, indigenous Latin Americans and Pacific Islanders, *extended families* are the basic family unit. Even in Western Europe, extended families (mostly of the stem type) were also clearly prevalent, England being a rare exception. Some have stated that the relative "uniqueness" of the traditional English family (the absolute nuclear family) was at least partly responsible for the birth of industrialization, free-market capitalism and liberalism in that country.

It is common for today's world to have older children in nuclear families to reach walking up to driving age ranges before meeting extended family members. Geographical isolation is common for middle-class families who move based on occupational opportunities while family branches "retain [their] basic independence". Some extended families hold family reunions or opportunities for gathering regularly, normally around holiday timc frames, to reestablish and integrate a stronger family connection. This allows individual nuclear families to connect with extended family members.

Australian Aborigines are another group for whom the concept of family extends well beyond the nuclear model. Aboriginal immediate families include aunts, uncles and a number of other relatives who would be considered "distant relations" in the context of the nuclear family. Aboriginal families have strict social rules regarding whom they can marry. Their family structure incorporates a shared responsibility for all tasks.

Where families consist of multiple generations living together, the family is usually headed by the oldest man. More often than not, it consists of grandparents, their sons and their sons' families.

Hindu Joint Family

A joint Hindu family, otherwise called a "Hindu undivided family", consists of all persons lineally descended from a common ancestor, and includes their wives and unmarried daughters. A daughter ceases to be a member of her father's family on marriage and becomes a member of her husband's family. The joint and undivided family is the normal condition of Hindu society. An undivided Hindu family is ordinarily joint not only in estate, but also in food and worship. The existence of a joint estate is not an essential prerequisite to constitute a joint family. A family that does not own any property may, nevertheless, be joint. Where there is joint estate, and the members of the family become separate in estate, the family ceases to be a joint family. Mere severance in food and worship does not operate as a separation. Businesses carried out by Hindu joint families in India are governed by the Hindu law, where the liability of the entire business is borne out by the oldest surviving male member, who is the manager of the family and is the head of family and is also the head of the business of the Hindu undivided family by default. He is called "Karta".

Recent Trend in the United States

In the early stages of the twentieth century, it was not very common to find many families with extended kin in their household, which may have been due to the idea that the young people in these times typically waited to establish themselves and start a household before they married and filled a home. As life expectancy becomes older and programs such as Social Security benefit the elderly, the old are now beginning to live longer than prior generations, which then may lead to generations mixing together. According to results of a study by Pew Research Centre in 2010, approximately 50 million (nearly one in six) Americans, including rising numbers of seniors, live in households with at least two adult generations, and often three. It has become an ongoing trend for elderly generations to move in and live with their children, as they can give them support and help with everyday living. The main reasons cited for this shift are an increase in unemployment and slumped housing prices and arrival of new immigrants from Asian and South American countries. In 2003, the number of U.S. "family groups" where one or more subfamilies live in a household (e.g. a householder's daughter has a child. The mother-child is a subfamily) was 79 million. 2.6 million of U.S. multigenerational family households in 2000 with a householder, the householder's children, and the householder's grandchildren. That's 65 percent of multigenerational family households in the U.S. So it is twice as common for a grandparent to be the householder than for adult children to bring parents into their home. The increase in the number of multigenerational households has created complex legal issues, such as who in the household has authority to consent to police searches of the family home or private bedrooms.

Economic Background

Economic background has become a very prominent factor in the likelihood of living in an extended family. Many families who live in low-income areas are beginning to move in with one another for financial and emotional support. The relative economic deprivation of racial and ethnic minorities leads to higher levels of extended family involvement; primarily because blacks and Latinos have less money and education than whites, they are more likely to give and receive help from kin. Having family on which one can rely is very important in times of economic hardship especially if there are children involved. Living in an extended family provides constant care for children and support for other members of the family as well. Analysis of the National Survey of Families and Households suggests there are differences between whites and other ethnic groups because of economic differences among racial groups: blacks and Latinos less often have the economic resources that allow the kind of privatization that the nuclear family entails. Extended kinship, then, is a survival strategy in the face of economic difficulties. Being able to rely on not only two parents but grandparents, aunts, uncles, brothers, and sisters helps to create a support system which in turn brings families closer together. Living in an extended family provides many things that a nuclear family does not.

The number of multigenerational households has been steadily rising because of the economic hardships people are experiencing today. According to the AARP, multigenerational households have increased from 5 million in 2000 to 6.2 million in 2008. "There's no question that with some ethnicities that are growing in America, it is more mainstream and traditional to have multigenerational households. We're going to see that increasing in the general population as well," says AARP's Ginzler. While high unemployment and housing foreclosures of the recession have played a key role in the trend, Pew Research Centre exec VP and co-author of its multigenerational household study Paul Taylor said it has been growing over several decades, fuelled by demographic and cultural shifts such as the rising number of immigrants and the rising average age of young-adult marriages. The importance of an extended family is one that many people may not realise, but having a support system and many forms of income may help people today because of the difficulties in finding a job and bringing in enough money.

Complex Family

"Complex family" is a generic term for any family structure involving more than two adults. The term can refer to any extended family, polyamorous or to a polygamy of any type. It is often used to refer to the group marriage form of polygamy.

Matrifocal Family

A matrifocal family structure is one where mothers head families and fathers play a less important role in the home and in bringing up children.

Definition

"A family or domestic group is matrifocal when it is centred on a woman and her children. In this case the father(s) of these children are intermittently present in the life of the group and occupy a secondary place. The children's mother is not necessarily the wife of one of the children's fathers." In general, according to Laura Hobson Herlihy citing P. Mohammed, women have "high status" if they are "the main wage earners", they "control ... the household economy", and males tend to be absent. The term was coined in 1956. Men's absences are often of long durations.

Alternative terms for 'matrifocal' or 'matrifocality' include *matricentric*, *matripotestal*, and *women-centred kinship networks*.

The matrifocal is distinguished from the matrilocal, the matrilineal, and matriarchy (the last because matrifocality does not imply that women have power in the larger community).

Characteristics and Distribution

According to anthropologist Maurice Godelier, matrifocality is "typical of Afro-Caribbean groups" and some African-American communities. These include families in which a father has a wife and one or more mistresses; in a few cases, a mother may have more than one lover. Matrifocality was also found, according to Rasmussen per Herlihy, among the Tuareg people in northern Africa; by Raymond T. Smith (according to Herlihy), in some Black Caribbean families in British Guyana; according to Herlihy citing other authors, in some Mediterranean communities; and, according to Herlihy quoting Scott, in urban Brazil.

Herlihy found matrifocality among the Miskitu people, in the village of Kuri, on the Caribbean coast of northeastern Honduras in the late 1990s. According to Herlihy, the "main power" of Kuri women lies "in their ability to craft everyday social identities and kinship relations .... Their power lies beyond the scope of the Honduran state, which recognises male surnames and males as legitimate heads of households." Herlihy found in Kuri a trend toward matriliny and a correlation with matrilineality, while some patriarchal norms also existed. Herlihy found that the "women knew more than most men about village histories, genealogies, and local folklore" and that "men typically did not know local kinship relations, the proper terms of reference, or reciprocity obligations in their wife's family" and concluded that Miskitu women "increasingly assume responsibility for the social reproduction of identities and ultimately for preserving worldwide cultural and linguistic diversity". The Nair community in Kerala and the Bunt community in Tulunadu in South India are prime examples of matrifocality. This can be attributed to the fact that if males were largely warriors by profession, a community was bound to lose male members at youth, leading to a situation where the females assumed the role of running the family.

History

In the 14th century, in Jiangnan, South China, under Mongol rule by the Yuan dynasty, Kong Qi kept a diary of his view of some families as practicing gynarchy, not defined as it is in major dictionaries but defined by Paul J. Smith as "the creation of short-term family structures dominated by women" and not as matrilineal or matriarchal. The gynarchy possibly could be passed down through generations. According to Paul J. Smith, it was to this kind of gynarchy that "Kong ascribed...the general collapse of society" and Kong believed that men in Jiangnan tended to "forfeit...authority to women".

Matrifocality arose, Godelier said, in some Afro-Caribbean and African American cultures as a consequence of enslavement of thousands. Slaves were forbidden to marry and their children belonged to the slavemasters. Women in slave families "often" sought impregnation by White masters so the children would have lighter skin colour and be more successful in life, lessening the role of Black husbands. Some societies, particularly Western European, allow women to enter the paid labour force or receive government aid and thus be able to afford to raise children alone while some other societies "oppose ... [women] living on their own."

In feminist belief (more common in the 1970s than in the 1990s–2000s and criticized within feminism and within archaeology, anthropology, and theology as lacking a scholarly basis), there was a "matrifocal (if not matriarchal) Golden Age" before patriarchy.

Matrilocal Residence

In social anthropology, matrilocal residence or matrilocality (also uxorilocal residence or uxorilocality) is a term referring to the societal system in which a married couple resides with or near the wife's parents. Thus, the female offspring of a mother remain living in (or near) the mother's house, thereby forming large clan-families, typically consisting of three or four generations living in the same place.

Description

Frequently, visiting marriage is being practiced, meaning that husband and wife are living apart in their separate families, seeing each other in their spare time. The children of such marriages are raised by the mother's extended matrilineal clan. The father does not have a significant role in the upbringing of his own children; he does, however, in that of his sisters' children (his nieces and nephews). In direct consequence, property is inherited from generation to generation, and, over all, remains largely undivided.

Matrilocal residence is found most often in horticultural societies. Examples of matrilocal societies include the people of Ngazidja, the Ancient Pueblo Peoples of Chaco Canyon, the Nair community in Kerala in South India, the Moso of Yunnan and Sichuan in southwestern China, the Siraya of Taiwan, and the Minangkabau of western Sumatra. In native Amazonia, this residence pattern is often associated with the customary practice of brideservice, as seen among the Urarina of northeastern Peru. In contemporary mainland China, matrilocal residence has been encouraged by the government in an attempt to counter the problem of unbalanced male-majority sex ratios caused by the abortion, infanticide and abandonment of girls. Because girls traditionally marry out in virilocal marriage (living with or near the husband's parents) they have been seen as "mouths from another family" or as a waste of resources to raise. During the Song Dynasty in medieval China, matrilocal marriage became common for wealthy non-aristocratic families.

In other regions of the world, such as Japan, during the Heian period, a marriage of this type was not a sign of high status, but rather an indication of the patriarchal authority of the woman's family (her father or grandfather), who was sufficiently powerful to demand it.

Another matrilocal society is the !Kung San of Southern Africa. They practice uxorilocality for the bride service period, which lasts until the couple has produced three children or they have been together for more than ten years. At the end of the bride service period, the couple has a choice of which clan they want to live with. (Technically, uxorilocality differs from matrilocality; uxorilocality means the couple settles with the wife's family, while matrilocality means the couple settles with the wife's lineage. Because the !Kung do not live in lineages, they cannot be matrilocal; they are uxorilocal.)

Early theories explaining the determinants of postmarital residence (by, for example, Lewis Henry Morgan, Edward Tylor, and George Peter Murdock) connected it with the sexual division of labour. However, for many years cross-cultural tests of this hypothesis using worldwide samples failed to find any significant relationship between these two variables. On the other hand, Korotayev's tests have shown that the female contribution to subsistence does correlate significantly with matrilocal residence in general; however, this correlation is masked by a general polygyny factor. Although an increase in the female contribution to subsistence tends to lead to matrilocal residence, it also tends simultaneously to lead to general non-sororal polygyny which effectively destroys matrilocality. If this polygyny factor is controlled (e.g., through a multiple regression model), division of labour turns out to be a significant predictor of postmarital residence. Thus, Murdock's hypotheses regarding the relationships between the sexual division of labour and postmarital residence were basically correct, though, as has been shown by Korotayev, the actual relationships between those two groups of variables are more complicated than he expected.

Matrilocality in the Arikari culture in the 17th–18th centuries was studied anew within feminist archaeology by Christi Mitchell, in a critique of a previous study, the critique challenging whether men were virtually the sole agents of societal change while women were only passive.

According to Barbara Epstein, anthropologists in the 20th century criticized feminist promatriarchal views and said that "the goddess worship or matrilocality that evidently existed in many paleolithic societies was not necessarily associated with matriarchy in the sense of women's power over men. Many societies can be found that exhibit those qualities along with female subordination. Furthermore, militarism, destruction of the natural environment, and hierarchical social structures can be found in societies in which goddess worship, matrilocality, or matriliny exist."

In sociobiology, matrilocality refers to animal societies in which a pair bond is formed between animals born or hatched in different areas or different social groups, and the pair becomes resident in the female's home area or group.

Nuclear Family

The nuclear family or elementary family is a term used to define a family group consisting of a pair of adults and their children. This is in contrast to a single-parent family, to the larger extended family, and to a family with more than two parents. Nuclear families typically centre on a married couple; the nuclear family may have any number of children. There are differences in definition among observers; some definitions allow only biological children that are full-blood siblings, while others allow for a stepparent and any mix of dependent children including stepchildren and adopted children.

Family structures of one married couple and their children were present in Western Europe and New England in the 17th century, influenced by church and theocratic governments. With the emergence of proto-industrialization and early capitalism, the nuclear family became a financially viable social unit. The term *nuclear family* first appeared in the early twentieth century. Alternative definitions have evolved to include family units headed by same-sex parents, and perhaps additional adult relatives who take on a cohabiting parental role; in this latter case it also receives the name of conjugal family.

The concept that a narrowly defined nuclear family is central to stability in modern society has been promoted by familialists who are social conservatives in the United States, and has been challenged as historically and sociologically inadequate to describe the complexity of actual family relations.

Usage of the Term

Merriam-Webster dates the term back to 1947, while the *Oxford English Dictionary* has a reference to the term from 1925; thus it is relatively new, although nuclear family structures themselves date back thousands of years. The term *nuclear* is used in its general meaning referring to a central entity or "nucleus" around which others collect. In its most common usage, the term *nuclear family* refers to a household consisting of a father, a mother and their children all in one household dwelling. The late George Murdock, an influential observer of families, offered an early description:

The family is a social group characterized by common residence, economic cooperation and reproduction. It contains adults of both sexes, at least two of whom maintain a socially approved sexual relationship, and one or more children, own or adopted, of the sexually cohabiting adults.

Many individuals are part of two nuclear families in their lives: the family of origin in which they are offspring, and the family of procreation in which they are a parent.

Compared to Extended Family

An extended family group consists of non-nuclear (or "non-immediate") family members considered together with nuclear (or "immediate") family members.

Changes to Family Formation

In 2005, information from the United States Census Bureau showed that 70% of children in the US live in traditional two-parent families, with 66% of those living with parents who were married, and

60% living with their biological parents, and that "the figures suggest that the tumultuous shifts in family structure since the late 1960s have leveled off since 1990".

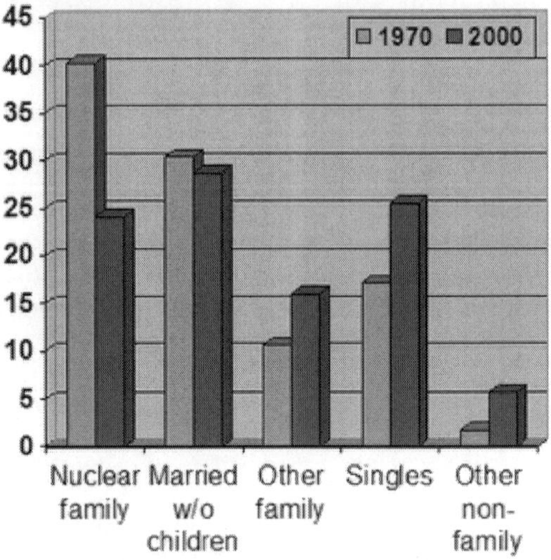

Figure: *From 1970 to 2000, family arrangements in the US became more diverse with no particular household arrangement prevalent enough to be identified as the "average"*

If considered separately from couples without children, single-parent families, and unmarried couples with children, in the United States traditional nuclear families appear to constitute a minority of households - with a rising prevalence of other family arrangements. In 2000, nuclear families with the original biological parents constituted roughly 24.1% of American households, compared to 40.3% in 1970. Roughly two-thirds of all children in the United States will spend at least some time in a single-parent household.

In the UK the number of nuclear families fell from 39% of all households in 1968 to 28% in 1992. The decrease accompanied an equivalent increase in the number of single-parent households and IN the number of adults living alone.

According to some sociologists, "[The nuclear family] no longer seems adequate to cover the wide diversity of household arrangements we see today." (Edwards 1991; Stacey 1996). A new term has been introduced, *postmodern family*, intended to describe the great variability in family forms, including single-parent families and couples without children."

Professor Wolfgang Haak of Adelaide University, detects traces of the nuclear family in prehistoric Central Europe. A 2005 archeological dig in Elau in Germany, analyzed by Haak, revealed genetic evidence suggesting that the 13 individuals found in a grave were closely related. Haak said, "By establishing the genetic links between the two adults and two children buried together in one grave, we have established the presence of the classic nuclear family in a prehistoric context in Central Europe.... Their unity in death suggest[s] a unity in life." This paper does not regard the nuclear family as "natural" or as the only model for human family life. "This does not establish the elemental family to be a universal model or the most ancient institution of human communities. For example, polygamous unions are prevalent in ethnographic data and models of household communities have apparently been involving a high degree of complexity from their origins." In this study evidence suggests that the nuclear family was embedded with an extended family. The remains of three children (probably siblings based on DNA evidence) were found buried with a woman who was not their mother but may have been an "aunt or a step-mother".

North American Conservatism

For social conservatism in the United States and in Canada, the idea that the nuclear family is traditional is an important aspect, where family is seen as the primary unit of society. These movements oppose alternative family forms and social institutions that are seen by them to undermine parental authority, like day care centres and sex education.

The Myth of the Nuclear Family

The ideal nuclear family is a myth because "across cultures, people live in all sorts of family groups." Examples of other family groups consist of polygamy when one person marries more than one wife. According to anthropological data, there is a lack of evidence that proves that the nuclear family has been around very long.

"The postwar nuclear family headed by a breadwinning man and homemaker wife that's become the "traditional" measuring stick against which today's families are judged is more mythical ideal than bygone reality"

To paraphrase Shannon Proudfoot, the ideal nuclear family is a myth because in today's society. In modern television shows, a balance between family love and family conflict is depicted.

Patrilocal Residence

In social anthropology, patrilocal residence or patrilocality (also virilocal residence or virilocality) is a term referring to the social system in which a married couple resides with or near the husband's parents. The concept of location may extend to a larger area such as a village, town, or clan area. This practice is found in about 69 percent of the world's cultures that have been described ethnographically. It has also been documented as well as among Neanderthals in Spain and ancient homonids in Africa.

Description

In a patrilocal society, when a man marries, his wife joins him in his father's home or compound, where they raise their children. These children will follow the same pattern. Sons will stay and daughters will move in with their husbands' families. Families living in a patrilocal residence generally assume joint ownership of domestic sources. The household is led by a senior member, who also directs the labour of all other members. Matrilocal residence may be regarded as the opposite of patrilocal residence. However, since the majority of societies exhibit at least some degree of patriarchy, in most matrilocal groups the brothers (or mothers' brothers) are the authority figures, not the wives or mothers themselves.

Early theories explaining the determinants of postmarital residence (e.g., Lewis Henry Morgan, Edward Tylor, or George Peter Murdock) connected it with the sexual division of labour. However, to date, cross-cultural tests of this hypothesis using worldwide samples have failed to find any significant relationship between these two variables. However, Korotayev's tests show that the female contribution to subsistence does correlate significantly with matrilocal (as opposed to patrilocal) residence in general; however, this correlation is masked by a general polygyny factor. Although an increase in the female contribution to subsistence tends to lead to matrilocal residence, it also tends simultaneously to lead to general non-sororal polygyny which effectively destroys matrilocality, and pushes a social system toward patrilocality. If this polygyny factor is controlled (e.g., through a multiple regression model), division of labour turns out to be a significant predictor of postmarital residence. Thus, Murdock's hypotheses regarding the relationships between the sexual division of labour and postmarital residence were basically correct, though, as has been shown by Korotayev, the actual relationships between those two groups of variables are more complicated than he expected.

Neanderthals and Early Hominins

It is claimed that the practice was also prevalent in some Neanderthal populations. A 49,000-year-old grave was found in Spain in 2010 which contained three related-to-each-other males, with three unrelated-to-each-other females, suggesting they were the partners of the males.

A 2011 study using ratios of strontium isotopes in teeth also suggested that roughly 2 million years ago, among Australopithecus and Paranthropus robustus groups in southern Africa, women tended to settle farther from their region of birth than men did.

Consanguinity

Consanguinity ("blood relation", from the Latin *consanguinitas*) is the property of being from the same kinship as another person. In that aspect, consanguinity is the quality of being descended from the same ancestor as another person. The laws of many jurisdictions set out degrees of consanguinity in relation to prohibited sexual relations and marriage parties or whether a given person inherits property when a deceased person has not left a will.

The degree of relative consanguinity can be illustrated with a consanguinity table, in which each level of lineal consanguinity (*i.e.*, generation or meiosis) appears as a row, and individuals with a collaterally consanguineous relationship share the same row. The Knot System is a numerical notation that defines consanguinity.

Legal Definitions

Modern Secular Law: Issues of consanguinity arise in several aspects of the law. It is directly relevant in determining whether a couple can marry. These are linked to a jurisdiction's definition of incest, so that couples in an incestuous relationship will not be permitted to marry. Some United States jurisdictions forbid first-cousins to marry, while others limit the prohibition to any direct ancestors or descendants, as well as siblings, half-siblings, aunts and uncles. However, marriage with aunts and uncles (avunculate marriage) is legal in Argentina, Australia, Austria, Brazil, France, Malaysia, and Russia, among other places in the world.

Several volumes of *Smith's Laws*, enacted from 1700 through 1829, contain certain public and private laws of the Province and Commonwealth of Pennsylvania. Several laws with a prescribed punishment against adultery, bigamy, incest and fornication and all combinations of those crimes were enacted in 1705.

Consanguinity is also relevant in issues of inheritance. In regard to the law of intestate succession (when a person dies without a will), under the Uniform Probate Code of the United States section 2-103, after a surviving spouse receives his or her share, the descendants (depending on the circumstances this may include children, grandchildren, or great grandchildren, either biological or adopted) receive the remainder of the intestate estate. If there are no children, the decedent's parent(s) receive the remainder of the estate. If there are neither descendants nor parents, the decedent's estate is distributed to descendants of the decedent's parents (again, depending on the circumstances, brothers and sisters, nieces and nephews, grand nieces and nephews and great grand nieces and nephews). If there are no descendants, parents, or descendants of parents, then the deceased's property passes to the decedent's grandparents, or if no grandparents, then the descendants of the grandparents of the decedent (uncles and aunts, first cousins, or first cousins once, twice, or thrice removed, second cousins, third cousins etc.).

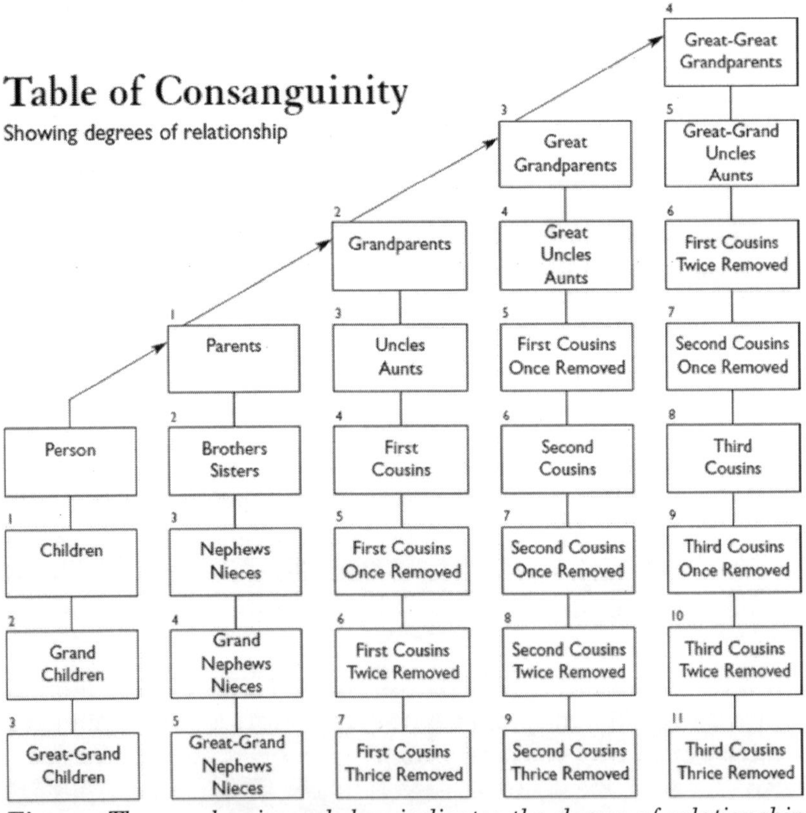

Figure: *The number in each box indicates the degree of relationship*

Also, some jurisdictions prohibit individuals from serving on a jury in which they have a certain degree of consanguinity with the defendant. Adoption may or may not be considered at law to create such a bond; in most Western societies, adoptive relationships are considered blood relationships for these purposes, but in others, including both Japan and ancient Rome, it was common for a couple with only daughters to adopt a son-in-law, making the marriage one between adoptive siblings.

Religious and Traditional Law

Under Roman civil law, which early canon law of the Catholic Church followed, couples were forbidden to marry if they were within four degrees of consanguinity. In the ninth century the church raised the number of prohibited degrees to seven and changed the method by which they were calculated. Eventually the nobility became too interrelated to marry as the pool of non-related prospective spouses became smaller. It was either defy the church's position or look elsewhere for eligible marriage candidates. In 1215 the Fourth Lateran Council made what they believed was a necessary change to canon law reducing the number of prohibited degrees of consanguinity from seven back to four. The method of calculating prohibited degrees was changed also. Instead of the former practice of counting up to the common ancestor then down to the proposed spouse, the new law computed consanguinity by counting back to the common ancestor. In the Roman Catholic Church, unknowingly marrying a closely consanguineous blood relative was grounds for an annulment, but during the eleventh and twelfth centuries dispensations were granted with increasing frequency due to the thousands of persons encompassed in the prohibition at seven degrees and the hardships this posed for finding potential spouses. After 1215 the general rule was that while fourth cousins could marry without dispensation, generally the need for dispensations was greatly reduced. In fourteenth century England, for example, papal dispensations for annulments due to consanguinity (and affinity) were relatively few.

The connotations of degree of consanguinity varies by context (e.g., Canon law, Roman law, etc.). Most cultures define a degree of consanguinity within which sexual interrelationships are regarded as incestuous (the "prohibited degree of kinship").

Among the Christian *Habesha* highlanders of Ethiopia and Eritrea (the predominantly orthodox Christian Amhara and Tigray-Tigrinya), it is a tradition to be able to recount one's paternal ancestors at least seven generations away starting from early childhood, because "those with a common patrilineal ancestor less than seven generations away are considered 'brother and sister' and may not marry." The rule is less strict on the mother's side, where the limit is about four generations back, but still determined patrilineally. This rule does not apply to

Muslims or other ethnic groups. Ayurveda clearly states that marriage within the Gotra is a consanguineous marriage which can lead to many gestational and genetic problems in the fetus. So it has become a common practice in the Hindu households during pre-marriage discussions to ask the couples' Gotra. Couples of the same Gotra are advised not to marry. The advisers of this system say that this practice definitely helps in reducing the gestational problems and ensures a healthy progeny.

Genetic Definitions

The percentage of consanguinity between any two individuals decreases fourfold as the most recent common ancestor recedes one generation. Consanguinity, as commonly defined, does not depend on the amount of shared DNA within two people's genome. It rather counts the number of meioses separating two individuals. Because of the effects of pedigree collapse, this does not directly translate into the amount of shared genetic substance.

It is common to distinguish first-degree cousins, second-degree cousins, and often also third-degree cousins. Since comparatively few people can trace their full family tree for more than four generations, the identity of fourth-degree cousins often cannot be established. Also, at a genetic level, half-fourth cousins typically do not exhibit greater genetic similarity with one another than with any other individual from the same population.

Double first cousins are descended from two pairs of siblings, and have the same genetic similarity as half-siblings.

Conventionally, genetic consanguinity is expressed as defined by Wright with the coefficient of relationship r, where r is defined as the fraction of homozygous due to the consanguinity under discussion. Thus, a parent and child pair has a value of r=0.5, siblings have a value of r=0.5, a parent's sibling has r=0.25, and first cousins have r=0.125.

As a working definition, unions contracted between persons biologically related as second cousins or closer ($r \geq 0.0156$) are categorized as consanguineous. This arbitrary limit has been chosen because the genetic influence in marriages between couples related to a lesser degree would usually be expected to differ only slightly from that observed in the general population.

Globally, the most common form of consanguineous union contracted is between first cousins, in which the spouses share 1/8 of their genes inherited from a common ancestor, and so their progeny are homozygous (or more correctly autozygous) at 1/16 of all loci (r =

0.0625). Due to variation in geographical and ethnic background and the loci chosen to genotype there is some 2.4% variation expected. In practice the technical factors involved are the design of the SNP genotyping platform was used (e.g. which SNP array or sequencing method) and which software cut-offs were applied.

Rates of Occurrence

Historically, some European nobles cited a close degree of consanguinity when they required convenient grounds for divorce, especially in contexts where religious doctrine forbade the voluntary dissolution of an unhappy or childless marriage. Conversely, the consanguinity law of succession requires the next monarch to be of the same blood of the previous one; allowing, for example, illegitimate children to inherit.

It is estimated that 55% of marriages between Pakistani Muslim immigrants in the United Kingdom are between first cousins, where "preferential patrilateral parallel cousin marriage" (where a boy marries the daughter of his father's brother) is often favoured.

Genetic Disorders

The phenomenon of inbreeding, or endogamy, increases the level of homozygotes for autosomal genetic disorders and generally leads to a decreased fitness of a population known as inbreeding depression, a major objective in clinical studies. The offspring of consanguineous relationships are at greater risk of certain genetic disorders. Autosomal recessive disorders occur in individuals who are homozygous for a particular recessive gene mutation. This means that they carry two copies (alleles) of the same gene. Except in certain rare circumstances (new mutations or uniparental disomy) both parents of an individual with such a disorder will be carriers of the gene.

Such carriers are not affected and will not display any signs that they are carriers, and so may be unaware that they carry the mutated gene. As relatives share a proportion of their genes, it is much more likely that related parents will be carriers of an autosomal recessive gene, and therefore their children are at a higher risk of an autosomal recessive disorder. The extent to which the risk increases depends on the degree of genetic relationship between the parents; so the risk is greater in mating relationships where the parents are close relatives, but for relationships between more distant relatives, such as second cousins, the risk is lower (although still greater than the general population). A study based on cognitive behaviours among children has revealed the cognitive impairments, more common among the subjects having greater value of inbreeding coefficients. The low genetic heterozygosity associated with increased consanguinity in a population (identified by microsatellite markers) increases its susceptibility to infectious pathogens such as tuberculosis and hepatitis. A notable historical example of the detrimental effects of consanguinous marriages is the now-extinct House of Habsburg.

Kinship Terminology

Kinship terminology is the systems used in languages to refer to the persons to whom an individual is related through kinship. Different societies classify kinship relations differently and therefore use different systems of kinship terminology - for example some languages distinguish between affinal and consanguine uncles, whereas others have only one word to refer to both a father and his brothers. Kinship terminologies include the terms of address used in different languages or communities for different relatives and the terms of reference used to identify the relationship of these relatives to ego or to each other.

Historical View

Anthropologist Lewis Henry Morgan (1818–1881) performed the first survey of kinship terminologies in use around the world. Though much of his work is now considered dated, he argued that kinship terminologies reflect different sets of distinctions. For example, most kinship terminologies distinguish between sexes (the difference between a brother and a sister) and between generations (the difference between a child and a parent). Moreover, he argued, kinship terminologies distinguish between relatives by blood and marriage (although recently some anthropologists have argued that many societies define kinship in terms other than blood).

However, Morgan also observed that different languages (and, by extension, societies) organise these distinctions differently. He proposed to describe kin terms and terminologies as either descriptive or classificatory. When a descriptive term is used, it can only represent one type of relationship between two people, while a classificatory term represents one of many different types of relationships. For example, the word *brother* in English-speaking societies indicates a son of the same parent; thus, English-speaking societies use the word *brother* as a descriptive term. But a person's male first cousin could be the mother's brother's son, mother's sister's son, father's brother's son, father's sister's son, and so on; English-speaking societies therefore use the word *cousin* as a classificatory term.

Morgan discovered that a descriptive term in one society can become a classificatory term in another society. For example, in some societies, one would refer to many different people as "mother" (the woman who gave birth to oneself, as well as her sister and husband's sister, and also one's father's sister). Moreover, some societies do not group together relatives which the English-speaking societies classify together. For example, some languages have no one-word equivalent to *cousin*, because different terms refer to mother's sister's children and to father's sister's children.

Armed with these different terms, Morgan identified six basic patterns of kinship terminologies:

- Hawaiian kinship: the most classificatory; only distinguishes between sex and generation. Thus, siblings and cousins are not distinguished (the same terms are used for both types of relatives).
- Sudanese kinship: the most descriptive; no two types of relatives share the same term. Siblings are distinguished from cousins, and different terms are used for each type of cousin (i.e. father's brother's children, father's sister's children, mother's sister's children and mother's brother's children).
- Eskimo kinship: has both classificatory and descriptive terms; in addition to sex and generation, it also distinguishes between lineal relatives (those related directly by a line of descent) and collateral relatives (those related by blood, but not directly in the line of descent). Lineal relatives have highly descriptive terms; collateral relatives have highly classificatory terms. Thus, siblings are distinguished from cousins, while all types of cousins are grouped together. The system of English-language kinship terms falls into the "Eskimo" type.
- Iroquois kinship: has both classificatory and descriptive terms; in addition to sex and generation, it also distinguishes between siblings of opposite sexes in the parental generation. A genealogical relationship traced through a pair of siblings of the same sex is classed as a blood relationship, but one traced though a pair of siblings of the opposite sex can be considered an in-law relationship. In other words, siblings are grouped together with parallel cousins, while separate terms are used for cross-cousins. Also, one calls one's mother's sister "mother" and one's father's brother "father". However, one refers to one's mother's brother and one's father's sister by separate terms (often the terms for "father-in-law" and "mother-in-law", since cross-cousins can be preferential marriage partners).

- Crow kinship: like Iroquois, but further distinguishes between mother's side and father's side. Relatives on the mother's side of the family have more descriptive terms, and relatives on the father's side have more classificatory terms. Thus, Crow kinship is like Iroquois kinship, with the addition that a number of relatives belonging to one's father's matrilineage are grouped together, ignoring generational differences, so that the same term is used for both one's father's sister and one's father's sister's daughter, etc.
- Omaha kinship: like Iroquois, but further distinguishes between mother's side and father's side. Relatives on the mother's side of the family have more classificatory terms, and relatives on the father's side have more descriptive terms. Thus, Omaha kinship is like Iroquois, with the addition that a number of relatives belonging to one's mother's patrilineage are grouped together, ignoring generational differences, so that the same term is used for both one's mother's brother and one's mother's brother's son, etc.

The basic principles of Crow and Omaha terminologies are symmetrical and opposite, with Crow systems having a matrilineal emphasis and Omaha systems a patrilineal emphasis.

Relative Age

Some languages, such as Bengali, Telugu, Tamil, Sinhalese, Chinese, Japanese, Korean, Cambodian, Vietnamese, Hungarian, Bulgarian and Nepalese add another dimension to some relations: relative age. Rather than one term for "brother", there exist, for example, different words for "older brother" and "younger brother". In Tamil, an older male sibling is referred to as *Annan* and a younger male sibling as *Thambi*, whereas older and younger female siblings are called *Akka* and *Thangai* respectively.

Identification of Alternating Generations

Other languages, such as Chiricahua, use the same terms of address for alternating generations. So a Chiricahua child (male or female) calls their paternal grandmother *-ch'iné*, and likewise this grandmother will call her son's child *-ch'iné*. Terms that recognise alternating generations and the prohibition of marriage within one's own set of alternate generation relatives (0, ±2, ±4, ±6, etc.) are common in Australian Aboriginal kinship.

The relative age and alternating-generations systems are combined in some languages. For instance Tagalog borrows the relative age system of the Chinese kinship and follows the generation system of kinship. Philippine Kinship distinguishes between generation, age and in some cases gender.

Discovery of Dravidian Kinship Terminology

Floyd Lounsbury (1964) discovered a seventh, Dravidian type of terminological system that had been conflated with Iroquois in Morgan's typology of kin-term systems because both systems distinguish relatives by marriage from relatives by descent, although both are classificatory categories rather than based on biological descent. Kay (1967), Scheffler (1971), and Tjon Sie Fat (1981) gave variant criteria for Dravidian classificatory logic, but the basic idea is that of applying an even/odd distinction to relatives that takes into account the gender of every linking relative for ego's kin relation to any given person. A MFBD(C), for example, is a mother's father's brother's daughter's child. If each female link (M,D) is assigned a 0 and each male (F,B) a 1, the number of 1s is either even or odd; in this case, even. In a Dravidian system with a patrilineal modulo-2 counting system, marriage is prohibited with this relative, and a marriageable relative must be modulo-2 odd. There exists also a version of this logic with a matrilineal bias. Discoveries of systems that use modulo-2 logic, as in South Asia, Australia, and many other parts of the world, marked a major advance in the understanding of kinship terminologies that differ from kin relations and terminologies employed by Europeans.

On Dravidian Kinship

The Dravidian kinship system involves selective "cousinhood." One's father's brother's children and one's mother's sister's children are NOT cousins but brothers and sisters "one step removed." They are considered "consanguinous" ("pangali") and marriage with them is strictly forbidden as it is "incestuous."

However, one's father's sister's children and one's mother's brother's children are considered cousins and potential mates ("muraicherugu"). Marriages between such cousins are allowed and encouraged. There is a clear distinction between cross cousins who are one's true cousins and parallel cousins who are in fact "siblings". Like Iroquois people, Dravidians refer to their father's sister as "mother-in-law" and their mother's brother as "father-in-law."

Abbreviations for Genealogical Relationships

The genealogical terminology used in many genealogical charts describes relatives of the subject in question. Using the abbreviations below, genealogical relationships may be distinguished by single or compound relationships, such as BC for a brother's children, MBD for a mother's brother's daughter, and so forth.

- B = Brother
- C = Child(ren)
- D = Daughter
- F = Father
- GC = Grandchild(ren)
- GP = Grandparent(s)
- H = Husband
- LA = In-law
- M = Mother
- P = Parent
- S = Son
- SI = Siblings
- SP = Spouse
- W = Wife
- Z = Sister
- (m.s.) = male speaking
- (f.s.) = female speaking

Roles

Most Western societies employ Eskimo kinship terminology. This kinship terminology commonly occurs in societies based on conjugal (or nuclear) families, where nuclear families have a degree of relative mobility. Members of the nuclear use descriptive kinship terms:

- Father: a male parent
- Mother: a female parent
- Son: a male child of the parent(s)
- Daughter: a female child of the parent(s)
- Brother: a male sibling
- Sister: a female sibling
- Grandfather: the father of a parent
- Grandmother: the mother of a parent
- Cousins: two people who share at least one grandparent in common, but neither the same parents.

Such systems generally assume that the mother's husband is also the biological father. In some families, a woman may have children with more than one man or a man may have children with more than one woman. The system refers to a child who shares only one parent with another child as a "half-brother" or "half-sister". For children who do not share biological or adoptive parents in common, English-speakers use the term "stepbrother" or "stepsister" to refer to their new relationship with each other when one of their biological parents marries one of the other child's biological parents. Any person (other than the biological parent of a child) who marries the parent of that child becomes the "stepparent" of the child, either the "stepmother" or "stepfather". The same terms generally apply to children adopted into a family as to children born into the family.

Typically, societies with conjugal families also favour neolocal residence; thus upon marriage a person separates from the nuclear family of their childhood (family of orientation) and forms a new nuclear family (family of procreation). However, in western society the single parent family has been growing more accepted and has begun to make an impact on culture. Single parent families are more commonly single mother families than single father. These families sometimes face difficult issues besides the fact that they have to rear their children on their own, for example low income making it difficult to pay for rent, child care, and other necessities for a healthy and safe home. Members of the nuclear families of members of one's own (former) nuclear family may class as lineal or as collateral. Kin who regard them as lineal refer to them in terms that build on the terms used within the nuclear family:

- Grandparent
  - Grandfather: a parent's father
  - Grandmother: a parent's mother
- Grandchild
  - Grandson: a child's son
  - Granddaughter: a child's daughter

For collateral relatives, more classificatory terms come into play, terms that do not build on the terms used within the nuclear family:

- Uncle: father's brother, mother's brother, father's sister's husband, mother's sister's husband
- Aunt: father's sister, mother's sister, father's brother's wife, mother's brother's wife
- Nephew: brother's son, sister's son, husband's brother's son, husband's sister's son, wife's brother's son, wife's sister's son
- Niece: brother's daughter, sister's daughter, husband's brother's daughter, husband's sister's daughter, wife's brother's daughter, wife's sister's daughter

When additional generations intervene (in other words, when one's collateral relatives belong to the same generation as one's grandparents or grandchildren), the prefixes "great-" or "grand-" modifies these terms. Also, as with grandparents and grandchildren, as more generations intervene the prefix becomes "great-grand-," adding another "great-" for each additional generation. Most collateral relatives have never had membership of the nuclear family of the members of one's own nuclear family.

- Cousin: the most classificatory term; the children of uncles or aunts. One can further distinguish cousins by degrees of collaterality and by generation. Two persons of the same generation who share a grandparent count as "first cousins" (one degree of collaterality); if they share a great-grandparent they count as "second cousins" (two degrees of collaterality) and so on. If two persons share an ancestor, one as a grandchild and the other as a great-grandchild of that individual, then the two descendants class as "first cousins once removed" (removed by one generation); if they shared ancestor figures as the grandparent of one individual and the great-great-grandparent of the other, the individuals class as "first cousins twice removed" (removed by two generations), and so on. Similarly, if they shared ancestor figures as the great-grandparent of one person and the great-great-grandparent of the other, the individuals class as "second cousins once removed". Hence one can refer to a "third cousin once removed upwards."

Cousins of an older generation (in other words, one's parents' first cousins), although technically first cousins once removed, are often classified with "aunts" and "uncles." Similarly, a person may refer to close friends of one's parents as "aunt" or "uncle," or may refer to close friends as "brother" or "sister," using the practice of fictive kinship. English-speakers mark relationships by marriage (except for wife/husband) with the tag "-in-law."

The mother and father of one's spouse become one's mother-in-law and father-in-law; the female spouse of one's child becomes one's daughter-in-law and the male spouse of one's child becomes one's son-in-law. The term "sister-in-law" refers to three essentially different relationships, either the wife of one's sibling, or the sister of one's spouse, or, in some uses, the wife of one's spouse's sibling. "Brother-in-law" expresses a similar ambiguity.

The terms "half-brother" and "half-sister" indicate siblings who share only one biological or adoptive parent.

History of Theories

Social Darwinists: Early scholars of family history applied Darwin's biological theory of evolution in their theory of evolution of family systems. American anthropologist Lewis H. Morgan published *Ancient Society* in 1877 based on his theory of the three stages of human progress from Savagery through Barbarism to Civilization. Morgan's book was the "inspiration for Friedrich Engels' book" *The Origin of the Family, Private Property and the State* published in 1884.

Engels expanded Morgan's hypothesis that economical factors caused the transformation of primitive community into a class-divided society. Engels' theory of resource control, and later that of Karl Marx, was used to explain the cause and effect of change in family structure and function. The popularity of this theory was largely unmatched until the 1980s, when other sociological theories, most notably structural functionalism, gained acceptance.

The Nuclear Family in Industrial Society

Contemporary society generally views the family as a haven from the world, supplying absolute fulfillment. Zinn and Eitzen discuss the image of the "family as haven [...] a place of intimacy, love and trust where individuals may escape the competition of dehumanizing forces in modern society". During industrialization, "[t]he family as a repository of warmth and tenderness (embodied by the mother) stands in opposition to the competitive and aggressive world of commerce (embodied by the father). The family's task was to protect against the outside world." However, Zinn and Eitzen note, "The protective image of the family has waned in recent years as the ideals of family fulfillment have taken shape. Today, the family is more compensatory than protective. It supplies what is vitally needed but missing in other social arrangements."

"The popular wisdom", according to Zinn and Eitzen, sees the family structures of the past as superior to those today, and families as more stable and happier at a time when they did not have to contend with problems such as illegitimate children and divorce. They respond to this, saying, "there is no golden age of the family gleaming at us in the far back historical past." "Desertion by spouses, illegitimate children, and other conditions that are considered characteristics of modern times existed in the past as well."

The Postmodern Family

Others argue that whether or not one views the family as "declining" depends on one's definition of "family". "Married couples have dropped below half of all American households. This drop is shocking from traditional forms of the family system. Only a fifth of households were following traditional ways of having married couples raising a family together." In the Western World, marriages are no longer arranged for economic, social or political gain, and children are no longer expected to contribute to family income. Instead, people choose mates based on love. This increased role of love indicates a societal shift toward favouring emotional fulfilment and relationships within a family, and this shift necessarily weakens the institution of the family.

Margaret Mead considers the family as a main safeguard to continuing human progress. Observing, "Human beings have learned, laboriously, to be human", she adds: "we hold our present form of humanity on trust, [and] it is possible to lose it" ... "It is not without significance that the most successful large-scale abrogations of the family have occurred not among simple savages, living close to the subsistence edge, but among great nations and strong empires, the resources of which were ample, the populations huge, and the power almost unlimited"

Oedipal Family Model and Fascism

The model, common in the western societies, of the family triangle, husband-wife-children isolated from the outside, is also called the *oedipal model of the family*, and it is a form of patriarchal family. Many philosophers and psychiatrists have analyzed such a model. In such a family, they argue, the young develop in a perverse relationship, wherein they learn to love the same person who beats and oppresses them. They believe that young children grow up and develop loving a person who is oppressing them physically or mentally, and that these children are not taught in a way that will raise affectionate children. Such philosophers claim that the family therefore constitutes the first cell of the fascist society, as the children will carry this attitude of love for oppressive figures in their adult life. They claim that fathers torment their sons. Deleuze and Guattari, in their analysis of the dynamics at work within a family, "track down all varieties of fascism, from the enormous ones that surround and crush us to the petty ones that constitute the tyrannical bitterness of our everyday lives".

As it has been explained by Deleuze, Guattari and Foucault, as well as other philosophers and psychiatrists such as Laing and Reich, the patriarchal-family conceived in the West tradition serves the purpose of perpetuating a propertarian and authoritarian society. The child grows according to the oedipal model, which is typical of the structure of capitalist societies, and he becomes in turn owner of submissive children and protector of the woman.

As the young undergoes physical and psychological repression from someone for whom they develop love, they develop a loving attitude towards authority figures. They will bring such attitude in their adult life, when they will desire social repression and will form docile subjects for society. Michel Foucault, in his systematic study of sexuality, argued that rather than being merely repressed, the desires of the individual are efficiently mobilized and used, to control the individual, alter interpersonal relationships and control the masses. Foucault believed organised religion, through moral prohibitions, and economic powers, through advertising, make use of unconscious sex drives. Dominating desire, they dominate individuals. According to the analysis of Michel Foucault, in the west:

> *the [conjugal] family organisation, precisely to the extent that it was insular and heteromorphous with respect to the other power mechanisms, was used to support the great "maneuvers" employed for the Malthusian control of the birthrate, for the populationist incitements, for the medicalization of sex and the psychiatrization of its nongenital forms.* —Michel Foucault, The History of Sexuality vol I, chap. IV, sect. Method, rule 3, p. 99

Descent

Descent Rules: In many societies where kinship connections are important, there are rules, though they may be expressed or be taken for granted. There are four main heading that anthropologists use to categorize rules of descent. They are bilateral, unilineal, ambilineal and double descent.

- Bilateral descent or two sided descent affiliates an individual more or less equally with relatives on his father's and mother's sides. A good example is the Yako of the Crossriver state of Nigeria.
- Unilineal rules affiliates an individual through the descent of one sex only, that is, either through males or through females. They are subdivided into two: patrilineal (male) and matrilineal (female). Most societies are patrilineal. Examples of a matrilineal system of descent are the Nyakyusa of Tanzania and the Nayar of Kerala, India. Many societies that practise a matrilineal system often have a patrilocal residence and men still exercise significant authority.

- Ambilineal (or Cognatic) rule affiliates an individual with kinsmen through the father's or mother's line. Some people in societies that practise this system affiliate with a group of relatives through their fathers and others through their mothers. The individual can choose which side he wants to affiliate to. The Samoans of the South Pacific are an excellent example of an ambilineal society. The core members of the Samoan descent group can live together in the same compound.
- Double Descent refers to societies in which both the patrilineal and matrilineal descent group are recognised. In these societies an individual affiliates for some purposes with a group of patrilineal kinsmen and for other purposes with a group of matrilineal kinsmen. The most widely known case of double descent is the Afikpo of Imo state in Nigeria. Although patrilineage is considered an important method of organisation, the Afikpo considers matrilineal ties to be more important.

Descent Groups

A descent group is a social group whose members talk about common ancestry. A unilineal society is one in which the descent of an individual is reckoned either from the mother's or the father's line of descent. With matrilineal descent individuals belong to their mother's descent group. Matrilineal descent includes the mother's brother, who in some societies may pass along inheritance to the sister's children or succession to a sister's son. With patrilineal descent, individuals belong to their father's descent group. Societies with the Iroquois kinship system, are typically uniliineal, while the Iroquois proper are specifically matrilineal.

In a society which reckons descent bilaterally (bilineal), descent is reckoned through both father and mother, without unilineal descent groups. Societies with the Eskimo kinship system, like the Eskimo proper, are typically bilateral. The egocentrid kindred group is also typical of bilateral societies. Some societies reckon descent patrilineally for some purposes, and matrilineally for others. This arrangement is sometimes called double descent. For instance, certain property and titles may be inherited through the male line, and others through the female line.

Societies can also consider descent to be ambilineal (such as Hawaiian kinship) where offspring determine their lineage through the matrilineal line or the patrilineal line. Lineages, clans, phratries, moieties, and matrimonial sides A lineage is a unilineal descent group that can demonstrate their common descent from a known apical ancestor. Unilineal lineages can be matrilineal or patrilineal, depending on whether they are traced through mothers or fathers, respectively. Whether matrilineal or patrilineal descent is considered most significant differs from culture to culture.

A clan is generally a descent group claiming common descent from an apical ancestor. Often, the details of parentage are not important elements of the clan tradition. Non-human apical ancestors are called totems. Examples of clans are found in Chechen, Chinese, Irish, Japanese, Polish, Scottish, Tlingit, and Somali societies.

A phratry is a descent group composed of two or more clans each of whose apical ancestors are descended from a further common ancestor.

If a society is divided into exactly two descent groups, each is called a moiety, after the French word for *half*. If the two halves are each obliged to marry out, and into the other, these are called matrimonial moieties. Houseman and White (1998b, bibliography) have discovered numerous societies where kinship network analysis shows that two halves marry one another, similar to matrimonial moieties, except that the two halves—which they call matrimonial *sides*—are neither named nor descent groups, although the egocentric kinship terms may be consistent with the pattern of sidedness, whereas the sidedness is culturally evident but imperfect.

The word *deme* refers to an endogamous local population that does not have unilineal descent. Thus, a deme is a local endogamous community without internal segmentation into clans.

House Society

In anthropology, a house society is a society where kinship and political relations are organised around membership in corporately organised dwellings rather than around descent groups or lineages, as in the "House of Windsor". The concept was originally proposed by Claude Lévi-Strauss who called them "*sociétés a maison*". The concept has been applied to understand the organisation of societies from Mesoamerica and the Moluccas to North Africa and medieval Europe.

The House society is a hybrid, transitional form between kin-based and class-based social orders, and is not one of Lévi-Strauss' 'elementary structures' of kinship. Lévi-Strauss introduced the concept as an alternative to 'corporate kinship group' among the cognatic kinship groups of the Pacific region. The socially significant groupings within these societies have variable membership because kinship is reckoned bilaterally (through both father's and mother's kin) and come together for only short periods. Property, genealogy and residence are not the basis for the group's existence.

House Societies and Kinship

Lévi-Strauss' most succinct definition of a House was that it is "a corporate body holding an estate made up of both material and immaterial wealth, which perpetuates itself through the transmission of its name, its goods and its titles down a real or imaginary line considered legitimate as long as this continuity can express itself in the language of kinship or of affinity and, most often, of both."

There are three elements to this definition:

1) The House is a corporate body ('moral person') holding an estate made up of both material and immaterial goods.
2) As a 'moral person' it is an alternate metaphor replacing 'blood' in defining the social identity of the group. As a symbol of the group, the House persists over generations and links the group to its sacred origins.
3) The House persists over time by transmitting its titles through conditional kinship principles: "patrilineal descent and matrilineal descent, filiation and residence, hypergamy and hypogamy, close marriage and distant marriage, heredity and election: all these notions which usually allow anthropologists to distinguish the various known types of society, are united in the house, as if, in the last analysis the spirit (in the eighteenth-century sense) of this institution expressed an effort to transcend, in all spheres of collective life, theoretically incompatible principles."

Only the core group (the highest-ranking members) will inhabit the House as a residence. The other House members (which Errington refers to as the "server group") will only come together on special ritual occasions, making this an "occasional kinship group." Other House members have multiple overlapping ties to other Houses as well, through both mother's and father's kin. Their ability to assert a claim to membership in a House will depend on a number of criteria, such as their parents' participation, their ability to contribute to the House's upkeep, and their participation in its rituals. Successful claims of membership may bring special benefits, such as the right to utilise House resources with the consent of the core members.

House Societies and Social Ranking

Most of the examples of 'sociétés à maison' cited by Lévi-Strauss, with the exception of the Kwakiutl Indians of the North-west coast of

Canada, were feudal. This has led some to ask if feudalism was an essential feature of House societies, and answering in the negative. Schrauwers, in contrast, has argued that House societies are characteristically organised around a system of social ranks, not feudalism. That is, the House is not an economic class but a socially ranked group (e.g. a nobility) in a society organised around a system of social ranks; while a House may own property, it is thus not tied to a feudal mode of production. Schrauwers gives, as an alternate example, societies organised around slavery where a noble group's property are its slaves (such as the Kwakiutl case).

Houses and Politics

Houses are political in three ways; there is an intra-House politics by which leadership is determined and resources are allocated within the House, as well as an inter-House politics between rival Houses. These two forms of political engagement may be connected through agonistic exchange institutions such as the Potlatch. There is, lastly, also a politics of struggle and incorporation between highly ranked noble Houses and those groups like slaves and commoners who lack the resources to maintain their organisation as a House.

Intra-House Political Struggle

Houses are tied together through oftentimes contradictory forms of kinship, whether descent or alliance. Given that Houses are not lineages, leadership is rarely ascribed by genealogical seniority alone (i.e. primogeniture). Leadership of a House is gained through status competition.

Inter-House Political Struggle

A number of traditional Southeast Asian kingdoms, such as those in Bali, or the kingdom of Luwu in Sulawesi, were dominated by noble Houses that competed with each other for control of the state. These states have alternately been described as mandala states.

Political Struggles Between Classes within a House Society

Although they may be referred to as House Societies, not all societies with Houses have those Houses uniformly distributed among all ranks and classes. The House in Bali, as well as in the kingdom of Luwu in Sulawesi, is an "optional" kinship group. Schrauwers has argued that class and House formation are linked. He points out, for example, that the inherited estate of some Sulawesi House societies in the kingdom of Luwu is composed of slaves; that is, the House's property is composed of another social rank of individuals. In this case, class and rank are synonymous. Because they are property, slaves are prevented from forming their own Houses. Commoners in those societies are of a different rank, but lack property, and therefore cannot form their own houses either. The way in which these lower classes were prevented from forming Houses was two-fold. On the one hand, they might be engaged in the agonistic exchange systems with Noble Houses that results in their using up and losing all of their House property. On the other hand, noble Houses at the centre of the state might engage in policies of divide and rule, urging different groups at the periphery to attack each other, take slaves, and these would form Houses which then intermarry with the Houses at the centre.

Chapter 7

Alliance Theory

The alliance theory (or general theory of exchanges) is the name given to the structural method of studying kinship relations. It finds its origins in Claude Lévi-Strauss's *Elementary Structures of Kinship* (1949), and is opposed to the functionalist theory of Radcliffe-Brown. Alliance theory has oriented most anthropological French works until the 1980s, and its influences were felt in various fields, including psychoanalysis (who shared the belief in a universal incest taboo), philosophy and political philosophy.

The hypothesis of a "marriage-alliance" emerged in this frame, pointing out towards the necessary interdependence of various families and lineages. Weddings themselves are thus seen as a form of communication, which anthropologists such as Lévi-Strauss, Louis Dumont or Rodney Needham described for us. Alliance theory hence tries to understand the basic questions about inter-individual relations, or what constitutes society.

Alliance theory is based on the incest taboo: according to it, only this universal prohibition of incest pushes human groups towards exogamy. Thus, inside a given society, certain categories of kin are forbidden to inter-marry. The incest taboo is thus a negative prescription; without it, nothing would push men to go searching for women outside of their inner kinship circle, or vice versa. This theory echoes with Freud's *Totem and Taboo* (1913). But the incest taboo of alliance theory, in which one's daughter or sister is offered to someone outside a family circle, starts a circle of exchange of women: in return, the giver is entitled to a woman from the other's intimate kinship group. Thus the negative prescriptions of the prohibition have positive counterparts The idea of the alliance theory is thus of a reciprocal or a generalized exchange which founds affinity. This global phenomena takes the form of a "circulation of women" which links together the various social groups in one whole: society.

Elementary Structures and Complex Structures

According to Lévi-Strauss's alliance theory, there are two different structural "models" of marriage exchange. Either the women of ego's group are offered to another group "explicitly defined" by social institutions: these are the "elementary structures of kinship". Or the group of possible spouses for the women in ego's group is "indetermined and always open", to the exclusion, however, of certain kin-people (nuclear family, aunts, uncles...), as in the Western world. Lévi-Strauss call these latter "complex structures of kinship".

Levi-Strauss' model attempted to offer a single explanation for cross-cousin marriage, sister-exchange, dual organisation and rules of exogamy. Marriage rules over time create social structures, as marriages are primarily forged between groups and not just between the two individuals involved. When groups exchange women on a regular basis they marry together, with each marriage creating a debtor/creditor relationship which must be balanced through the "repayment" of wives, either directly or in the next generation. Levi-Strauss proposed that the initial motivation for the exchange of women was the incest taboo, which he deemed to be the beginning and essence of culture, as it was the first rule to check natural impulses; and secondarily the sexual division of labour. The former, by prescribing exogamy, creates a distinction between marriageable and tabooed women and thus necessitates a search for women outside one's own kin group ("marry out or die out"), which fosters exchange relationships with other groups; the latter creates a need for women to do "women's tasks". By necessitating wife-exchange arrangements, exogamy therefore promotes inter-group alliances and serves to form structures of social networks.

Levi-Strauss also discovered that a wide range of historically unrelated cultures had the rule that individuals should marry their cross-cousin, meaning children of siblings of the opposite sex - from a male perspective that is either the FZD (father's sister's daughter in kinship abbreviation) or the MBD (mother's brother's daughter in kinship abbreviation). Accordingly, he grouped all possible kinship systems into a scheme containing three basic kinship structures, constructed out of two types of exchange. He called the three kinship structures elementary, semi-complex and complex.

Elementary structures are based on positive marriage rules that specify whom a person must marry, while complex systems specify negative marriage rules (whom one must not marry), thus leaving a certain amount of room for choice based on preference. Elementary structures can operate based on two forms of exchange: restricted (or direct) exchange, a symmetric form of exchange between two groups (also called moieties) of wife-givers and wife-takers; in an initial restricted exchange FZ marries MB, with all children then being bilateral cross-cousins (the daughter is both MBD and FZD). Continued restricted exchange means that the two lineages marry together. Restricted exchange structures are generally quite uncommon.

The second form of exchange within elementary structures is called generalised exchange, meaning that a man can only marry either his MBD (matrilateral cross-cousin marriage) or his FZD (patrilateral cross-cousin marriage). This involves an asymmetric exchange between at least three groups. Matrilateral cross-cousin marriage arrangements where the marriage of the parents is repeated by successive generations are very common in parts of Asia (e.g. amongst the Kachin). Levi-Strauss considered generalised exchange to be superior to restricted exchange because it allows the integration of indefinite numbers of groups. Examples of restricted exchange are found in some tribes residing in Amazonia. These tribal societies are made up of multiple moieties which often split up, thus rendering them comparatively unstable. Generalised exchange is more integrative but contains an implicit hierarchy, for instance amongst the Kachin where wife-givers are superior to wife-takers. Consequently, the last wife-taking group in the chain is significantly inferior to the first wife-giving group to which it is supposed to give its wives. These status inequalities can destabilise the entire system or can at least lead to an accumulation of wives (and in the case of the Kachin also of bridewealth) at one end of the chain.

From a structural perspective, matrilateral cross-cousin marriage is superior to its patrilateral counterpart; the latter has less potential to produce social cohesion since its exchange cycles are shorter (the direction of wife exchange is reversed in each successive generation). Levi-Strauss' theory is supported by fact that patrilateral cross-cousin marriage is in fact the rarest of three types. However, matrilateral generalised exchange poses a risk, as group A depends on being given a woman from a group that it has not itself given a woman to, meaning that there is a less immediate obligation to reciprocate compared to a restricted exchange system. The risk created by such a delayed return is obviously lowest in restricted exchange systems.

Levi-Strauss proposed a third structure between elementary and complex structures, called the semi-complex structure, or the Crow-Omaha system. Semi-complex structures contain so many negative marriage rules that they effectively come close to prescribing marriage to certain parties, thus somewhat resembling elementary structures. These structures are found amongst societies such as the Crow and Omaha native Indians in North America.

In Levi-Strauss' order of things, the basic building block of kinship is not just the nuclear family, as in structural-functionalism, but the so-called kinship atom: the nuclear family together with the wife's brother. This "mother's brother" (from the perspective of the wife-seeking son) plays a crucial role in alliance theory, as he is the one who ultimately decides whom his daughter will marry. Moreover, it is not just the nuclear family as such but alliances between families that matter in regard to the creation of social structures, reflecting the typical structuralist argument that the position of an element in the structure is more significant than the element itself. Descent theory and alliance theory therefore look at two different sides of the same coin: the former emphasising bonds of consanguinity (kinship by blood), the latter stressing bonds of affinity (kinship by law or choice).

History of Kinship Studies

One of the foundational works in the anthropological study of kinship was Morgan's *Systems of Consanguinity and Affinity of the Human Family* (1871). As is the case with other social sciences, Anthropology and kinship studies emerged at a time when the understanding of the Human species' comparative place in the world was somewhat different from today's. Evidence that life in stable social groups is not just a feature of humans, but also of many other primates, was yet to emerge and society was considered to be a uniquely human affair. As a result, early kinship theorists saw an apparent need to explain not only the details of *how* human social groups are constructed, their patterns, meanings and obligations, but also *why* they are constructed at all. The *why* explanations thus typically presented the fact of life in social groups (*which appeared to be unique to humans*) as being largely a result of human ideas and values.

Morgan's Early Influence

Morgan's explanation was largely based on the notion that all humans have an inherent *natural valuation* of genealogical ties (an unexamined assumption that would remain at the heart of kinship studies for another century), and therefore also an inherent desire to construct social groups around these ties. Even so, Morgan found that members of a society who are *not* close genealogical relatives may nevertheless use what he called *kinship terms* (which he considered to be originally based on genealogical ties). This fact was already evident in his use of the term *affinity* within his concept of the *system of kinship.* The most lasting of Morgan's contributions was his discovery of the difference between descriptive and classificatory kinship terms, which situated broad kinship classes on the basis of imputing abstract social patterns of relationships having little or no overall relation to genetic closeness but instead cognition about kinship, social distinctions as they affect linguistic usages in kinship terminology, and strongly relate, if only by approximation, to patterns of marriage.

Kinship Networks and Social Process

A more flexible view of kinship was formulated in British social anthropology. Among the attempts to break out of universalizing assumptions and theories about kinship, Radcliffe-Brown (1922, The Andaman Islands; 1930, The social organisation of Australian tribes) was the first to assert that kinship relations are best thought of as concrete networks of relationships among individuals. He then described these relationships, however, as typified by interlocking interpersonal roles. Malinowski (1922, Argonauts of the Western Pacific) described patterns of events with concrete individuals as participants stressing the relative stability of institutions and communities, but without insisting on abstract systems or models of kinship. Gluckman (1955, The judicial process among the Barotse of Northern Rhodesia) balanced the emphasis on stability of institutions against processes of change and conflict, inferred through detailed analysis of instances of social interaction to infer rules and assumptions. John Barnes, Victor Turner, and others, affiliated with Gluckman's Manchester school of anthropology, described patterns of actual network relations in communities and fluid situations in urban or migratory context, as with the work of J. Clyde Mitchell (1965, Social Networks in Urban Situations). Yet, all these approaches clung to a view of stable functionalism, with kinship as one of the central stable institutions.

"Kinship System" as Systemic Pattern

The concept of "system of kinship" tended to dominate anthropological studies of kinship in the early 20th century. Kinship systems as defined in anthropological texts and ethnographies were seen as constituted by patterns of behaviour and attitudes in relation to the differences in terminology, listed above, for referring to relationships as well as for addressing others. Many anthropologists went so far as to see, in these patterns of kinship, strong relations between kinship categories and patterns of marriage, including forms of marriage, restrictions on marriage, and cultural concepts of the boundaries of incest. A great deal of inference was necessarily involved in such constructions as to "systems" of kinship, and attempts to construct systemic patterns and reconstruct kinship evolutionary histories on these bases were largely invalidated in later work. However, anthropologist Dwight Read later argued that the way in which kinship categories are defined by individual researchers are substantially inconsistent. This occurs when working within a systemic cultural model that can be elicited in fieldwork, but also allowing considerable individual variability in details, such as when they are recorded through relative products.

Conflicting Theories of the Mid 20th Century

In trying to resolve the problems of dubious inferences about kinship "systems", George P. Murdock (1949, Social Structure) compiled kinship data to test a theory about universals in human kinship in the way that terminologies were influenced by the behavioural similarities or social differences among pairs of kin, proceeding on the view that the psychological ordering of kinship systems radiates out from ego and the nuclear family to different forms of extended family. Lévi-Strauss (1949, Les Structures Elementaires), on the other hand, also looked for global patterns to kinship, but viewed the "elementary" forms of kinship as lying in the ways that families were connected by marriage in different fundamental forms resembling those of modes of exchange: symmetric and direct, reciprocal delay, or generalized exchange.

Recognition of Fluidity in Kinship Meanings and Relations

Building on Lévi-Strauss's (1949) notions of kinship as caught up with the fluid languages of exchange, Edmund Leach (1961, Pul Eliya) argued that kinship was a flexible idiom that had something of the grammar of a language, both in the uses of terms for kin but also in the fluidities of language, meaning, and networks. His field studies criticized the ideas of structural-functional stability of kinship groups as corporations with charters that lasted long beyond the lifetimes of individuals, which had been the orthodoxy of British Social Anthropology. This sparked debates over whether kinship could be resolved into specific organised sets of rules and components of meaning, or whether kinship meanings were more fluid, symbolic, and independent of grounding in supposedly determinate relations among individuals or groups, such as those of descent or prescriptions for marriage. Work on symbolic kinship by David M. Schneider in his (1984, A Critique of The Study of Kinship) reinforced this view. In response to Schneider's 1984 work on Symbolic Kinship, Janet Carsten re-developed the idea of "relatedness" from her initial ideas, looking at what was socialized and biological, from her studies with the Malays (1995, The substance of kinship and the heat of the hearth; feeding, personhood and relatedness among the Malays in Pulau Langkawi, *American Ethnologist*). She uses the idea of relatedness to move away from a pre-constructed analytic opposition which exists in anthropological thought between the biological and the social. Carsten argued that relatedness should be described in terms of indigenous statements and practices, some of which fall outside what anthropologists have conventionally understood as kinship (Cultures of Relatedness, 2000). This kind of approach – recognising relatedness in its concrete and variable cultural forms – exemplifies the ways that anthropologists have grappled with the fundamental importance of kinship in human society without imprisoning the fluidity in behaviour, beliefs, and meanings in assumptions about fixed patterns and systems.

Beyond Biological Relationships

Ideas about kinship do not necessarily assume any biological relationship between individuals, rather just close associations. Malinowski, in his ethnographic study of sexual behaviour on the Trobriand Islands noted that the Trobrianders did not believe pregnancy to be the result of sexual intercourse between the man and the woman, and they denied that there was any physiological relationship between father and child. Nevertheless, while paternity was unknown in the "full biological sense", for a woman to have a child without having a husband was considered socially undesirable. Fatherhood was therefore recognised as a social role; the woman's husband is the "man whose role and duty it is to take the child in his arms and to help her in nursing and bringing it up"; "Thus, though the natives are ignorant of any physiological need for a male in the constitution of the family, they regard him as indispensable socially".

As social and biological concepts of parenthood are not necessarily coterminous, the terms "pater" and "genitor" have been used in anthropology to distinguish between the man who is socially recognised as father (pater) and the man who is believed to be the physiological parent (genitor); similarly the terms "mater" and "genitrix" have been used to distinguish between the woman socially recognised as mother (mater) and the woman believed to be the physiological parent (genitrix). Such a distinction is useful when the individual who is considered the legal parent of the child is not the individual who is believed to be the child's biological parent. For example, in his ethnography of the Nuer, Evans-Pritchard notes that if a widow, following the death of her husband, chooses to live with a lover outside of her deceased husband's kin group, that lover is only considered genitor of any subsequent children the widow has, and her deceased husband continues to be considered the pater. As a result, the lover has no legal control over the children, who may be taken away from him by the kin of the pater when they choose. The terms "pater" and "genitor" have also been used to help describe the relationship between children and their parents in the context of divorce in Britain. Following the divorce and remarriage of their parents, children find themselves using the term "mother" or "father" in relation to more than one individual, and the pater or mater who is legally responsible for the child's carc, and whose family name the child uses, may not be the genitor or genitrix of the child, with whom a separate parent-child relationship may be maintained through arrangements such as visitation rights or joint custody.

It is important to note that the terms "genitor" or "genetrix" do not necessarily imply actual biological relationships based on consanguinity, but rather refer to the socially held belief that the individual is physically related to the child, derived from culturally held ideas about how biology works. So, for example, the Ifugao may believe that an illegitimate child might have more than one physical father, and so nominate more than one genitor. J.A. Barnes therefore argued that it was necessary to make a further distinction between genitor and genitrix (the supposed biological mother and father of the child), and the actual genetic father and mother of the child.

Legal Ramifications

Kinship and descent have a number of legal ramifications, which vary widely between legal and social structures. Next of Kin traditionally and in common usage refers to the person closest related to you by blood, such as a parent or your children. In legal terms, for example in intestacy, it has come to mean the person closest to you, which is generally the spouse if married, followed by the natural children of the deceased.

Whilst someone is alive they may nominate any person close to them to be their next of kin. The next of kin is usually asked for as a contact in case of accident, emergency or sudden death. It does not involve completing any forms or registration in the UK, and may be a friend or carer unrelated to you by blood or marriage.

Most human groups share a taboo against incest; relatives are forbidden from marriage but the rules tend to vary widely when one moves beyond the nuclear family. At common law, the prohibitions are typically phrased in terms of "degrees of consanguinity."

More importantly, kinship and descent enters the legal system by virtue of intestacy, the laws that at common law determine who inherits the estates of the dead in the absence of a will. In civil law countries, the doctrine of legitime plays a similar role, and makes the lineal descendants of the dead person forced heirs. Rules of kinship and descent have important public aspects, especially under monarchies, where they determine the order of succession, the heir apparent and the heir presumptive.

Compatibility with Other Sciences

Within the biological sciences, there are theoretical approaches to understanding under what conditions some species live in groups (typically due to the distribution of key food resources and patterns of predation), and in particular, under what conditions significant social behaviours can evolve to become a typical feature of a species (Kin selection theory). Because these characteristics are common to most primates, including humans, biologists maintain that these theories should in principle be generally applicable. The question arises as to how these ideas can be applied to the human species whilst fully taking account of the extensive ethnographic evidence that has emerged from anthropological research on kinship patterns.

Early derivations of Kin selection theory and the related field of Sociobiology, encouraged some biologists such as Darwinian anthropologists and evolutionary psychologists to approach human kinship with the assumption that kin selection theory predicts that kinship relations in humans *are indeed* expected to depend on genetic relatedness, which they readily connected with the *genealogy* approach of early anthropologists such as Morgan.

This biological position, coming at a time (the 1970s) when anthropologists were starting to reject the *genealogical* basis of human kinship patterns provoked criticism from ethnographers including notably, Marshall Sahlins who strongly critiqued the approach through reviews of ethnographies in his 1976 *The Use and Abuse of Biology*. Such counter evidence and critiques did not dissuade the program however, and fundamental and heated disagreements between the two sides continued. These early disagreements over the nature of human kinship and cooperative behaviour have formed an important core of the continuing controversies related to evolutionary psychology and sociobiology ever since..

There have since been two approaches that seek to reconcile the anthropological and biological perspectives. Holland argued that biologists themselves have not sufficiently recognised that kin selection theory does not in fact require that genetic relatedness *per se* is the condition that mediates social bonding and social cooperation in any species. Holland speculates that in ancestral environments, social cooperation mediated through ties of familiarity and attachments would typically have increased the inclusive fitness of genes (the key criterion in kin selection theory) without any form of detection of actual genetic relationships. Kin selection theory in this view is seen as specifying an ultimate cause rather than a proximate cause of social bonding and cooperation. Holland thus argues that properly understood, the findings of cultural anthropologists and the theories of evolutionary biologists are compatible.

Fitting with this approach, Nurture kinship emphasizes that social relationships, and the cooperation that accompanies them, are commonly built upon emotional bonds and attachments. This perspective re-unites current ethnographic findings both with the work of earlier anthropologists such as Audrey Richards, and also with John Bowlby and colleagues' foundational work on emotional attachment theory. In this perspective, biological theories are indeed compatible with ethnographic data on human kinship, though their explanatory scope is much narrower than the approaches of sociobiology and evolutionary psychology had typically assumed. Biology's relevant application is limited to theorizing the ultimate causes of the (non-deterministic) proximate mechanisms of cooperation such as emotional attachments. Bowlby himself emphasized the compatibility of his own work with kin selection theory. Anthropological kinship data is also thus considered compatible with current psychological theory of social bonding and relationships. In this perspective, whilst theoretical approaches are unified across biology, psychology and anthropology, for a full account of *specific* kinship patterns in any *particular* human society, ethnographic methods, including the analysis of historical contingencies, symbolic systems, economic and other influences, remain central.

The other approach, that of Evolutionary psychology, continues to take the view that genetic relatedness (or genealogy) is key to understanding human kinship patterns. A current view is that humans have an inborn but culturally affected system for detecting certain forms of genetic relatedness. One important factor for sibling detection, especially relevant for older siblings, is that if an infant and one's mother are seen to care for the infant, then the infant and oneself are assumed to be related. Another factor, especially important for younger siblings who cannot use the first method, is that persons who grew up together see one another as related. Yet another may be genetic detection based on the major histocompatibility complex. This kinship detection system in turn affects other genetic predispositions such as the incest taboo and a tendency for altruism towards relatives.

One issue within this approach is why many societies organise according to descent and not exclusively according to kinship. An explanation is that kinship does not form clear boundaries and is centred differently for each individual. In contrast, descent groups usually do form clear boundaries and provide an easy way to create cooperative groups of various sizes.

According to an evolutionary psychology hypothesis that assumes that descent systems are optimized to assure genetic high genetic probability of relatedness between lineage members, males should prefer a patrilineal system if paternal certainty is high; males should prefer a matrilineal system if paternal certainty is low. Some research supports this association with one study finding no patrilineal society with low paternity confidence and no matrilineal society with high paternal certainty. Another association is that pastoral societies are relatively more often patrilineal compared to horticultural societies. This may be because wealth in pastoral societies in the form of mobile cattle can easily be used to pay bride price which favour concentrating resources on sons so they can marry.

Inheritance

Inheritance is the practice of passing on property, titles, debts, rights and obligations upon the death of an individual. It has long played an important role in human societies. The rules of inheritance differ between societies and have changed over time.

Terminology

In law, an *heir* is a person who is entitled to receive a share of the deceased's (the person who died) property, subject to the rules of inheritance in the jurisdiction where the deceased (decedent) died or owned property at the time of death. A person does not become an heir before the death of the deceased, since the exact identity of the persons entitled to inherit is determined only then. Members of ruling noble or royal houses expected to become heirs are called heirs apparent if first in line and incapable of being displaced from inheriting by another claim; otherwise, they are heirs presumptive. There is a further concept of joint inheritance, pending renunciation by all but one, which is called coparceny.

In modern law, the terms *inheritance* and *heir* refer exclusively to succession to property by descent from a deceased dying intestate. Takers in property succeeded to under a will are termed generally *beneficiaries,* and specifically *devisees* for real property, *bequestees* for personal property, or *legatees* for money.

History

Detailed anthropological and sociological studies have been made about customs of patrilineal inheritance, where only male children can inherit. Some cultures also employ matrilineal succession, where property can only pass along the female line, most commonly going to the sister's sons of the decedent; but also, in some societies, from the mother to her daughters. Some ancient societies and most modern states employ egalitarian inheritance, without discrimination based on gender and/or birth order.

Islamic Laws of Inheritance

The Quran introduced a number of different rights and restrictions on matters of inheritance, including general improvements to the treatment of women and family life compared to the pre-Islamic societies that existed in the Arabian Peninsula at the time. The Quran also presented efforts to fix the laws of inheritance, and thus forming a complete legal system. This development was in contrast to pre-Islamic societies where rules of inheritance varied considerably. Furthermore, the Quran introduced additional heirs that were not entitled inheritance in pre-Islamic times, mentioning nine relatives specifically of which six were female and three were male. In addition to the above changes, the Quran imposed restrictions on testamentary powers of a Muslim in disposing his or her property. In their will, a Muslim can only give out a maximum of one third of their property.

The Quran contains only three verses that give specific details of inheritance and shares, in addition to few other verses dealing with testamentary. But this information was used as a starting point by Muslim jurists who expounded the laws of inheritance even further using Hadith, as well as methods of juristic reasoning like Qiyas. Nowadays, inheritance is considered an integral part of Shariah Law and its application for Muslims is mandatory, though many peoples, despite being Muslim, have other inheritance customs.

Jewish Laws of Inheritance

The inheritance is patrilineal. The father —that is, the owner of the land— bequeaths only to his male descendants, so the Promised Land passes from one Jewish father to his sons.

If there were no living sons and no descendants of any previously living sons, daughters could inherit. In Numbers 27:1-4, the daughters of Zelophehad (Mahlah, Noa, Hoglah, Milcah, and Tirzah) of the tribe of Manasseh come to Moses and ask for their father's inheritance, as they have no brothers. The order of inheritance is set out in Numbers 27:7-11: a man's sons inherit first, daughters if no sons, brothers if he has no children, and so on.

Later, in Numbers 36, some of the heads of the families of the tribe of Manasseh come to Moses and point out that, if a daughter inherits and then marries a man not from her paternal tribe, her land will pass from her birth-tribe's inheritance into her marriage-tribe's. So a further rule is laid down: if a daughter inherits land, she must marry someone within her father's tribe. (The daughters of Zelophehad marry the sons' of their father's brothers. There is *no* indication that this was not their choice.)

The tractate Baba Bathra, written during late Antiquity in Babylon, deals extensively with issues of property ownership and inheritance according to Jewish Law. Other works of Rabbinical Law, such as the Hilkhot na%alot : mi-sefer Mishneh Torah leha-Rambam, and the Sefer ha-yerushot: »im yeter ha-mikhtavim be-divre ha-halakhah be-»Aravit uve-»Ivrit uve-Aramit also deal with inheritance issues. The first, often abbreviated to Mishneh Torah, was written by Maimonides and was very important in Jewish tradition. All these sources agree that the firstborn son is entitled to a double portion of his father's estate: Deuteronomy 21:17. This means that, for example, if a father left five sons, the firstborn receives a third of the estate and each of the other four receives a sixth. If he left nine sons, the firstborn receives a fifth and each of the other eight receive a tenth. If the eldest surviving son is not the firstborn son, he is not entitled to the double portion.

Philo of Alexandria and Josephus also comment on the Jewish laws of inheritance, praising them above other law codes of their time. They also agreed that the firstborn son must receive a double portion of his father's estate.

Inheritance Inequality

The distribution of the inherited wealth is often unequal. The majority might receive little while only a small number inherit a larger amount, with the lesser amount given to daughter in the family. The amount of inheritance is often far less than the value of a business initially given to the son, especially when a son takes over a thriving multi-million dollar business, yet the daughter is given the balance of the actual inheritance amounting to far less than the value of business that was initially given to the son. This is especially seen in old world cultures, but continues in many families to this day.

Arguments for eliminating the disparagement of inheritance inequality include the right to property and the merit of individual allocation of capital over government wealth confiscation and redistribution, but this does not resolve the problem of unequal inheritance. In terms of inheritance inequality, some economists and sociologists focus on the inter generational transmission of income or wealth which is said to have a direct impact on one's mobility (or immobility) and class position in society. Nations differ on the political structure and policy options that govern the transfer of wealth.

According to the American federal government statistics compiled by Mark Zandi, currently of "Moody's Economy.com", back in 1985, the average inheritance was $39,000. In subsequent years, the overall amount of total annual inheritance was more than doubled, reaching nearly $200 billion. By 2050, there is an estimated $25 trillion average inheritance transmitted across generations. Some researchers have attributed this rise to the baby boomer generation. Historically, the baby boomers were the largest influx of children conceived after WW2. For this reason, Thomas Shapiro suggests that this generation "is in the midst of benefiting from the greatest inheritance of wealth in history."

Inherited wealth may help explain why many Americans who have become rich may have had a "substantial head start". In September 2012, according to the Institute for Policy Studies, "over 60 percent" of the Forbes richest 400 Americans "grew up in substantial privilege".

Inheritance and Social Stratification

Inheritance inequality has a significant effect on stratification. Inheritance is an integral component of family, economic, and legal institutions, and a basic mechanism of class stratification. It also affects the distribution of wealth at the societal level. The total cumulative effect of inheritance on stratification outcomes takes three forms. The first form of inheritance is the inheritance of cultural capital (i.e. linguistic styles, higher status social circles, and aesthetic preferences). The second form of inheritance is through familial interventions in the form of *inter vivos* transfers (i.e. gifts between the living), especially at crucial junctures in the life courses. Examples include during a child's milestone stages, such as going to college, getting married, getting a job, and purchasing a home. The third form of inheritance is the transfers of bulk estates at the time of death of the testators, thus resulting in significant economic advantage accruing to children during their adult years. The origin of the stability of inequalities is material (personal possessions one is able to obtain) and is also cultural, rooted either in varying child-rearing practices that are geared to socialization according to social class and economic position. Child-rearing practices among those who inherit wealth may centre around favouring some groups at the expense of others at the bottom of the social hierarchy.

Sociological and Economic Effects of Inheritance Inequality

The degree to which economic status and inheritance is transmitted across generations determines one's life chances in society. Although many have linked one's social origins and educational attainment to life chances and opportunities, education cannot serve as the most influential predictor of economic mobility. In fact, children of well-off parents generally receive better schooling and benefit from material, cultural, and genetic inheritances. Likewise, schooling attainment is often persistent across generations and families with higher amounts of inheritance are able to acquire and transmit higher amounts of human capital. Lower amounts of human capital and inheritance can perpetuate inequality in the housing market and higher education. Research reveals that inheritance plays an important role in the accumulation of housing wealth. Those who receive an inheritance are more likely to own a home than those who do not regardless of the size of the inheritance.

Often, minorities and individuals from socially disadvantaged backgrounds receive less inheritance and wealth. As a result, mixed races might be excluded in inheritance privilege and are more likely to rent homes or live in poorer neighbourhoods, as well as achieve lower educational attainment compared whites in America, but this is not always the case, as many interracial marriages exist that redistributes wealth among non-whites. Individuals with a substantial amount of wealth and inheritance often intermarry with others of the same social class to protect their wealth and ensure the continuous transmission of inheritance across generations; thus perpetuating a cycle of privilege. For this reason, it can even be argued that one's inheritance places them in a specific social class position that requires a level of participation in certain activities that promote the oppression of lower-class individuals in terms of the social hierarchy and system of stratification.

Nations with the highest income and wealth inequalities often have the highest rates of homicide and disease (such as obesity, diabetes, and hypertension). A New York Times article reveals that the U.S. is the world's wealthiest nation, but "ranks twenty-ninth in life expectancy, right behind Jordan and Bosnia." This has been regarded as highly attributed to the significant gap of inheritance inequality in the country, although there are clearly other factors such as the healthcare system. When social and economic inequalities centred on inheritance are perpetuated by major social institutions such as family, education, religion, etc., these differing life opportunities are transmitted from each generation. As a result, this inequality becomes part of the overall social structure.

Taxation: Many states have inheritance taxes or death duties, under which a portion of any estate goes to the government.

Social Constructionism

Social constructionism or the social construction of reality (also social concept) is a theory of knowledge in sociology and communication theory that examines the development of jointly constructed understandings of the world. It assumes that understanding, significance, and meaning are developed not separately within the individual, but in coordination with other human beings. The elements most important to the theory are (a) the assumption that human beings rationalize their experience by creating a model of the social world and how it functions and, (b) that language is the most essential system through which humans construct reality.

Definition

Social constructs are the by-products of countless human choices, rather than laws related to human judgment. Social constructionism is not related to anti-determinism, though. Social constructionism is typically positioned in opposition to essentialism, which sees phenomena in terms of inherent, transhistorical essences independent of human judgement. A major focus of social constructionism is to uncover the ways in which individuals and groups participate in the construction of their perceived social reality. It involves looking at the ways social phenomena are created, institutionalized, known, and made into tradition by humans. The social construction of reality is an ongoing, dynamic process that is (and must be) reproduced by people acting on their interpretations and their knowledge of it. Because social constructs as facets of reality and objects of knowledge are not "given" by nature, they must be constantly maintained and re-affirmed in order to persist. This process also introduces the possibility of change: what "justice" is and what it means shifts from one generation to the next.

Ian Hacking noted in *The Social Construction of What?* that social construction talk is often in reference not only to worldly items, like things and facts – but also to beliefs about them.

Origins

Although the precise origin of social constructionism is debatable, it is generally considered that within the context of social theory, social constructionism emerged during the 1980s and further developed during the 1990s. This is evident from the list of academic works with the words "Social Construction of" in their title which Ian Hacking lists on the first page of his book "The Social Construction of What?". Hacking lists two titles from 1970s, eight from the 1980s, and twenty-one from the 1990s This chronology is corroborated by Dave Elder-Vass in his book "The Reality of Social Construction"

Dave Elder-Vass cites the Berger and Luckmann book "The Social Construction of Reality", originally published in 1966, as the work "which introduced the term social construction to sociologists and began the trajectory. . .[of the development of social constructionism].

Andy Lock and Tom Strong trace some of the fundamental tenets of social constructionism back to the work of the 18th century Italian political philosopher, rhetorician, historian, and jurist Giambattista Vico.

According to Lock and Strong, other influential thinkers whose work has had an impact on the development of social constructionism are: Edmund Husserl, Alfred Schutz, Maurice Merleau-Ponty, Martin Heidegger, Hans-Georg Gadamer, Paul Ricoeur, Jürgen Habermas, Emmanuel Levinas, Mikhail Bakhtin, Valentin Volosinov, Lev Vygotsky, George Herbert Mead, Ludwig Wittgenstein, Gregory Bateson, Harold Garfinkel, Erving Goffman, Anthony Giddens, Michel Foucault, Ken Gergen, Mary Gergen, Rom Harre, and John Shotter.

Based on the above, it could be surmised that the intellectual foundations of social constructionism span phenomenology, hermeneutics, poststructuralism, symbolic interactionism, as well as some strands of literary criticism and social psychology.

Social Constructionist Analysis

"Social construction" may mean many things to many people. Ian Hacking, having examined a wide range of books and articles with titles of the form "The social construction of X" or "Constructing X", argues that when something is said to be "socially constructed", this is shorthand for at least the following two claims:

(0) In the present state of affairs, X is taken for granted; X appears to be inevitable.

(1) X need *not* have existed, or need *not* be at all as it is. X, or X as it is at present, is *not* determined by the nature of things; it is *not* inevitable.

Hacking adds that the following claims are also often, though not always, implied by the use of the phrase "social construction":

(2) X is quite bad as it is.

(3) We would be much better off if X were done away with, or at least radically transformed.

Thus a claim that gender is socially constructed probably means that gender, as currently understood, is not an inevitable result of biology, but highly contingent on social and historical processes. In addition, depending on who is making the claim, it may mean that our current understanding of gender is harmful, and should be modified or eliminated, to the extent possible.

According to Hacking, "social construction" claims are not always clear about exactly what isn't "inevitable", or exactly what "should be done away with." Consider a hypothetical claim that quarks are "socially constructed". On one reading, this means that quarks themselves are not "inevitable" or "determined by the nature of things." On another reading, this means that our *idea* (or conceptualization, or understanding) of quarks is not "inevitable" or "determined by the nature of things". The distinction between "quarks themselves" and "our idea (or conceptualization, or understanding) of quarks" will undoubtedly trouble some with a philosophical bent. Hacking's distinction is based on intuitive metaphysics, with a split between things out in the world, on one hand, and ideas thereof in our minds, on the other. Hacking is less advocating a serious, particular metaphysics than he is suggesting a useful way to analyze claims about "social construction".

Hacking is much more sympathetic to the second reading than the first. Furthermore, he argues that, if the second reading is taken, there need not always be a conflict between saying that quarks are "socially constructed" and saying that they are "real". In our gender example, this means that while a legitimate biological basis for gender may exist, *some* of society's perceptions of gender may be socially constructed.

The stronger first position, however, is more-or-less an inevitable corollary of Willard Van Orman Quine's concept of ontological relativity, and particularly of the Duhem-Quine thesis. That is, according to Quine and like-minded thinkers (who are not usually characterized as social constructionists) there is no single privileged explanatory framework that is closest to "the things themselves"—every theory has merit only in proportion to its explanatory power.

As we step from the phrase to the world of human beings, "social construction" analyses can become more complex. Hacking briefly examines Helène Moussa's analysis of the social construction of "women refugees". According to him, Moussa's argument has several pieces, some of which may be implicit:

1. Canadian citizens' idea of "the woman refugee" is not inevitable, but historically contingent. (Thus the idea or category "the woman refugee" can be said to be "socially constructed".)
2. Women coming to Canada to seek asylum are profoundly affected by the category of "the woman refugee". Among other things, if a woman does not "count" as a "woman refugee" according to the law, she may be deported, and forced to return to very difficult conditions in her homeland.
3. Such women may modify their behaviour, and perhaps even their attitudes towards themselves, in order to gain the benefits of being classified as a "woman refugee".
4. If such a woman does not modify her behaviour, she should be considered un-Canadian and as such should not be admitted to citizenship.

Hacking suggests that this third part of the analysis, the "interaction" between a socially constructed category and the individuals that are actually or potentially included in that category, is present in many "social construction" analyses involving types of human beings.

Applications

Personal Construct Psychology

Since its appearance in the 1950s, personal construct psychology (PCP) has mainly developed as a constructivist theory of personality and a system of transforming individual meaning-making processes, largely in therapeutic contexts. It was based around the notion of persons as scientists who form and test theories about their worlds. Therefore, it represented one of the first attempts to appreciate the constructive nature of experience and the meaning persons give to their experience. Social constructionism (SC), on the other hand, mainly developed as a form of a critique, aimed to transform the oppressing effects of the social meaning-making processes. Over the years, it has grown into a cluster of different approaches, with no single SC position. However, different approaches under the generic term of SC are loosely linked by some shared assumptions about language, knowledge, and reality.

A usual way of thinking about the relationship between PCP and SC is treating them as two separate entities that are similar in some aspects, but also very different in others. This way of conceptualizing this relationship is a logical result of the circumstantial differences of their emergence. In subsequent analyses these differences between PCP and SC were framed around several points of tension, formulated as binary oppositions: personal/social; individualist/relational; agency/structure; constructivist/constructionist. Although some of the most important issues in contemporary psychology are elaborated in these contributions, the polarized positioning also sustained the idea of a separation between PCP and SC, paving the way for only limited opportunities for dialogue between them.

Reframing the relationship between PCP and SC may be of use in both the PCP and the SC communities. On one hand, it extends and enriches SC theory and points to benefits of applying the PCP "toolkit" in constructionist therapy and research. On the other hand, the reframing contributes to PCP theory and points to new ways of addressing social construction in therapeutic conversations.

Educational Psychology

Social constructivism has been studied by many educational psychologists, who are concerned with its implications for teaching and learning.

Environmental Leftist Social Constructionism

The Postmodern social construction of nature is a theory of postmodernist continental philosophy that poses an alternative critique of previous mainstream, promethean dialogue about environmental sustainability and ecopolitics. Whereas traditional criticisms of environmentalism come from the more conservative "right" of politics, leftist critiques of nature pioneered by postmodernist constructionism highlight the need to recognise "the other". The implicit assumption made by theorists like Wapner is that a new "response to ecocriticism would require critics to acknowledge the ways in which they themselves silence nature and then to respect the sheer otherness of the nonhuman world."

This is because postmodernism prides itself on criticizing the urge toward mastery that characterizes modernity. But mastery is exactly what postmodernism is exerting as it captures the nonhuman world within its own conceptual domain. That in turn implies postmodern cultural criticism can deepen the modernist urge toward mastery by eliminating the ontological weight of the nonhuman world. "What else could it mean to assert that there is no such thing as nature?". Thus, the issue becomes an existentialist query about whether nature can exist in a humanist critique, and whether we can discern the "other's" views in relation to our actions on their behalf. This theorem has come to be known as "The Wapner Paradigm."

Systemic Therapy

Systemic therapy is a form of psychotherapy which seeks to address people as people in relationship, dealing with the interactions of groups and their interactional patterns and dynamics.

Teleology of Social Construction

The concepts of *weak* and strong as applied to opposing philosophical positions, "isms", inform a teleology – the goal-oriented, meaningful or "final end" of an interpretation of reality. "Isms" are not personal opinions, but the extreme, modal, formulations that actual persons, individuals, can then consider, and take a position between. There are opposing philosophical positions concerning the feasibility of co-creating a common, shared, social reality, called *weak* and strong.

John R. Searle does not elucidate the terms strong and *weak* in his book *The Construction of Social Reality*, but he clearly uses them in his Chinese room argument, where he debates the feasibility of creating a computing machine with a sharable understanding of reality, and he adds "We are precisely such machines." Strong artificial intelligence (Strong AI) is the bet that computer programmers will somehow eventually achieve a computing machine with a mind of its own, and that it will eventually be more powerful than a human mind. Weak AI bets they won't.

David Deutsch in his book *The Fabric of Reality* uses a form of strong Turing principle to share Frank Tipler's view of the final state of the universe as an omnipotent (but not omniscient), Omega point, computer. *But this computer is a society of creative thinkers, or people* (albeit posthuman transhuman persons), having debates in order to generate information, in the never-ending attempt to attain omniscience of this physics—its evolutionary forms, its computational abilities, and the methods of its epistemology—having an eternity to do so. (p. 356)

Because both the Chinese room argument and the construction of social reality deal with Searle and his debates, and because they both use *weak* and strong to denote a philosophical position, and because both debate the programmability of "the other", it is worth noting the correspondence that "strong AI" is strong social constructionism, and "weak AI" is weak social constructivism.

Strong social constructiv"ism" says "none are able to *communicate* either a full reality or an accurate ontology, therefore my position must impose, by a sort of divine right, my observer-relative epistemology", whereas weak social constructiv*ism* says "none are able to *know* a full reality, therefore *we must* cooperate, informing and conveying an objective ontology as best we can."

Weak Teleology

Weak social constructionism sees the underlying, objective, "brute fact" elements of the class of languages and functional assignments of human, metaphysical, reality. Brute facts are all facts that are not institutional (metaphysical, social agreement) facts. The skeptic portrays the *weak* aspect of social constructivism, and wants to spend effort debating the institutional realities.

Harvard psychologist Steven Pinker writes that "some categories really are social constructions: they exist only because people tacitly agree to act as if they exist. Examples include money, tenure, citizenship, decorations for bravery, and the presidency of the United States."

In a similar vein, Stanley Fish has suggested that baseball's "balls and strikes" are social constructions.

Both Fish and Pinker agree that the sorts of objects indicated here can be described as part of what John Searle calls "social reality." In particular, they are, in Searle's terms, ontologically subjective but epistemologically objective.. "Social facts" are temporally, ontologically, and logically dependent on "brute facts." For example, "money" in the form of its raw materials (rag, pulp, ink) as constituted socially for barter (for example by a banking system) is a social fact of "money" by virtue of (i) collectively willing and intending (ii) to impose some particular function (purpose for which), (iii) by constitutive rules atop the "brute facts." "Social facts have the remarkable feature of having no analogue among physical brute facts" (34). The existence of language is itself constitutive of the social fact (37), which natural or brute facts do not require. Natural or "brute" facts exist independently of language; thus a "mountain" is a mountain in every language and in no language; it simply is what it is..

Searle illustrates the evolution of social facts from brute facts by the constitutive rule: X counts as Y in C. "The Y terms has to assign a new *status* that the object does not already have just in virtue of satisfying the Y term; and there has to be collective agreement, or at least acceptance, both in the imposition of that status on the stuff referred to by the X term and about the function that goes with that status. Furthermore, because the physical features brute facts specified by the X term are insufficient by themselves to guarantee the fulfillment of the assigned function specified by the Y term, the new status and its attendant functions have to be the sort of things that can be constituted by collective agreement or acceptance."

It is true that language is not a "brute fact," that it is an institutional fact, a human convention, a metaphysical reality (that happens to be physically uttered), but Searle points out that there are language-independent thoughts "noninstitutional, primitive, biological inclinations and cognitions not requiring any linguistic devices," and that there are many "brute facts" amongst both humans and animals that are truths that should not be altered in the social constructs because language does not truly constitute them, despite the attempt to institute them for any group's gain: money and property are language dependent, but desires (thirst, hunger) and emotions (fear, rage) are not. (Descartes describes the difference between imagination as a sort of vision, or image, and intellect as conceptualizing things by symbolic manipulation.) Therefore, there is doubt that society or a computer can be completely programmed by language and images, (because there is a programmable, emotive effect of images that derives from the language of judgment towards images).

Finally, against the strong theory and for the weak theory, Searle insists, "it could not be the case, as some have maintained, that all facts are institutional [i.e., social] facts, that there are no brute facts, because the structure of institutional facts reveals that they are logically dependent on brute facts. To suppose that all facts are institutional [i.e., social] would produce an infinite regress or circularity in the account of institutional facts. In order that some facts are institutional, there must be other facts that are brute [i.e., physical, biological, natural]. This is the consequence of the logical structure of institutional facts."

Ian Hacking, Canadian philosopher of science, insists, "the notion that everything is socially constructed has been going the rounds. John Searle [1995] argues vehemently (and in my opinion cogently) against universal constructionism." "Universal social constructionism is descended from the doctrine that I once named linguistic idealism and attributed, only half in jest, to Richard Nixon [Hacking, 1975, p. 182]. Linguistic idealism is the doctrine that only what is talked about exists, nothing has reality until it is spoken of, or written about. This extravagant notion is descended from Berkeley's idea-ism, which we call idealism: the doctrine that all that exists is mental." "They are a part of what John Searle [1995] calls social reality. His book is titled the *Construction of Social Reality,* and as I explained elsewhere [Hacking, 1996], that is not a *social* construction book at all."

Hacking observes, "the label 'social constructionism' is more code than description" of every Leftist, Marxist, Freudian, and Feminist PostModernist to call into question every moral, sex, gender, power, and deviant claim as just another essentialist claim—including the claim that members of the male and female sex are inherently different, rather than historically and socially constructed. Hacking observes that his 1995 simplistic dismissal of the concept actually revealed to many readers the outrageous implications of the theorists: Is child abuse a real evil, or a social construct, asked Hacking? His dismissive attitude, "gave some readers a way to see that there need be no clash between construction and reality," inasmuch as "the metaphor of social construction once had excellent shock value, but now it has become tired."

Informally, they require human practices to sustain their existence, but they have an effect that is (basically) universally agreed upon. The disagreement lies in whether this category should be called "socially constructed." Ian Hacking argues that it should not. Furthermore, it is not clear that authors who write "social construction" analyses ever mean "social construction" in Pinker's sense. ". If they never do, then Pinker (probably among others) has misunderstood the point of a social constructionist argument.

To understand how weak social constructionism can conclude that metaphysics (a human affair) is not the entire "reality," see the arguments against the study metaphysics. This inability to accurately share the *full* reality, even given time for a rational conversation, is similarly proclaimed by *weak artificial intelligence.*

Strong Teleology

Strong social constructionism sees everything as a social construction, everything as metaphysical. This is not to say that it sees the outer world as having beings in a non-reality, as unreal. Rather, it proposes that the notions of "real" and "unreal" are themselves social constructs, so that the question of whether anything is "real" is just a matter of social convention. The conservative proponent of institutions the way they are progressing, would, in Rudolf Carnap's words "pretend to teach knowledge which is of a higher level than that of empirical science." Everyone else has *their own* reality, and take the stance that "if you have to ask, you would not understand."

Strong social constructionists oppose the existence of "brute" facts. That a mountain is a *mountain* (as opposed to just another undifferentiated clump of earth) is socially engendered, and not a *brute* fact. That the concept of mountain is universally admitted in all human languages reflects near-universal human consensus, but does not make it an objective reality; similarly for all apparently real objects and events: trees, cars, snow, collisions. It reasons that all reality is thought, all thought is in a language, all language is a convention, and that all convention is socially acceptable, hence, it uses language to socially program.

A *Strong social constructionism* entity convenes and forms the conventions of consensus reality, a real, human operated set of social programs, whose subjects participate in operating on the "real" to the extent they conform democratically and politely. If its ontology is accused, the pragmatic answer is "read the minutes of the meeting", both because the strong social constructionism is busy creating programs, and because sharing a reality accurately and completely is futile.

Also, in regards to Broadcast History, 'social construction' refers to the way in which the media form has been created. This relates both to its structure and regulation. It's the way that the social media outlet is constructed by our society.

History and Development

Berger and Luckmann

Constructionism became prominent in the U.S. with Peter L. Berger and Thomas Luckmann's 1966 book, *The Social Construction of Reality*. Berger and Luckmann argue that all knowledge, including the most basic, taken-for-granted common sense knowledge of everyday reality, is derived from and maintained by social interactions. When people interact, they do so with the understanding that their respective perceptions of reality are related, and as they act upon this understanding their common knowledge of reality becomes reinforced. Since this common sense knowledge is negotiated by people, human typifications, significations and institutions come to be presented as part of an objective reality, particularly for future generations who were not involved in the original process of negotiation. For example, as parents negotiate rules for their children to follow, those rules confront the children as externally produced "givens" that they cannot change. Berger and Luckmann's social constructionism has its roots in phenomenology. It links to Heidegger and Edmund Husserl through the teaching of Alfred Schutz, who was also Berger's PhD adviser.

Narrative Turn

During the 1970s and 1980s, social constructionist theory underwent a transformation as constructionist sociologists engaged with the work of Michel Foucault and others as a narrative turn in the social sciences was worked out in practice. This had a particular impact on the emergent sociology of science and the growing field of science and technology studies. In particular, Karin Knorr-Cetina, Bruno Latour, Barry Barnes, Steve Woolgar, and others used social constructionism to relate what science has typically characterized as objective facts to the processes of social construction, with the goal of showing that human subjectivity imposes itself on those facts we take to be objective, not solely the other way around. A particularly provocative title in this line of thought is Andrew Pickering's *Constructing Quarks: A Sociological History of Particle Physics*. At the same time, Social Constructionism shaped studies of technology – the Sofield, especially on the Social construction of technology, or SCOT, and authors as Wiebe Bijker, Trevor Pinch, Maarten van Wesel, etc. Despite its common perception as objective, mathematics is not immune to social constructionist accounts. Sociologists such as Sal Restivo and Randall Collins, mathematicians including Reuben Hersh and Philip J. Davis, and philosophers including Paul Ernest have published social constructionist treatments of mathematics.

Postmodernism

Social constructionism can be seen as a source of the postmodern movement, and has been influential in the field of cultural studies. Some have gone so far as to attribute the rise of cultural studies (the cultural turn) to social constructionism. Within the social constructionist strand of postmodernism, the concept of socially constructed reality stresses the ongoing mass-building of worldviews by individuals in dialectical interaction with society at a time. The numerous realities so formed comprise, according to this view, the imagined worlds of human social existence and activity, gradually crystallised by habit into institutions propped up by language conventions, given ongoing legitimacy by mythology, religion and philosophy, maintained by therapies and socialization, and subjectively internalised by upbringing and education to become part of the identity of social citizens.

In the book *The Reality of Social Construction*, the British sociologist Dave Elder-Vass places the development of social constructionism as one outcome of the legacy of postmodernism. He writes "Perhaps the most widespread and influential product of this process coming to terms with the legacy of postmodernism is social constructionism, which has been booming within the domain of social theory since the 1980s."

Criticisms

Social constructionism falls toward the nurture end of the spectrum of the larger nature and nurture debate. Consequently critics have argued that it generally ignores biological influences on behaviour or culture, or suggests that they are unimportant to achieve an understanding of human behaviour. In contrast, most psychologists and social scientists believe that behaviour is a very complex interaction of both biological and cultural influences. Other disciplines, such as evolutionary psychology, behaviour genetics, behavioural neuroscience, epigenetics, etc., take a nature-nurture interactionism approach to understand behaviour or cultural phenomena.

In 1996, to illustrate what he believed to be the intellectual weaknesses of social constructionism and postmodernism, physics professor Alan Sokal submitted an article to the academic journal *Social Text* deliberately written to be incomprehensible but including phrases and jargon typical of the articles published by the journal. The submission, which was published, was an experiment to see if the journal would "publish an article liberally salted with nonsense if (a) it sounded good and (b) it flattered the editors' ideological preconceptions." The Postmodernism Generator is a computer program that is designed to produce similarly incomprehensible text. In 1999, Sokal, with coauthor Jean Bricmont published the book *Fashionable Nonsense*, which criticized postmodernism and social constructionism.

Philosopher Paul Boghossian has also written against social constructionism. He follows Ian Hacking's argument that many adopt social constructionism because of its potentially liberating stance: if things are the way that they are only because of our social conventions, as opposed to being so naturally, then it should be possible to change them into how we would rather have them be. He then states that social constructionists argue that we should refrain from making absolute judgements about what is true and instead state that something is true in the light of this or that theory. Countering this, he states:

> *"But it is hard to see how we might coherently follow this advice. Given that the propositions which make up epistemic systems are just very general propositions about what absolutely justifies what, it makes no sense to insist that we abandon making absolute* particular *judgements about what justifies what while allowing us to* accept *absolute* general *judgements about what justifies what. But in effect this is what the epistemic relativist is recommending"*

Later in the same work, Boghossian severely constrains the requirements of relativism. He states that instead of believing that any world view is just a true as any other (cultural relativism), we should believe that:

> *"If we were to encounter an* actual, *coherent, fundamental, genuine alternative to our epistemic system, C2, whose track record was* impressive *enough to make us doubt the correctness of our own system, C1, we would not be able to justify C1 over C2 even by our own lights.*

Woolgar and Pawluch argue that constructionsts tend to 'ontological gerrymander' social conditions in and out of their analysis. Following this point, Thibodeaux argued that constructionism can both separate and combine a subject and their effective environment. To resolve this he argued that objective conditions should be used when analyzing how perspectives are motivated.

Social constructionism has been criticized by evolutionary psychologists, including Steven Pinker in his book *The Blank Slate*. John Tooby and Leda Cosmides used the term "standard social science model" to refer to social-science philosophies that they argue fail to take into account the evolved properties of the brain.

Coefficient of Relationship

The coefficient of relationship is a measure of the degree of consanguinity (or biological relationship) between two individuals. A coefficient of inbreeding can be calculated for an individual, as a measure for the amount of pedigree collapse within that individual's genealogy. The term coefficient of relationship was defined by Sewall Wright in 1922, and was derived from his definition of the coefficient of inbreeding of 1921. The measure is most commonly used in genetics and genealogy.

In general, the higher the level of inbreeding the closer the coefficient of relationship approaches a value of 1, expressed as a percentage, and approaches a value of 0 for individuals with arbitrarily remote common ancestors.

Coefficient of Inbreeding

The coefficient of inbreeding ("f") is a measure of the likelihood of genetic effects due to inbreeding to be expected based on a known pedigree (i.e. a fully documented genealogy e.g. due to a fixed system of breeding). The measure expresses the expected percentage of homozygosity arising from a given system of breeding.

For a given gene with equally common dominant and recessive variants *A* and *a*, a random-bred stock will be 50% homozygous (25% *AA* and 25% *aa*), while a closely inbred population will be 100% homozygous (100% *AA* or 100% *aa*). The coefficient of inbreeding f is thus designed to run from 0 for an expected 50% homozygosis to 1 for an expected 100% homozygosis, f=2h-1, where h is the chance of finding homozygosis in this gene.

Note that f is an expectation value for an unspecified, hypothetical, perfectly Mendelian gene. Its definition holds regardless of whether the organism's genome actually contains such a gene. Therefore, the coefficient of inbreeding is a statistical value derived from the individual's pedigree and cannot be verified or "measured" exactly by looking at the individual's genome.

The coefficient of relationship ("r") between two individuals B and C is obtained by a summation of coefficients calculated for every line by which they are connected to their common ancestors. Each such line connects the two individuals via a common ancestor, passing through no individual which is not a common ancestor more than once. A path coefficient between an ancestor A and an offspring O separated by n generations is given as:

$$p_{AO} = 2^{-n}.((1+f_A)/(1+f_O))^{½}$$

where f_A and f_O are the coefficients of inbreeding for A and O, respectively.

The coefficient of relationship r_{BC} is now obtained by summing over all path coefficients:

$$r_{BC} = \Sigma\, p_{AB}.p_{AC}.$$

By assuming that the pedigree can be traced back to a sufficiently remote population of perfectly random-bred stock (f_A=0) the definition of r may be simplified to

$$r_{BC} = \Sigma_p\, 2^{-L(p)},$$

where p enumerates all paths connecting B and C with unique common ancestors (i.e. all paths terminate at a common ancestor and may not pass through a common ancestor to a common ancestor's ancestor), and L(p) is the length of the path p.

To given an (artificial) example: Assuming that two individuals share the same 32 ancestors of n=5 generations ago, but do not have any common ancestors at four or less generations ago, their coefficient of relationship would be

$$r = 2^n.2^{-2n} = 2^{-n} = 3\%.$$

Individuals for which the same situation applies for their 1024 ancestors of ten generations ago would have a coefficient of $r = 2^{-10}$ = 0.1%. If follows that the value of r can be given to an accuracy of a few percent if the family tree of both individuals is known for a depth of five generations, and to an accuracy of a tenth of a percent if the known depth is at least ten generations. The contribution to r from common ancestors of 20 generations ago (corresponding to roughly 500 years in human genealogy, or the contribution from common descent from a medieval population) falls below one part-per-million.

Human Relationships

The coefficient of relationship is sometimes used to express degrees of kinship in numerical terms in human genealogy.

In human relationships, the value of the coefficient of relationship is usually calculated based on the knowledge of a full family tree extending to a comparatively small number of generations, perhaps of the order of three or four. As explained above, the value for the coefficient of relationship so calculated is thus a lower bound, with an actual value that may be up to a few percent higher. The value is accurate to within 1% if the full family tree of both individuals is known to a depth of seven generations.

Degree of relationship	*Relationship*	*Coefficient of relationship (r)*
	Inbred strain	99%
0	identical twins; clones	100%
1	parent-offspring	50% (2^{-1})
2	full siblings	50% ($2^{-2}+2^{-2}$)
2	3/4 siblings or sibling-cousins	37.5% ($2^{-2}+2.2^{-4}$)
2	grandparent-grandchild	25% (2^{-2})

Contd...

Degree of relationship	***Relationship***	***Coefficient of relationship (r)***
2	half siblings	25% (2^{-2})
3	aunt/uncle-nephew/niece	25% (2.2^{-3})
4	double first cousins	25% ($2^{-3}+2^{-3}$)
3	great grandparent-great grandchild	12.5% (2^{-3})
4	first cousins	12.5% (2.2^{-4})
6	quadruple second cousins	12.5% (8.2^{-6})
6	triple second cousins	9.38% (6.2^{-6})
4	half-first cousins	6.25% (2^{-4})
5	first cousins once removed	6.25% (2.2^{-5})
6	double second cousins	6.25% (4.2^{-6})
6	second cousins	3.13% ($2^{-6}+2^{-6}$)
8	third cousins	0.78% (2.2^{-8})
10	fourth cousins	0.20% (2.2^{-10})

Most legally prohibited degree of kinship regarding incestuous relationships concern relations of $r = 25\%$ or higher (3 or 4 degrees of relationship or lower), while most permit unions of individuals with $r = 12.5\%$ or lower. An exception are a number of US states where cousin marriage is prohibited. Also, most legislations make no provision for the rare case of marriage between double first cousins.

It should also be noted that incest laws also include prohibitions of unions between biologically unrelated individuals if there is a close legal relationship such as adoption or affinity. It also covers relationships where there is no likelihood of birth of children.

Social Processes Affecting Family

An elementary family can be defined as a social group consisting of father, mother and their children. Bohannan in his definition of the family emphasized the functional as well as the structural roles of the family. According to him a family contains people who are linked by sexual and affinal relationships as well as those linked by descent who are linked by secondary relationships that is by chains of primary relationships.

According to William J Goode at least two adult persons of opposite sex reside together. They engage in some kind of division of labour i.e they both do not perform exactly the same tasks. They engage in many types of economic and social exchanges i.e. they do things for one another. They share many things in common such as food, sex, residence and both goods and social activities. The adults have parental relations with their children as their children have filial relations with them; the parents have some authority over their children and both share with one another while also assuming some obligations for protection, cooperation and nurture. There are sibling relations among the children themselves with a range of obligations to share, protect and help one another. Individuals are likely to create various kinds of relations with each other but if their continuing social relations exhibit some or all of the role patterns, in all probability they would be viewed as the family.

A host of inter-related factors like economic, educational, legal and demographic like population growth, migration and urbanization etc have been affecting the structure of the family in India. There are many published accounts demonstrating that changes have taken place in the structure of the family due to exposures to the forces of industrialization. Nuclear status of family is considered as the outcome of its impact. Such an interpretation presupposes existence of non-nuclear family structure in such societies. Empirical evidence sometimes does not support this position. Further industrial establishments have their own requirements of human groups for their efficient functioning. As a result people are migrating to industrial areas and various kinds of family units have been formed added extraordinary variety to overall situation.

Due to the influences of urbanization the joint family structure is under severe stress and in many cases it has developed a tendency toward nuclear family. When there is no disagreement on the authenticity of such a tendency the traditional ideal joint family was perhaps not the exclusive type before such influences came into existence. Both modernisation and urbanization are considered as the major contributing factors toward modernisation. In fact modernisation as a social â€"psychological attribute can be in operation independent of industrialization and urbanization.

With the passage of time through exposures to the forces of modernisation family structure underwent multiple changes. One of the important features of the family studies in India has been concerned with the question of whether the joint family system is disintegrating and a new nuclear type of family pattern is emerging. According to Augustine it seems almost unrealistic that we think of a dichotomy between the joint and nuclear family. This is especially true given the rapidity of social change that has swept our country. In the context of industrialization, urbanization and social change it is very difficult to think of a dichotomy between the joint and the nuclear family in India. In the present context these typologies are not mutually exclusive. Social change is an inevitable social process that can be defined as observable transformations in social relationships. This transformation is most evident in the family system. However because of structures our traditionally these transformations are not easily observable.

According to Augustine the concept of transitionality has two dimensions â€" retrospective and prospective. The retrospective dimension implies the traditional past of our family and social system while the prospective one denotes the direction in which change is taking place in our family system. Transitionality is thus an attempt to discuss the crux of the emergent forms of family. The studies conducted in several parts of the country show that the joint family system in India is undergoing a process of structural transformation due to the process of modernisation, industrialization and urbanization. A nuclear family develops into a joint family after the marriage of a son and hence the process of fission and fusion take place in the family system due to various reasons. In most parts of India where patriarchal families exist sons are expected to stay put together with the parents till the marriage of the children. After this they tend to separate. Thus the process of fission take place and the joint family is broken into relatively smaller number of units sometimes into nuclear units. Nicolas on the basis of his study in rural West Bengal concludes that if a joint family between a father and his married sons divides a joint family among brothers rarely survive. The father seems to be the keystone of the joint family structure. Despite the solidarity among the male siblings after the father's death many forces tend to break the joint family into separate units.

Significant numbers of studies have been conducted on the urban family structure in India. T.K Oomen in his article Urban family in Transition points out that most of these studies have been obsessed with a single question is the joint family in India breaking down and undergoing a process of nuclear due to urbanization? Scholars point out that industrial urbanization has not brought disintegration in the joint family structure. Milton Singer studies the structure of the joint family among the industrialists of Madras City. He finds that joint family system has not been a blockade for entrepreneurship development. Rather it has facilitated and adapted to industrialization. Ramakrishna Mukherjee in 'Sociologists and Social Change in India Today' finds that the joint family is over represented in the trade and commerce sector of national economy and in the high and middle grade occupations and nuclear family is over represented in the rural rather than in the urban areas. Based on his study on the family structure in West Bengal he concludes that the central tendency in the Indian society is to pursue the joint family organisation. T.K Oomen is of the opinion that so far urban family has been viewed from within as a little society .To him for a proper understanding the urban family should be placed in a broad social context. For this purpose the urban families should be placed in a broad social context. The urban families are to be distinguished through the mode of earning a livelihood and sources of income, structure of authority, urban social milieu and social ecology and the emerging value patterns.

The socio-ecological factors like the settlement patterns, cultural environments of the urban migrants and associations to various occupational, political, ideological, cultural, economic groups influence and reorient the style and pattern of urban families. The urban centres are melting pots of traditional and modern values. Individualism is growing at a significant speed in the urban areas. Individualism is against the spirit of the joint family and questions the established authority of the patriarchal set up.

In the context of rapid technological transformation, economic development and social change the pattern of family living has been diverse in urban India. Life is complex both in the rural and in the urban areas .In the urban areas and even in the rural areas many couples are in gainful employment. They depend on others for childcare. With the structural break down of the joint family they face lot of difficulties in raising their children. For employment many rural men come out of the village leaving behind their wives and children.

In the process of structural transformation the old structure of authority and value has been challenged. The growing individualism questions the legitimacy of the age-old hierarchic authority. The old value system also changes significantly. However this system of transformation has minimized the importance of mutual respect, love and affection among the family members belonging to various generations. The lack of emotional support in the family often leads the youth to the path of alcoholism and drug addiction.

Fictive Kinship

Fictive kinship is a term used by anthropologists and ethnographers to describe forms of kinship or social ties that are based on neither consanguinal (blood ties) nor affinal ("by marriage") ties, in contrast to *true kinship* ties. To the extent that consanguinal and affinal kinship ties might be considered *real* or *true* kinship, the term *fictive kinship* has in the past been used to refer to those kinship ties that are *fictive*, in the sense of *not-real*. Invoking the concept as a cross-culturally valid anthropological category therefore rests on the presumption that the inverse category of "(true) kinship" built around consanguinity and affinity is similarly cross-culturally valid. Use of the term was common until the mid-to-late twentieth century, when anthropology effectively deconstructed and revised many of the concepts and categories around the study of kinship and social ties. In particular, anthropologists established that a consanguinity basis for kinship ties is not universal across cultures, and that—on the contrary—it may be a culturally specific symbol of kinship only in particular culture.

Stemming from anthropology's early connections to legal studies, the term *fictive kinship* may also be used in a legalistic sense, and this use continues in societies where these categories and definitions regarding kinship and social ties have legal currency; e.g. in matters of inheritance. As part of the deconstruction of kinship mentioned above, anthropologists now recognise that—cross-culturally—the kinds of social ties and relationships formerly treated under the category of "kinship" are very often not necessarily predicated on blood ties or marriage ties, and may rather be based on shared residence, shared economic ties, nurture kinship, or familiarity via other forms of interaction.

Examples

Types of relations often described by anthropologists as *fictive kinship* include compadrazgo relations, foster care, common membership in a unilineal descent group, and legal adoption. A noted Gurung tradition is the institution of "Rodi", where teenagers form fictive kinship bonds and become Rodi members to socialize, perform communal tasks, and find marriage partners. In Western culture, a person may refer to close friends of one's parents as "aunt" or "uncle" (and their children as "cousin"), or may refer to close friends as "brother" or "sister". In particular, college fraternities and sororities in some North American cultures usually use "brother" and "sister" to refer to members of the organisation. Monastic, Masonic, and Lodge organisations also use the term "Brother" for members. "Nursing Sister" is used to denote a rank of nurse, and the term "Sisterhood" may be used for feminists. Fictive kinship was discussed by Jenny White in her work on female migrant workers in Istanbul. In her work, she draws on ideas of production and the women she works with being drawn together through "webs of indebtedness" through which the women refer to each other as kin.

- Compadrazgo is a form of fictive kinship that is rooted in Central Mexico history for many years. Literally meaning "co-parenthood", compadrazgo is a term to describe the set of relationships between a child, their parents, and their godparents. It has been hypothesized that these relationships evolved after the Spanish conquest in 1521 to help deal with stressful situations. These fictive kinships still exist in modern day Mexican societies, and are established by providing some form of aid throughout the child's life.
- Undocumented immigrants have also demonstrated fictive kin relationships. Undocumented restaurant workers are known to form pseudo-families in which they cooperate within living and working situations. These relationships benefit the workers by creating a support system that would otherwise be unavailable to those living far from home.
- Some fictive kin relationships have been discovered in Israel in relation to organ transplants. Hospital committees are formed to assess whether the organ donation is from a true family member or from a friend. In order to obtain organ transplants, some individuals are forced to find strangers and pay them compensation for the procedure. However, the relationship between the donor and recipient must be invented as a familial relationship in order to pass through the hospital committee. In this case, fictive kinship is created knowingly to both parties in order to achieve their goals, and is mutualistic in nature.
- Adoption and foster care have always been grouped into the fictive kinship category (in cases where the child shares no genetic relatedness to the caregivers). The children are normally treated as the adopters' biological kin, receiving a lot of parental investment despite not having family ties. This view has been chastised by some who claim that notions of kinship are not always based on biological determinants.
- The military has also been an avenue to propagate fictive kinship, such as the sense of brotherhood felt by the soldiers. Fictive kinship has been demonstrated among the spouses of military men and women as well. These relationships may facilitate close bonds that are beneficial during times of hardship.
- Other times, relationships can appear from the outside to be fictive kinship relationships, but the reality is that this appearance is just the result of kinship terminology. Members

of the Shanti Nagar village in North India refer to everyone—even strangers—in familial terms. A man would address another man of a similar in age as "brother", and would address an older man as "uncle". Although these terms used in addressing one another appear fictive kinship in nature, they do not actually suggest the existence of ritual kin relationships.

Critiques

Recently, many anthropologists have abandoned a distinction between "real" and "fictive" kin, because many cultures do not base their notion of kinship on genealogical relations. This was argued most forcefully by David M. Schneider, in his 1984 book *A critique of the study of kinship*. In response to this insight, Janet Carsten developed the idea of "relatedness". She developed her initial ideas from studies with the Malays in looking at what was socialized and biological. Here she uses the idea of relatedness to move away from a pre-constructed analytics opposition which exists in anthropological thought between the biological and the social. Carsten argued that relatedness should be described in terms of indigenous statements and practices, some of which fall outside what anthropologists have conventionally understood as kinship.

Use in Sociobiology

In the biological and animal behavioural sciences, the term "kinship" has a different meaning from the current anthropological usage of the term, and more in common with the former anthropological usage that assumed that blood ties are ontologically prior to social ties. In these sciences, "kinship" is commonly used as a shorthand for "the regression coefficient of (genetic) relatedness", which is a metric denoting the proportion of shared genetic material between any two individuals relative to average degrees of genetic variance in the population under study. This coefficient of relationship is an important component of the theory of inclusive fitness, a treatment of the evolutionary selective pressures on the emergence of certain forms of social behaviour. Confusingly, inclusive fitness theory is more popularly known through its narrower form, kin selection theory, whose name clearly resonates with former conceptions of "kinship" in anthropology.

Whilst inclusive fitness theory thus describes one of the necessary conditions for the evolutionary emergence of social behaviours, the details of the proximate conditions mediating the expression of social bonding and cooperation have been less investigated in sociobiology. In particular, the question of whether genetic relatedness (or "blood ties") must necessarily be present for social bonding and cooperation to be expressed has been the source of much confusion, partly due to thought experiments in W. D. Hamilton's early theoretical treatments. In addition to setting out the details of the evolutionary selection pressure, Hamilton roughly outlined two possible mechanisms by which the expression of social behaviours might be mediated:

> The selective advantage which makes behaviour conditional in the right sense on the discrimination of factors which correlate with the relationship of the individual concerned is therefore obvious. It may be, for instance, that in respect of a certain social action performed towards neighbours indiscriminately, an individual is only just breaking even in terms of inclusive fitness. If he could learn to recognise those of his neighbours who really were close relatives and could devote his beneficial actions to them alone an advantage to inclusive fitness would at once appear. Thus a mutation causing such discriminatory behaviour itself benefits inclusive fitness and would be selected. In fact, the individual may not need to perform any discrimination so sophisticated as we suggest here; a difference in the generosity of his behaviour according to whether the situations evoking it were encountered near to, or far from, his own home might occasion an advantage of a similar kind.

Traditional sociobiology did not consider the divergent consequences between these basic possibilities for the expression of social behaviour, and instead assumed that the expression operates in the "recognition" manner, whereby individuals are behaviourally primed to discriminate which others are their "true" genetic relatives, and engage in cooperative behaviour with them. But when expression has evolved to be primarily location-based or context-based—depending on a society's particular demographics and history—social ties and cooperation may or may not coincide with "blood ties". Reviews of the mammal, primate, and human evidence demonstrate that expression of social behaviours in these species are primarily location-based and context-based, and examples of what used to be labelled as "fictive kinship" are readily understood in this perspective.

Nurture Kinship

The concept of nurture kinship in the anthropological study of human social relationships (kinship) highlights the extent to which such relationships are brought into being through the performance of various acts of nurture between individuals. The concept stands in contrast to the earlier anthropological concepts of human kinship relations being fundamentally based on "blood ties", some other form of shared substance, or a proxy for these (as in fictive kinship). This conception of the ontology of social ties has become stronger in the wake of Schneider's influential *Critique of the Study of Kinship* and Holland's subsequent *Social Bonding and Nurture Kinship*, demonstrating that as well as the ethnographic record, *biological theory and evidence* also more strongly support the *nurture* perspective than the *blood* perspective. Both argue that the earlier *blood* theory of kinship derived from an unwarranted extension of symbols and values from anthropologists' own cultures.

Intellectual Background

Reports of kinship ties being based on various forms of shared nurture date back at least to William Robertson Smith's (1889) compiled *Lectures on The Religion of the Semites*:

According to antique ideas, those who eat and drink together are by this very act tied to one another by a bond of friendship and mutual obligation... The idea that kinship is not purely an affair of birth, but may be acquired, has quite fallen out of our circle of ideas. (Robertson Smith 1889, 265, 273)

At this stage, Robertson Smith interpreted the kinship ties emerging from the sharing of food as constituting an alternative form of the sharing of substance, aside from the sharing of blood or genetic substance. However, later observations focused on the *nurturing* qualities of food-sharing behaviour, allowing a potential distinction between the earlier emphasis on kinship as shared *substance* (e.g. food or blood) and kinship as *performance* (of care-giving or nurturing behaviours):

I want to examine the human relationships of a primitive society as determined by nutritional needs, showing how hunger shapes the sentiments which bind together the members of each social group. By what means is this fundamental biological want fulfilled in a given environment; and what forms of human activities and social groupings are so derived? (Richards 1932, 23)

Sometimes the line between conceiving of kinship as *substance* or as *nurture* is blurred by using both concepts. For example, the substance of food or milk may be conceived as the medium or vehicle through which the nurturing behaviour is performed (e.g. Strathern 1973). The notion that it is *the nurturing acts themselves* that create social ties between people has developed most noticeably since the 1970s:

The Navajo never mention common substance in finding or invoking kinship ties or norms. Kinship is defined in terms of the acts of giving birth and sharing sustenance. The primary bond in the Navajo kinship system is the mother-child bond, and it is in this bond that the nature and meaning of kinship become clear. In Navajo culture, kinship means intense, diffuse, and enduring solidarity, and this solidarity is realised in actions and behaviour befitting the cultural definitions of kinship solidarity. Just as a mother is one who gives life to her children through birth and sustains their life by providing them with loving care, assistance, protection, and sustenance, kinsmen are those who sustain each other's life by helping one another, protecting one another, and by the giving or sharing of food and other items of subsistence. Where this kind of solidarity exists, kinship exists; where it does not, there is no kinship. (Witherspoon 1975, 21-22)

The term "nurture kinship" may have been first used in the present context by Watson (1983), who contrasted it with "nature kinship" (kinship concepts built upon shared substance of some kind). Since the 1970s, an increasing number of ethnographies have documented the extent to which social ties in various cultures can be understood to be built upon nurturant acts.

Ethnographic Examples

Marshall on the Truk (now known as the Chuuk) of Micronesia: All sibling relationships – natural or created – involve the height of sharing and "feelings of strong sentimental attachment." ... In Trukese kinship, actions speak louder than words; ttong must be demonstrated by nurturant acts. Trukese kinship pivots on the fulcrum of nurturance, a fact partially understood by Ruth Goodenough (1970:331) who noted the "intense concentration on problems of nurture – taking care of and being cared for by others" in GTS. Nurture is the nature of Trukese kinship. (Marshall 1977, 656)

Gow on the Piro of Amazonia: As a child begins to eat real food, and to walk and eventually to talk, its relationship to its parents changes from one in which the parents take care that their physical connection to the body of the child does not harm it, into one in which gifts of food, given out of love for the child, evoke the child's love for its parents and other kin. Older siblings are very important here. From birth, the baby is frequently picked up and held (marcar, "to hold in the arms") by its older brothers and sisters. As it learns to walk and talk, its closest physical ties are with such siblings, for they are its constant companions and they eat and sleep together. Such intimate ties with siblings replace the earlier one with parents as the child grows. (Gow, 1991, 157)

Thomas on the Temanambondro of Madagascar: Yet just as fathers are not simply made by birth, neither are mothers, and although mothers are not made by "custom" they, like fathers, can make themselves through another type of performatively constituted relation, the giving of "nurture". Relations of ancestry are particularly important in contexts of ritual, inheritance and the defining of marriageability and incest; they are in effect the "structuring structures" (Bourdieu 1977) of social reproduction and intergenerational continuity. Father, mother and children are, however, also performatively related through the giving and receiving of "nurture" (fitezana). Like ancestry, relations of "nurture" do not always coincide with relations by birth; but unlike ancestry, "nurture" is a largely ungendered relation, constituted in contexts of everyday practical existence, in the intimate, familial and familiar world of the household, and in ongoing relations of work and consumption, of feeding and farming. (Thomas 1999, 37)

Storrie on the Hoti of Venezuelan Guiana: It was my Hoti friends who, through their rejection of my expectations that I would be able to "collect" genealogical information, brought me to the idea that dwelling together and particularly the notions of consumption and ingestion are, for them, fundamental to social identity. Whenever I attempted to discover if there were ideas of genealogical relatedness between kin, I was told that there is nothing that links a parent to their children, or siblings to each other, apart from the bonds of affection and sentiment that they feel for each other. In other words, there is nothing more to "relatedness" than those things that link "all people" together. (Storrie 2003, 420)

Viegas on a Bahian Amerinidian Community in Brazil: Adults who early in their lives had been taken to become raised children [fostered] state clearly that the situation had never displeased them. They maintain that they belong to the woman who cared for or raised them, and it is to her that they want their children to become attached. Although they recognise who their *pais legítimos* are, it is those who have cared for a person for a longer period of their childhood that are considered mother and father.

It is in this sense that kinship is constituted as memory of being related through caring and feeding, along the lines developed in large part by Peter Gow and within other South Amerindian contexts. (de Matos Viegas 2003, 32)

Link with Attachment Theory

It can be seen from the ethnographies that several anthropologists have found that describing social ties in terms of emotional attachments is appropriate. This has prompted some to suggest that an interdisciplinary collaboration might be useful:

> Bowlby argued that *attachment behaviour in humans and other animals is instinctive,* i.e. that evolutionary pressures have selected this psychological trait.... Now: might Bowlby's realist approach – which defines these behaviours as universal and instinctive, which examines their consequences through naturalistic observation, and which stresses their central role in intensifying human relatedness – be a useful starting point for anthropologists?... Extrapolating from the work of Myers [on emotions], one could make the case that *all* anthropological discussions of relatedness – e.g. the accounts by Malinowsky, Mauss, and a great many others of the ways in which gift exchange and reciprocity, or commensality and the sharing of "substance", help to constitute human relatedness – are also by definition, dealing with intractable problems of attachment and separation in social life. (Stafford 2000, 12,24; emphasis in original)

> Within the discipline of psychology, the formation of social and emotional ties are treated by attachment theory. Drawing on animal studies from the 1950s onwards, John Bowlby and colleagues described how—for all primates, including humans—the reliable provision of nurture and care leads to strong bonds of attachment between the carer and cared-for. Attachment theorists now suggest that infants are biologically predisposed to emit signals such as tracking visually, crying, smiling, vocalising, clinging, etc., to elicit nurturance and proximity not only to their mother, but also to their father or any other caregiver (Ainsworth, Bell & Stayton, 1974; Lamb, 1978b). Consistent and prompt responding to infants' signals leads to infants' perception of adults as concerned, predictable, and reliable, and to the formation of secure attachment. Mothers, fathers and other caregivers, by their different styles of responding, create a different set of expectations and an array of attachment relationships of various qualities and flavours (Bretherton, 1985; Bridges, Connell & Belsky, 1988; Stroufe, 1988). (Geiger 1996, 6)

Following the nurture kinship approach thus allows a synthesis between the extensive cross-cultural data of ethnographers and the long-standing findings of psychology on the nature of human bonding and emotional ties.

Link with Evolutionary Biology

David Schneider suspected that the the traditional anthropological models of *blood kinship* were not mirrored by the "scientific facts of biology".

The last few pages of my book, American Kinship, make the point that the biological elements have a symbolic significance. They constitute an integrated set of symbols in the sense that they are a model for how life, in certain of its aspects, is constituted and should be lived. The symbols are 'biological' in the sense that the culturally given definition of the symbol system is that it is derived from the facts of biology as a process of nature itself. But it is fundamental to our understanding that we appreciate that these biological elements are symbols and that their symbolic referents are not biology as a natural process at all.

It is even a moot question as to whether the symbols derive from the facts of nature and the facts of biology as these can be determined scientifically. What is indisputable is that the symbols are formed of elements which in native culture are defined as biological, particularly as aspects of the reproductive process. What is disputable is whether they in fact derive from, or mirror, or are models formed after the scientific facts of biology. I do not think that they are, but this subject is best left to another time. (Schneider 1972, 45, 62)

Holland subsequently showed that Schneider's intuition in regard to the 'scientific facts' was correct. In evolutionary biology, the theory treating the evolution of social cooperation emerged in a formal version in the 1960s and 1970s in the form of inclusive fitness theory, and a related theory, kin selection. The theory specifies that one criterion for the evolution of certain kinds of social traits is a statistical association of identical genes, as would exist when close genetic relatives associate with one another. Early applications of the theory applied to humans (darwinian anthropology) took as their starting position the former anthropological perspective that human kinship is fundamentally "based on" blood-ties. However, these extensions emerged at precisely the time that anthropology was reflexively critiquing this "blood" assumption behind traditional kinship theorizing. This reversion to "blood" led some anthropologists to strongly attack the emerging biological perspectives as suffering the same ethnocentric assumptions (e.g., "blood is thicker than water") that the anthropologists themselves had recently eschewed.

This clash of perspectives led to something of a stand-off and a lack of communication between the disciplines, resulting in little cooperation and progress for three decades. The stand-off was resolved by Holland's Social Bonding and Nurture Kinship which re-visited biological inclusive fitness theory to draw a distinction between the evolutionary mechanisms for the emergence of social traits and the proximate mechanisms through which they are expressed. In a strict interpretation of the theory, a statistical association of related genes (as would be present in the interactions of close genetic relatives) is understood as a necessary (though not sufficient) condition for the evolutionary emergence of certain traits relating to social cooperation. However, this does not entail that the proximate mechanisms governing the *expression* of such social traits in primates and humans necessarily depends on conditions of genetic relatedness *per se*. For the vast majority of social mammals—including primates and humans—the formation of social bonds (and the resulting social cooperation) are based on familiarity from an early developmental stage, and the same kinds of mechanisms that attachment theorists have outlined. In short, in humans and in other primates, genetic relatedness is not necessary for the attachment bonds to develop, and it is the performance of nurture that underlies such bonds and the enduring social cooperation that typically accompanies them.

Therefore, the nurture kinship perspective leads to the synthesis of evolutionary biology, psychology, and socio-cultural anthropology on the topic of social bonding and cooperation, without reductionism or positing a deterministic role to genes or genetic relatedness in the mechanisms through which social behaviours are expressed.

Milk Kinship

Milk kinship, formed during nursing by a non-biological mother, was a form of fostering allegiance with fellow community members. This particular form of kinship did not exclude particular groups, such that class and other hierarchal systems did not matter in terms of milk kinship participation.

Traditionally speaking, this practice predates the Early Modern Era, though it became a widely used mechanism for developing alliances in many hierarchical societies during the Early Modern Period. Milk kinship used the practice of breast feeding by a wet nurse to feed a child either from the same community, or a neighbouring one. This wet nurse played the strategic role in forging relations between her family and the family of the child she was nursing, as well as their community.

In Islamic Societies

In the early modern period, milk kinship was widely practiced in many Arab countries for both religious and strategic purposes. Like the Christian practice of godparenting, milk kinship established a second family that could take responsibility for a child whose biological parents came to harm. "Milk kinship in Islam thus appears to be a culturally distinctive, but by no means unique, institutional form of adoptive kinship." A child in one of these societies would be breastfed by a woman of a lower class, enabling the child's biological mother to maintain her modesty.

The childhood of the prophet Muhammad illustrates the practice of traditional Arab milk kinship. In his early childhood, he was sent away to foster-parents amongst the Bedouin. By nursing him, Halimah bint Abdullah became his "milk-mother." The rest of her family was drawn into the relationship as well: her husband al-Harith became Muhammad's "milk-father," and Muhammad was raised alongside their biological children as a "milk-brother." This case suggests that it was typical for a child's wet nurse to be responsible for raising him.

Sunni Islam prohibits marriage between milk-brothers and milk-sisters, or milk-children and milk-parents. This stricture was sometimes deployed for strategic purposes such as blocking undesirable marriages. Shi'ite Islam goes further in this restriction by also prohibiting marriage to the consanguineous kin of a milk-parent. In early modern Shi'ite societies, though, the wet nurse was always from a subordinate group, so that marriage to her kin would not have been likely.

Strategic Reasons for Milk Kinship

"Colactation links two families of unequal status and creates a durable and intimate bond; it removes from 'clients' their outsider status but excludes them as marriage partners...it brings about a social relationship that is an alternative to kinship bonds based on blood." People of different races and religions could be brought together strategically through the bonding of the milk mother and their milk 'children'.

Lower Class in Society

Milk kinship was as relevant for peasants as 'fostering' or as 'hosting' other children, in that it secured the good will from their masters and their wives. As previously mentioned the milk women's family is the 'core range' to the child she is nursing and they become milk kin, which may strategically be useful for the future if the child is from a higher class family, as the milk women's children will become 'milk-brothers' and 'milk-sisters.' Thus peasant women would most often play the role of the 'milk' mother to her non-biological children, and they held an important role in maintaining the connection between herself and the master whose baby she is nursing. It is also important to note that it was also a practical way to assist families who were of a very ill mother or whose mother died in childbirth. This would have been helpful in many societies where, especially in times of war, if families perished, other members of society would end up co-parenting through the link of milk-kinship.

Higher Class in Society

Noble offspring were often sent to milk kin fosterers that would foster them to maturity so that the children would be raised by their successive status subordinates. The purpose of this was for political importance to build milk kin as bodyguards. This was a major practice in the Hindu Kush society.

Conflicting Theories/ideas/myths About Milk Kinship

One particular theory mentioned by Peter Parkes is an Arab folk-analogy that breast milk is supposed to be "transformed male semen" that arises from Hertiers Somatic Scheme. There is no evidence that Arabs ever considered a mothers milk to be 'transformed sperm'. Another suggested analogy is that breast milk was a refinement of uterine blood. It is also suggested since that milk is of the woman, her moods and dispositions are transferred through the breast milk. Peter Parkes mentions that milk-kinship was "further endorsed as a canonical impediment to marriage by several eastern Christian churches". This gives us evidence that this was widely practiced among numerous religious communities, and not just Islamic communities, in the early modern Mediterranean.

Hertiers Somatic Scheme

Hertiers Somatic Scheme states that marriage between milk kin is forbidden because 'the milk is from the man'. However, the rules of Sunni marital incest show that this is in fact incorrect as these rules apply through a standard of adoptive kin relations. Hertiers Somatic Scheme is where the misconception that milk is considered transformed sperm comes from. This idea is incorrect, and was deduced generally from an Arab saying that the milk is from the man.

Practice in Eastern Christianity

Weisner-Hanks mentions the introduction in the fifteenth century of prohibitions in the Christian Canon Law, in which one is not allowed to marry any one suspected to be of respective kin. Individuals who shared godparents, and great grandparents were prohibited against marrying. The prohibitions against marriage also extended to that of natural godparents. This was because both natural and 'foster' or 'spiritual' parents had an investment on the child's spiritual well being, which would not be achieved by going against Canon Law. The practice of milk kinship is paralleled quite frequently, among scholarly works, with that of Christian godparent-hood or spiritual kinship. Parkes states that in both milk kinship and god-or co-parenthood "we deal with a fictitious kinship relationship between people of unequal status that is embedded in a long-term exchange of goods and services that we know as patronage". Iranians seemed to have "taken care to confine delegated suckling to subordinate non-kin - particularly those with whom marriage would be undesirable in any event". Marriage taboos due to milk kinship were taken very seriously since some regarded breast milk to be refined female blood from the womb, thus conveying a 'uterine substance' of kinship. Children who were milk kin to each other were prohibited to marry as well as two children from different parents who were suckled by the same woman. It was as much of a taboo to marry your milk-brother or -sister, as it was to marry a biological brother or sister. It is extremely important to understand that in all cases "What is forbidden by blood kinship is equally forbidden by milk kinship".

Chapter 8

Interpersonal Relationship

An interpersonal relationship is a strong, deep, or close association or acquaintance between two or more people that may range in duration from brief to enduring.

This association may be based on inference, love, solidarity, regular business interactions, or some other type of social commitment. Interpersonal relationships are formed in the context of social, cultural and other influences.

The context can vary from family or kinship relations, friendship, marriage, relations with associates, work, clubs, neighbourhoods, and places of worship. They may be regulated by law, custom, or mutual agreement, and are the basis of social groups and society as a whole.

Field of Study

The study of interpersonal relationships involves several branches of the social sciences, including such disciplines as sociology, psychology, anthropology, and social work. Interpersonal skills are vital when trying to develop a relationship with another person.

The scientific study of relationships evolved during the 1990s and came to be referred to as 'relationship science', which distinguishes itself from anecdotal evidence or pseudo-experts by basing conclusions on data and objective analysis. Interpersonal ties are also a subject in mathematical sociology.

Importance

Human beings are innately social and are shaped by their experiences with others. There are multiple perspectives to understand this inherent motivation to interact with others.

Need to Belong

According to Maslow's hierarchy of needs, humans need to feel love(sexual/nonsexual) and acceptance from social groups (family, peer groups). In fact, the need to belong is so innately ingrained that it may be strong enough to overcome physiological and safety needs, such as children's attachment to abusive parents or staying in abusive romantic relationships. Such examples illustrate the extent to which the psychobiological drive to belong is entrenched.

Social Exchange

Another way to appreciate the importance of relationships is in terms of a reward framework. This perspective suggests that individuals engage in relations that are rewarding in both tangible and intangible ways. The concept fits into a larger theory of social exchange. This theory is based on the idea that relationships develop as a result of cost-benefit analyses. Individuals seek out rewards in interactions with others and are willing to pay a cost for said rewards. In the best-case scenario, rewards will exceed costs, producing a net gain. This can lead to "shopping around" or constantly comparing alternatives to maximize the benefits (rewards) while minimizing costs.

Relational Self

Relationships are also important for their ability to help individuals develop a sense of self. The relational self is the part of an individual's self-concept that consists of the feelings and beliefs that one has regarding oneself that develops based on interactions with others. In other words, one's emotions and behaviours are shaped by prior relationships. Thus, relational self theory posits that prior and existing relationships influence one's emotions and behaviours in interactions with new individuals, particularly those individuals that remind him or her of others in his or her life. Studies have shown that exposure to someone who resembles a significant other activates specific self-beliefs, changing how one thinks about oneself in the moment more so than exposure to someone who does not resemble a significant other.

Stages

Interpersonal relationships are dynamic systems that change continuously during their existence. Like living organisms, relationships have a beginning, a lifespan, and an end. They tend to grow and improve gradually, as people get to know each other and become closer emotionally, or they gradually deteriorate as people drift apart, move on with their lives and form new relationships with others.

One of the most influential models of relationship development was proposed by psychologist George Levinger. This model was formulated to describe heterosexual, adult romantic relationships, but it has been applied to other kinds of interpersonal relations as well. According to the model, the natural development of a relationship follows five stages:

1. *Acquaintance and acquaintanceship* – Becoming acquainted depends on previous relationships, physical proximity, first impressions, and a variety of other factors. If two people begin to like each other, continued interactions may lead to the next stage, but acquaintance can continue indefinitely. Another example is association.
2. *Buildup* – During this stage, people begin to trust and care about each other. The need for intimacy, compatibility and such filtering agents as common background and goals will influence whether or not interaction continues.
3. *Continuation* – This stage follows a mutual commitment to quite a strong and close long-term friendships, romantic relationship, or even marriage. It is generally a long, relative stable period. Nevertheless, continued growth and development will occur during this time. Mutual trust is important for sustaining the relationship.
4. *Deterioration* – Not all relationships deteriorate, but those that do tend to show signs of trouble. Boredom, resentment, and dissatisfaction may occur, and individuals may communicate less and avoid self-disclosure. Loss of trust and betrayals may take place as the downward spiral continues, eventually ending the relationship. (Alternately, the participants may find some way to resolve the problems and reestablish trust and belief in others.)
5. *Termination* – The final stage marks the end of the relationship, either by breakups, death, or by spatial separation for quite some time and severing all existing ties of either friendship or romantic love.

Friendships may involve some degree of transitivity. In other words, a person may become a friend of an existing friend's friend. However, if two people have a sexual relationship with the same person, they may become competitors rather than friends. Accordingly, sexual behaviour with the sexual partner of a friend may damage the friendship. Sexual activities between two friends tend to alter that relationship, either by "taking it to the next level" or by severing it.

A List of Interpersonal Skills Includes

- Verbal communication – What we say and how we say it.
- Nonverbal communication – What we communicate without words, body language is an example.
- Listening skills – How we interpret both the verbal and non-verbal messages sent by others.
- Negotiation – Working with others to find a mutually agreeable outcome.
- Problem solving – Working with others to identify, define and solve problems.
- Decision making – Exploring and analysing options to make sound decisions.
- Assertiveness – Communicating our values, ideas, beliefs, opinions, needs and wants freely.

Flourishing, Budding, Blooming, Blossoming Relationships

Positive psychologists use the various terms "flourishing, budding, blooming, blossoming relationships" to describe interpersonal relationships that are not merely happy, but instead characterized by intimacy, growth, and resilience. Flourishing relationships also allow a dynamic balance between focus on the intimate relationships and focus on other social relationships.

Background

While traditional psychologists specialising in close relationships have focused on relationship dysfunction, positive psychology argues that relationship health is not merely the absence of relationship dysfunction. Healthy relationships are built on a foundation of secure attachment and are maintained with love and purposeful positive relationship behaviours. Additionally, healthy relationships can be made to "flourish." Positive psychologists are exploring what makes existing relationships flourish and what skills can be taught to partners to enhance their existing and future personal relationships. A social skills approach posits that individuals differ in their degree of communication skill, which has implications for their relationships. Relationships in which partners possess and enact relevant communication skills are more satisfying and stable than relationships in which partners lack appropriate communication skills.

Adult Attachment and Attachment Theory

Healthy relationships are built on a foundation of secure attachments. Adult attachment models represent an internal set of expectations and preferences regarding relationship intimacy that guide behaviour. Secure adult attachment, characterized by low attachment-related avoidance and anxiety, has numerous benefits. Within the context of safe, secure attachments, people can pursue optimal human functioning and flourishing. This is because social acts that reinforce feelings of attachment also stimulate the release of neurotransmitters such as oxytocin and endorphin, which alleviate stress and create feelings of contentment. Attachment theory can also be used as a means of explaining adult relationships.

Romantic Love

The capacity for love gives depth to human relationships, brings people closer to each other physically and emotionally, and makes people think expansively about themselves and the world.

Stages of romantic interpersonal relationships can also be characterized more generally by the following: attraction; initiation; development; sustaining vs. terminating.

- Attraction – Premeditated or automatic, attraction can occur between acquaintances, coworkers, lovers, etc., be based on sexual arousal, intellectual stimulation, or respect. Studies have shown that attraction can be susceptible to influence based on context and externally induced arousal, with the caveat that participants be unaware of the source of their arousal. A study by Cantor, J. R., Bryant, J., & Zillmann, D. (1975), induced arousal through physical exercise and found that participants rated erotic pictures highly 4 min post-exercise (when no longer realised aroused by exercise) than either immediately after (when arousal and awareness were greater) or 10 minutes later (when exercise-induced arousal had dissipated). As supported by a series of studies, Zillman and colleagues showed that a preexisting state of arousal can heighten reactions to affective stimuli. A classic study by Dutton & Aron (1974) showed that fear arousal from suspension bridges leads to higher attraction ratings by males of a female confederate.
- Initiation – There are several catalysts in the initiation of a new relationship. One commonly studied factor is physical proximity (also known as propinquity). The MIT Westgate studies famously showed that greater physical proximity between incoming students in a university residential hall led to greater relationship initiation. More specifically, only 10% of those living on opposite ends of Westgate West considered

each other friends while more than 40% of those living in adjacent apartments considered each other friends. The theory behind this effect is that proximity facilitates chance encounters, which lead to initiation of new relationships. This is closely related to the mere exposure effect, which states that the more an individual is exposed to a person or object, the more s/he likes it. Another important factor in the initiation of new relationships is similarity. Put simply, individuals tend to be attracted to and start new relationships with those who are similar to them. These similarities can include beliefs, rules, interests, culture, education, etc. Individuals seek relationships with like others because like others are most likely to validate shared beliefs and perspectives, thus facilitating interactions that are positive, rewarding and without conflict.

- Development – Development of interpersonal relationships can be further split into committed versus non-committed romantic relationships, which have different behavioural characteristics. In a study by Miguel & Buss (2011), men and women were found to differ in a variety of mate-retention strategies depending on whether their romantic relationships were committed or not. More committed relationships by both genders were characterized by greater resource display, appearance enhancement, love and care, and verbal signs of possession. In contrast, less committed relationships by both genders were characterized by greater jealousy induction. In terms of gender differences, men used greater resource display than women, who used more appearance enhancement as a mate-retention strategy than men.
- Sustaining vs. terminating – After a relationship has had time to develop, it enters into a phase where it will be sustained if it is not otherwise terminated. Some important qualities of strong, enduring relationships include emotional understanding and effective communication between partners. Research has also shown that idealization of one's partner is linked to stronger interpersonal bonds. Idealization is the pattern of overestimating a romantic partner's positive virtues or underestimating a partner's negative faults in comparison to the partner's own self-evaluation. In general, individuals who idealize their romantic partners tend to report higher levels of relationship satisfaction. Other research has examined the impact of joint activity on relationship quality. In particular, studies have shown that romantic partners that engage in a

novel and exciting physical activity together are more likely to report higher levels of relationship satisfaction than partners that complete a mundane activity.

In his triangular theory of love, psychologist Robert Sternberg theorizes that love is a mix of three components: some (1) passion, or physical attraction; (2) intimacy, or feelings of closeness; and (3) commitment, involving the decision to initiate and sustain a relationship. The presence of all three components characterizes consummate love, the most durable type of love. In addition, the presence of intimacy and passion in marital relationships predicts marital satisfaction. Also, commitment is the best predictor of relationship satisfaction, especially in long-term relationships. Positive consequences of being in love include increased self-esteem and self-efficacy.

Referring to the emotion of love, Psychiatrist Daniel Casriel defined the "logic of love" as "the logic of pleasure and pain" in the concept of a "Relationship Road Map" that became the foundation of PAIRS' relationship education classes.

> *"We are drawn to what we anticipate will be a source of pleasure and will look to avoid what we anticipate will be a source of pain. The emotion of love comes from the anticipation of pleasure."*

Based on Casriel's theory, sustaining feelings of love in an interpersonal relationship requires "effective communication, emotional understanding and healthy conflict resolution skills."

Theories and Empirical Research

Confucianism

Confucianism is a study and theory of relationships especially within hierarchies. Social harmony—the central goal of Confucianism—results in part from every individual knowing his or her place in the social order, and playing his or her part well. Particular duties arise from each person's particular situation in relation to others.

The individual stands simultaneously in several different relationships with different people: as a junior in relation to parents and elders, and as a senior in relation to younger siblings, students, and others. Juniors are considered in Confucianism to owe their seniors reverence and seniors have duties of benevolence and concern toward juniors. A focus on mutuality is prevalent in East Asian cultures to this day.

Minding Relationships

The mindfulness theory of relationships shows how closeness in relationships may be enhanced. Minding is the "reciprocal knowing process involving the nonstop, interrelated thoughts, feelings, and behaviours of persons in a relationship." Five components of "minding" include:

1. Knowing and being known: seeking to understand the partner
2. Making relationship-enhancing attributions for behaviours: giving the benefit of the doubt
3. Accepting and respecting: empathy and social skills
4. Maintaining reciprocity: active participation in relationship enhancement
5. Continuity in minding: persisting in mindfulness

Culture of Appreciation

After studying married couples for many years, psychologist John Gottman has proposed the theory of the "magic ratio" for successful marriages. The theory says that for a marriage to be successful, couples must average a ratio of five positive interactions to one negative interaction. As the ratio moves to 1:1, divorce becomes more likely. Interpersonal interactions associated with negative relationships include criticism, contempt, defenciveness, and stonewalling. Over time, therapy aims to turn these interpersonal strategies into more positive ones, which include complaint, appreciation, acceptance of responsibility, and self-soothing. Similarly, partners in interpersonal relationships can incorporate positive components into difficult subjects in order to avoid emotional disconnection.

In addition, Martin Seligman proposes the concept of Active-Constructive Responding, which stresses the importance of practicing conscious attentive listening and feedback skills. In essence, practicing this technique aims to improve the quality of communication between members of the relationship, and in turn the gratitude expressed between said members.

Capitalizing on Positive Events

People can capitalize on positive events in an interpersonal context to work toward flourishing relationships. People often turn to others to share their good news (termed "capitalization"). Studies show that both the act of telling others about good events and the response of the person with whom the event was shared have personal and interpersonal consequences, including increased positive emotions, subjective well-being, and self-esteem, and relationship benefits including intimacy, commitment, trust, liking, closeness, and stability. Studies show that the act of communicating positive events was associated with increased positive affect and well-being (beyond the impact of the positive event itself). Other studies have found that relationships in which partners responded to "good news" communication enthusiastically were associated with higher relationship well-being.

Other Perspectives

Neurobiology of Interpersonal Connections

Humans are social creatures, and there is no other behavioural process that is more important than attachment. Attachment requires sensory and cognitive processing that lead to intricate motor responses. As humans, the end goal of attachment is the motivation to acquire love, which is different from other animals who just seek proximity. There is an emerging body of research across multiple disciplines investigating the neurological basis of attachment and the prosocial emotions and behaviours that are the prerequisites for healthy adult relationships. The social environment, mediated by attachment, influences the maturation of structures in a child's brain. This might explain how infant attachment affects adult emotional health. Researchers are currently investigating the link between positive caregiver–child relationships and the development of hormone systems, such as the Hypothalamic–pituitary–adrenal axis (HPA axis) and Oxytocinergic system. In order to accurately study the neurobiology of interpersonal connection, the behaviour must fulfill three requirements. The first is that the behaviour must have a noticeable onset so that researchers are able to examine the formation of the attachment bond or how it is inhibited. Second, the behaviour must be selective in order differentiate it from normal social interaction. Lastly, the behaviour being studied has to be testable so it can be measured and manipulated, in order to establish reliability.

- The mother–infant attachment – Key biological factors have emerged that can explain the motivation behind maternal caregiving behaviour in humans and mammals. However, it does differ from species to species; due to that some species only exhibit maternal care postpartum, others exhibit it only slightly and some are very maternal. Two main neuroendocrine systems that revolved around Oxytocin and Dopamine, and another neuropeptide, prolactin are directly involved as mediators of maternal care. The mother–infant bond is so complex and strong due to these biological systems, that a response to maternal separation exists. The response to separation is due to the withdrawal of several different components from behavioural and biological systems. Separation anxiety, the psychological term that describes when the response that occurs infant is separated from the mother, causes loss of those components, as seen in studies done with rats.

1. *Oxytocinergic system* – Oxytocin is a peptide hormone produced in the hypothalamus that is passed through the posterior pituitary gland into the bloodstream. Oxytocin acts on the mammary glands and uterine muscles to stimulate the secretion of milk and uterine contractions during childbirth. However, it is a crucial factor in many aspects of social bonding, specifically the onset of the mother–infant attachment bond. It acts on the medial preoptic area (MPOA) and the ventral tegmental area (VTA) in the brain which are critical for integration of sensory information in maternal care. Oxytocin plays a key role in physical proximity and nurturing care and leads (as shown in studies with rats) the mother to go from avoiding behaviour to caring for their young. Oxytocin knockout rats or injection of an oxytocin receptor antagonist will lead to neglect of the infant or pup. In mammals, the development of the Oxytocinergic system has led to the basis of the mother–infant attachment.
2. *Dopaminergic system* – Dopamine is a neurotransmitter that affects behaviour in not just the mother but in the offspring as well. Dopamine is essential in for reinforcing behaviour that gives us pleasure because it is part of the limbic system that deals with emotion. Therefore, it is able to stimulate responsive maternal care and reinforce attachment. Understanding the dopaminergic system is important because it could make the difference between maternal neglect and nurture.
3. *Prolactin* – As seen in lesion studies of rats prolactin, which is also involved in lactation, is important in encouraging maternal behaviour. Decreasing the levels of prolactin or lack of the receptor of prolactin leads to inhibition of maternal care in rats.

- Adult–adult pair bond formation – Oxytocin and vasopressin play a crucial part in the process of bond formation of mates.

Vasopressin is a peptide hormone whose main function is to retain water in the body, and is also known as antidiuretic hormone (ADH). Pair bonding is studied using voles and it has been found that injection of both hormones stimulates the behavioural responses needed in pair bond formation, even when mating hasn't occurred. These results are also proven when injection of receptor antagonists of this hormones inhibits mating and necessary behaviours.

The ability to study the biological processes behind attachment allows scientists to be able to understand the fundamental levels to makeup a psychological construct. It provides a link between a psychological concept and it's physiological foundation.

Applications

Researchers are developing an approach to couples therapy that moves partners from patterns of repeated conflict to patterns of more positive, comfortable exchanges. Goals of therapy include development of social and interpersonal skills. Expressing gratitude and sharing appreciation for a partner is the primary means for creating a positive relationship. Positive marital counselling also emphasizes mindfulness. The further study of "flourishing relationships could shape the future of premarital and marital counselling as well."

Controversies

Some researchers criticize positive psychology for studying positive processes in isolation from negative processes. Positive psychologists argue that positive and negative processes in relationships may be better understood as functionally independent, not as opposites of each other.

Family Estrangement

Family estrangement is the physical and or emotional distancing between at least two family members in an arrangement which is considered unsatisfactory by at least one involved party. Family estrangements can be attributed to any of several factors within the family, such as attachment disorders, differing values and beliefs, disappointment, major life events or change, parental alienation, or poor communication.

In one typical scenario, an adult child shuns his or her parents and possibly other family members as the adult child transitions into adulthood. In another scenario, an intolerant parent might cast out an adult child because of life choices. In either case, the family estrangement may create an intergenerational rift that persists for decades and replicates itself in subsequent generations

Estrangement is synonymous with alienation: the replacement of love, affection, or friendliness with enmity, cruelty, or indifference.

Overview

Family estrangements are broken relationships between parents, grandparents, siblings and children. In common usage, family estrangement generally refers to an alienation between good or good enough parents who fulfilled their parental responsibilities and an adolescent or adult child who shuns them, generational rifts between grandparents and their families, and siblings who do not speak. Family estrangements differ from realistic or reasonable estrangements where family life is characterized by violence or neglect and the estrangement is a reasonable act of self-protection. Although a family estrangement can begin at any stage of life, it often begins during late adolescence and early adulthood. Characteristics of estrangement include a lack of empathy or warmth on the part of the individual initiating the estrangement. This pattern of behaviour causes psychological pain in the rejected family and heightened levels of stress in all parties. In many cases, estrangements are also characterized by another party intruding on the family dynamic. The outsider provides emotional support to the party initiating the estrangement, providing the estranger with an alternate social support system and thus enabling the deepening of the estrangement.

Health Implications

Those rejected by one or more family members in a family estrangement experience a decline in psychological and physical health. The social rejection in family estrangement is the equivalent of ostracism which undermines four fundamental human needs; the need to belong, the need for control in social situations, the need to maintain high levels of self-esteem, and the need to have a sense of a meaningful existence. The rejected parties suffer adverse psychological consequences such as loneliness, low self-esteem, aggression, and depression. Family estrangement activates the grief response. However, the rejected family may not achieve the final grief stage of acceptance, given that the social death of the relationship is potentially reversible. The prolonged suffering of the rejected party, together with a perceived or real stigma of having been rejected by a family member, results in isolation and behavioural changes in the rejected party. The rejected parties typically try a number of strategies to repair the rift. In some cases, apologies and amends for harsh words or circumstances created by divorce improves the relationship. In some cases, the initiator of the estrangement attempts to control the family with conditions for maintaining limited contact, a type of emotional blackmail which rarely if ever results in any good resolution. In other cases, the initiator is unable or unwilling to consider any type of reconciliation.

The health impact on estrangers is less obvious than on their families. Avoidance and bullying are the coping mechanisms of estrangers when under stress. They react emotionally and without sufficient self-regulation. They manufacture additional stress in their lives by being perfectionists or procrastinators. Estrangers are also more likely to binge drink. Consequently, estrangers are likely to have difficulties in future intimate relations as a result of their failure to resolve their family issues in a healthy manner.

Culture

The separation of young adults from their families of origin in order to create families of their own is part of normal human development. According to Bowen theory, this separation can be achieved in a healthy and gradual manner that preserves the intergenerational relationships of the family of origin, providing both the new family and family of origin with a sense of continuity and support. Alternately, a traumatic schism can differentiate these life stages. Familial estrangement falls into the second category.

A 2010 analysis of parent and adult-child relationships in England, Germany, Israel, Norway, Spain and the United States revealed that those relationships are most disharmonious in the US. The United States has the highest rating on individualism on the Hofestede Cultural Dimensions Model. The emphasis on the individual over a collective family unit is regarded as contributing to estrangement, as well as a rationale for estrangement. In individualistic cultures, the estranger typically justifies the estrangement with broad generalizations about a dysfunctional family or toxic family member. Estrangers often receive emotional support for their portrayal of themselves as victims who rescued themselves, a celebration of individualism and power. The estranged are often stigmatized as probably deserving of their treatment, an example of victim blaming. The estranged may also become less socially acceptable because of lowered self-regulation, a reaction to the social rejection.

Scenarios

Humans are fallible and no family is without its problems. Although working through stressful issues with communication, consideration and compassion should be the default coping mechanism, that effort can be demanding. When any family member dismisses another family member, ranking personal expectations over the family relationship, emotional cutoff and family estrangement is likely.

Values

A family member's sexual orientation, choice of spouse, or change in religion may challenge the social values of a family. Life choices regarding education, profession, and geography are other emotionally laden topics that reflect social values. Working through feelings to reach an understanding that accommodates the individual within the family unit challenges each individual's sense of identity as part of a society. When one or more family members rank their expectations and emotions as more important than those of another family member, then the conversation becomes a zero-sum game. This is known as a social trap in social psychology, a situation where the long term consequences of decisions result in a culminative loss to all parties. In these instances, estrangement is more likely than flexible accommodation. When a parent or grandparent initiates the emotional cut-off based on non-conformity, the estrangement may manifest in disownment .

Violence

Verbal abuse, physical abuse and emotional abuse are triggers for a reasonable estrangement. However, deciding what is abusive and what is within an acceptable range of human behaviour is not always clear and differs culturally. A recurring pattern of malicious denigration is considered grounds for a reasonable estrangement in many cultures. However, a recurring pattern of abuse is not the equivalent of a few harsh words spoken in anger by an otherwise loving person. Similarly, labelling a person narcissistic because he or she holds a different point of view may be a case of the accuser being intolerant of opposing viewpoints, rather than a case of needing to permanently remove oneself for self-protection.

Substance Abuse & Mental Illness

Estrangement over substance abuse or alcohol abuse may or may not be justifiable self-protection. Mental illness also poses a gray area when it comes to the reasonableness of estranging from a family member. In some cases, enforcing ground rules and boundaries may be an alternative to a familial estrangement. In either case, substance abuse and mental illness are significant family stressors. The most highly predictive domain of social estrangement for both alcohol and drug dependency is homelessness.

Post Traumatic Stress Disorder (PTSD) is correlated with family estrangement. The trauma resulting in PTSD can be anything, including but not limited to a sexual assault, imprisonment, bullying, battered person syndrome, physical assault or war experience. Although it is sometimes unclear whether a failure on the part of the family to be sufficiently supportive or the behaviours of the PTSD survivor lead to the estrangement, it is clear that feelings of emotional distancing from the family is a characteristic the PTSD victim introduces into the family dynamic. Ultimately, both family and victim are blameless. The fact of the PTSD can be a insurmountable family stressor. Studies on soldiers with PTSD have concluded that families with a PTSD warrior require more support to facilitate healing and prevent estrangement.

Betrayal

From disputes over inheritances to perceived insults in public settings, a sense of betrayal weakens the trust bonds of the family. According to Erik Erikson, trust is the foundation of any relationship.

Explanations

There are underlying psychological factors that explain family estrangement beyond the surface rationale of the scenario.

Environment of Evolutionary Adaptedness

Humans have evolved to adapt to separation from their families and social units by bonding with new social units. This psychology was particularly valuable to the young women in hunter-gatherer societies who were kidnapped as brides. Being able to rapidly bond with a new family unit was a matter of survival for the captives, and consequently has become a universal human trait. This trait is exploited by various organisations seeking to indoctrinate new recruits and in so doing replace the family as the key support system for the individual. The ability to essentially change an entire mindset in response to environmental changes suggests that exposure to other persons and a different environment restructure the brain and thinking patterns of individuals. Patty Hearst is a modern woman who experienced capture-bonding. Attachment theorist John Bowlby coined the term Environment of Evolutionary Adaptedness (EEA) to explain the psychology that creates this type of behavioural change.

Bowen Theory

In Bowen family systems theory, emotional cutoff and avoidance are unhealthy coping mechanisms for dealing with anxiety and stress. These coping mechanisms represent emotional and intellectual systems that are fused rather than differentiated, so that emotion overwhelm objective thought process and govern behaviour. Poor differentiation is associated with continued relationship problems in life. Poor differentiation is also contagious in that it creates high stress in others, as well as models poor behaviour. High differentiation is associated with emotional interdependence and multi-generational cooperation. Triangulation is when a third party enters the dynamic. A third party increases tension and often triggers a rebellion. Bowen theory is part of attachment theory.

Victim - Persecutor – Rescuer

The Karpman drama triangle is precipitated by a familial estrangement that involves a third party. A family member plays the victim role, casting the family as the persecutor. The new romantic interest, close friend or another family, for psychological motivations of their own, come to the victim's rescue and in so doing validates the dynamic for the victim. A sensationalistic 2014 family estrangement involving a cheerleader in New Jersey is an example of this dynamic. Another family not only provided refuge to the 18 year old high school student who was battling her parents over curfew, drinking and a boyfriend, but also funded a lawsuit on the teen's behalf seeking child support and other material considerations from the parents. The family reunited only after international media attention that, although split, in the majority harshly rejected the teen's complaints.

Faulty Thought Patterns

Splitting refers to the idolization or vilification of a person. At any point in time, a person is regarded as either 100% good or 100% bad, notwithstanding any evidence to the contrary. Splitting is an unhealthy coping mechanism that evokes a type of emotional amnesia. There are no shades of grey, no compassion, no acknowledgment of fallibility, and little forgiveness in splitting. Splitting is used by many people in various life circumstances. It is a characteristic of polarized ideology and naivete. Splitting is also a defining characteristic in both narcissistic and borderline personality disorders. Personality disorders can occur in individuals of any age. However, therapists hesitate to diagnose a personality disorder until the individual is fully grown and brain maturation is achieved. Accurate interpretation of the environment and others is a function of thinking processes in the cerebellum and a differentiation between emotional and rational thought. According to Dr. Jay Giedd, Chief of the Unit on Brain Imaging in the Child Psychiatry Branch at the NIMH, this part of the brain is not fully developed until the mid to late twenties.

Overindulgence

The combination of Dr. Spock's 1946 publication *The Common Sense Book of Baby and Child Care*, the post-war baby-boom and a prosperous economy transformed the American family. Building a child's self-esteem became central in modern child-rearing practices and education. Social welfare offices and court systems became more tolerant of youthful offenders, citing bad parenting or non-supportive environments as the root cause of bad behaviour in adolescents. The 1960s and 1970s ushered in an increased focus on rights and a decreased emphasis on responsibilities. Murray Bowen called this pattern a *societal* or *cultural regression*. In 1974, Bowen predicted that societal regression would increase polarization between groups, weaken the interdependence of families, and generally erode societal functioning by the mid-21st century. A survey of college graduates published in 2011 shows that two-thirds of college graduates score above the mean on a narcissism survey, a 30% increase between 1979 and 2006.

Kindergarchy is a term that refers to a culture that revolves around the wants and needs of the youngest members, an unintended consequence of post WWII child-rearing philosophy. Dan Kindlon, educational psychologist specialising in the cognitive and emotional development of children and adolescents, states that when the ego of the child is over-indulged throughout childhood, the young adult becomes prideful, envious and greedy. When that young adult finds his sense of entitlement thwarted, the resulting conflict is out of proportion with the precipitating event. Over-indulgence, regardless of the socio-economic status of the family, is a contributing factor in familial estrangement.

Social scientists and psychologists, such as Dr. Ron Taffel, claim that the parent – child relationship is fundamentally different from those relationships in previous generations due to the complexity of and rapid changes in the modern world. There is a growing belief that current "good" parenting practices in this social context are a mismatch. That mismatch manifests in troubling paradoxes and family estrangement. Social change may be the proximate cause of the increasing incidences of family estrangement.

Substitute Families

Both the estranger and the estranged may use social and work relationships to create substitute families. Support groups and other highly emotional organisations also provide a conduit for emotional energy from unresolved issues with parents, siblings and other family members. Becoming passionate about a cause or hobby, or even estrangement itself as an issue, is another coping mechanism.

The Future

Social workers working with the elder population are at the forefront of a new fallout from the family estrangement. Non-supportive or absent family members during parent or sibling end of life acutely increase the pain and stress of this transition. Additional stress in financial, medical and welfare sectors requires a re-evaluation of the social policy regarding family expectations versus governmental support systems.

Patrilineality

Patrilineality (agnatic kinship) is a system in which an individual belongs to his or her father's lineage. It generally involves the inheritance of property, names, or titles through the male line.

One's patriline (lit. *father line*) is one's father and his father and his father... and so on. Adjective forms are patrilineal, agnatic, and *male-line*. One's patriline is thus a record of descent from an ancestor to a descendant (of either sex) in which the individuals in all intervening generations are male. In cultural anthropology, a patrilineage is a consanguineal male and female kin group, each of whose members is descended from the common ancestor through male forebears. A person's family name (in most cultures) and a man's genetic Y-DNA have descended down this same line from father to son. In a patrilineal (or agnatic) descent system, an individual is considered to belong to the same descent group as his or her father from which the members' family name is commonly derived, although matrilineality has also been used as the descent group in some cultures. An *agnate* is one's genetic relative, male or female, exclusively through male ancestors.

Salic Law

Commonly understood in modern times to mean exclusion of women as hereditary monarchs, in parts of medieval and later Europe, the Salic Law was purported to be the grounds for males alone being eligible to inherit thrones, fiefs or land. The true scope and sway of the Salic Law was never defined rigidly, the original 6th century text being both ambiguously worded and originating in a kingdom long extinct. Although observance of, or disregard for, the law varied, it was broadly understood to prevail in domains that were originally Frankish or had at some time accepted Salian Frankish legal principles. Strict Salic inheritance has been officially revoked in all extant European monarchies except the Principality of Liechtenstein. However it still prevails in the transmission of most European titles of nobility, notably excepting Spain.

Genetic Genealogy

The fact that human Y-chromosome DNA (Y-DNA) is paternally inherited enables patrilines, and agnatic kinships, of men to be traced through genetic analysis.

Y-chromosomal Adam (Y-MRCA) is the patrilineal most recent common ancestor from whom all Y-DNA in living men is descended. An identification of a very rare and previously unknown Y-chromosome variant in 2012 led researchers to estimate that Y-chromosomal Adam lived 338,000 years ago (237,000 to 581,000 years ago with 95% confidence), judging from molecular clock and genetic marker studies. Before this discovery, estimates of the date when Y-chromosomal Adam lived were much more recent.

Early Medical Theories

In ancient medicine, there was a dispute between the one-seed theory, expounded by Aristotle, and the two-seed theory of the 2nd century A.D. Roman physician Galen. According the one-seed theory, the germ of every embryo is contained entirely in the male seed, and the role of the mother is simply as an incubator and provider of food: on this view only a patrilineal relative is genetically related. By the two-seed theory, the embryo is not conceived unless the male and female seed meet: this implies a bilineal, or cognatic, theory of relationship. It may be significant that Galen lived at about the same time (129 – 199/ 217 AD) that Roman law changed from the agnate to the cognate system of relationships.

Common to both theories was the mistaken belief that the female emits seed, rather not an egg, and that a seed is only produced when she comes to orgasm. Given that assumption, the evidence for the one-seed theory is the fact that a woman can conceive without coming to orgasm (though this was still a matter of dispute in the ancient world and the Middle Ages.) The evidence for the two-seed theory was the observable reality that individuals often resembled maternal relatives. These two pieces of evidence could not be reconciled until the discovery of ovulation in the early 19th century, confirming the two-seed theory as biological and dissociating the production of female seed from the occurrence of the orgasm.

In early Greek and Roman history, a few philosophers claimed that although every child has one absolute mother, it did not follow that every child had one absolute father ("mater semper certa est"). They suggested that a child's character could be influenced by the seed of two or more men if they had inseminated the same mother. This was considered a fringe theory even in its time, however, and never became widely accepted. Traces of such a theory appear to underline various myths of a hero (such as Heracles) with both a human and a divine father.

Roman Law

In Roman law, *agnati* were persons related through males only, as opposed to *cognati*. Agnation was founded on the idea of the family being held together by the *patria potestas*; *cognatio* involves simply the modern idea of kinship.

In Roman times, all citizens were divided by *gens* (clan) and *familia* (sept), determined on a purely patrilineal basis, in the same way as the modern inheritance of surnames. (The *gens* was the larger unit, and was divided into several *familiae*: a person called "Gaius Iulius Caesar" belonged to the Julian *gens* and the Caesar family.)

In the early Roman Republic, inheritance could occur only within the family, and was therefore purely agnatic. Women were largely excluded from inheritance until the Middle Republic, but suffered a legal setback in the passage of the *Lex Voconia* in 169 BC. This was however evaded by careful planning, and by 42 BC, many women had inherited large wealth.

In Imperial times, the system favouring patrilineal inheritance was changed by the Praetorian edict, giving paternal and maternal relatives equal rights.

In the Bible

The line of descent for monarchs and main personalities is almost exclusively through males. Tribal descent, such as whether one is a kohen or a Levite, is still inherited patrilineally in Judaism, as is communal identity as a Sephardi or Ashkenazi. This contrasts with the rule for inheritance of Jewish status in Orthodox and Conservative Judaism, which is matrilineal. Karaite Judaism interprets the Tanakh to indicate that Jewish status is only inherited patrilineally.

Agnatic Succession

Agnatic succession is the formal attempt to limit inheritance of a throne or fief (succession) to heirs descended from the original title holder through males only, excluding all descendants through females. Traditionally, agnatic succession is applied in determining the names and membership of European dynasties, often with reference to the tenets of Salic law, which emphasized male primogeniture. The most common forms of agnatic succession are agnatic primogeniture and agnatic seniority.

Agnatic Primogeniture

Under *agnatic primogeniture*, or patrilineal primogeniture, kinship (of males and females) is determined by tracing through only male ancestors to commonality: Those who share agnatic kinship are termed *agnates*. When an agnatic primogeniture system altogether excludes females from inheritance of the family's main possessions, it is known in Europe as application of the Salic law. Under Salic law an agnatic successor to a throne or title can still be female, provided that the kinship is calculated patrilineally and there are no living men of male-line descent.

As an example, because Queen Victoria of the United Kingdom was married to a prince of Saxe-Coburg and Gotha, her son and successor, Edward VII, was a member of that dynasty, and is considered the first British king of the House of Saxe-Coburg-Gotha (changed in 1917 to House of Windsor), as are his descendants in the male line. Victoria is reckoned to have belonged to her father's House of Hanover, despite the fact that, upon marriage in 1840, she legally became a member of the Saxon dynasty and acquired the surname of that family, Wettin. Agnatically, she was Hanoverian and is considered the last member of that dynasty to reign over Britain.

A roughly similar situation occurred on the accession of Elizabeth II, agnatically a Windsor, married to Prince Philip of Greece and Denmark, who had adopted the surname Mountbatten but whose actual patriline is of the House of Schleswig-Holstein-Sonderburg-Glücksburg. On 9 April 1952, Queen Elizabeth officially declared "that I and My children shall be styled and known as the House and Family of Windsor, and that my descendants who marry and their descendants, shall bear the name of Windsor." On 8 February 1960, the Queen confirmed that she and her children would continue to be known as the House and Family of Windsor, while those of her descendants not entitled to the title of Prince or Princess and the style of Royal Highness would bear that of Mountbatten-Windsor.

Agnatic Seniority

A variant to agnatic succession through primogeniture is agnatic seniority in which inheritance passes to the eldest male member of the family, typically the eldest surviving brother, rather than the eldest son of the deceased father.

Some European dynasties have had their traditional agnatic succession replaced with absolute primogeniture, meaning that the first child born to a monarch becomes the heir to the throne, regardless of the sex of the child. Great Britain and the Commonwealth recently made a move towards this form of succession. After reaching an agreement in principle at a meeting of the heads of the 16 remaining Commonwealth monarchies in Perth, Australia in 2011, the law's passage took on a new sense of urgency in December 2012 when it was announced that the Duchess of Cambridge was pregnant (although, in the event, the child turned out to be male). The Succession to the Crown Act 2013 was passed into British law on 25 April 2013 but will only come into force once all 15 other Commonwealth Realms also approve it.

Matrilineality

Matrilineality is a system in which descent is traced through the mother and maternal ancestors. Matrilineality is also a societal system in which one belongs to one's *matriline* or mother's lineage, which can involve the inheritance of property and/or titles. A matriline is a line of descent from a female ancestor to a descendant (of either sex) in which the individuals in all intervening generations are mothers – a mother line. In a matrilineal descent system an individual is considered to belong to the same *descent group* as her or his mother. This matrilineal descent pattern is in contrast to the more common pattern of patrilineal descent from which a family name is usually derived. The *matriline* of historical nobility was also called her or his enatic or uterine ancestry, corresponding to the patrilineal *agnatic* ancestry.

In some ancient cultures, membership in their groups was (and still is if in bold) inherited matrilineally. Example cultures or societies include the Cherokee, Choctaw, Gitksan, Haida, Hopi, Iroquois, Lenape, Navajo, and Tlingit of North America; the Minangkabau people of West Sumatra, Indonesia and Negeri Sembilan, Malaysia; the Nairs of Kerala and the Bunts and Billava of Karnataka in south India; the Khasi, Jaintia and Garo of Meghalaya in northeast India; eastern Sri Lanka; the Mosuo of China; the Basques of Spain and France; the Akan including the Ashanti of west Africa; the Tuaregs of west and north Africa; most Jewish communities; and the Serer of Senegal, the Gambia and Mauritania.

Feminist economists consider women in Sri Lanka as being in a relatively favourable position, shown in local matrilineality, even while matrilineality coexists with patriarchy. However, feminists have also criticized a custom in the same culture by which a woman raped is expected to live with the rapist.

Matrilineal Surname

Matrilineal surnames or *mother-line* surnames are inherited or handed down from mother to daughter (to daughter) in some matrilineal cultures, similar to the more familiar *patrilineal surnames* which are inherited or handed down from father to son (to son) in some patrilineal cultures (or societies). The terms *family name* or *surname* are used here interchangeably. For clarity and for brevity, the scientific terms *patrilineal surname* and *matrilineal surname* are usually abbreviated as *patriname* and *matriname.*

The test of whether a particular surname is a matriname is to determine whether it is actually being handed down from mother to daughter (to daughter) in a matriline.

The usual lack of matrinames to hand down in patrilineal cultures makes *traditional genealogy* more difficult in the mother-line case than in the more typical (father-line) case. After all, *father-line* surnames originated partly "to identify individuals clearly" and/or were adopted partly "for administrative reasons"; and these *patri*names help now in searching for facts and documentation from centuries ago.

Genetic Genealogy

The fact that mitochondrial DNA (mtDNA) is inherited maternally enables the matrilineal lines (or lineages) of individuals to be traced scientifically through genetic analysis. That is, all members of a *matriline,* of either sex, have inherited the same mtDNA, proof positive of their membership.

Mitochondrial Eve (mt-mrca) is the name given by researchers to the woman who, by matrilineal reckoning, is the most recent common ancestor (mrca) for all living humans. She is the person from whom all mtDNA in living humans is derived.

She is believed by some to have lived about 150,000 years ago in East Africa, in or near present-day Tanzania. The time she lived is calculated scientifically, based on the molecular clock technique of correlating elapsed time with observed genetic drift of the mtDNA.

Genetic genealogy builds upon (and helps) *traditional genealogy* – the latter was touched upon in the above section Matrilineal surname.

Early Human Kinship

In the late nineteenth century, almost all prehistorians and anthropologists believed, following Lewis H. Morgan's influential book *Ancient Society*, that early human kinship was everywhere matrilineal. This idea was taken up by Friedrich Engels in his book The Origin of the Family, Private Property and the State. The Morgan-Engels thesis that humanity's earliest domestic institution was not the family but the matrilineal clan soon became incorporated into communist orthodoxy. In reaction, most twentieth-century social anthropologists considered the theory of matrilineal priority untenable, although feminist scholars often attempted to revive it.

In recent years, evolutionary biologists, geneticists and palaeoanthropologists have been reassessing the issues, many citing genctic and other evidence that early human kinship may have been matrilineal after all. One crucial piece of indirect evidence has been genetic data suggesting that over thousands of years, women among sub-Saharan African hunter-gatherers have chosen to reside postmaritally not with their husbands' family but with their own mother and other natal kin.

Various Cultural Patterns

There appears to be some evidence for the presence of matrilineality in *pre*-Islamic Arabia, in a very limited number of the Arabian peoples (first of all among the Amirites of Yemen, and among some strata of Nabateans in Northern Arabia); on the other hand, there does not seem to be any reliable evidence for the presence of matrilineality in Islamic Arabia, although the Fatimid Caliphate claimed succession from the Islamic Prophet Mohammad via his daughter Fatima.

A modern example from South Africa is the order of succession to the position of the Rain Queen in a culture of matrilineal primogeniture: Not only is dynastic descent reckoned through the female line, but only females are eligible to inherit.

Clan Names vs. Surnames

Most of the example cultures in this article are based on (matrilineal) clans. Any clan might possibly contain from one to several or many *descent groups* or *family groups* – i.e., any matrilineal clan might be descended from one or several or many unrelated female ancestors. Also, each such descent group might have its own family name or *surname*, as one possible cultural pattern. The following two example cultures each follow a different pattern, however:

Example 1. Members of the (matrilineal) clan culture Minangkabau do not even have a *surname* or *family name*. In contrast, members do have a *clan name*, which is important in their lives although not included in the member's name. Instead, one's name is just one's given name.

Example 2. Members of the (matrilineal) clan culture Akan, also do not have matrilineal *surnames* and likewise their important *clan name* is not included in their name. However, members' names do commonly include second names which *are called surnames* but which are *not* routinely passed down from either father or mother to all their children as a *family name*.

Note well that if a culture did include one's *clan name* in one's name and routinely handed it down to all children in the *descent group* then it would automatically be the *family name* or *surname* for one's descent group (as well as for all other descent groups in one's clan).

Care of Children

While a *mother* normally takes care of her own children in all cultures, in some matrilineal cultures an "uncle-father" will take care of his nieces and nephews instead: in other words *social fathers* here are uncles. There is a disconnection between the role of father and genitor (who in the general case may be unknown anyway). In such matrilineal cultures, especially where residence is also matrilocal, a man will exercise guardianship rights not over the children he fathers but exclusively over his sisters' children, who are viewed as 'his own flesh'. These children's biological father – unlike an uncle who is their mother's brother and thus their caregiver – is in some sense a 'stranger' to them, even when affectionate and emotionally close. This may be true for the traditional Akan culture below, for example.

According to Steven Pinker, attributing to Kristen Hawkes, among foraging groups matrilocal societies are less likely to commit female infanticide than are patrilocal societies.

Matrilineality in Specific Ethnic Groups

In America

Lenape: Occupied for 10,000 years by Native Americans, the land that would become New Jersey was overseen by clans of the Lenape or Lenni Lenape or Delaware, who farmed, fished, and hunted upon it. The pattern of their culture was that of a matrilineal agricultural and mobile hunting society that was sustained with fixed, but not permanent, settlements in their *clan* territories.

Villages were established and relocated as the clans farmed new sections of the land when soil fertility lessened and when they moved among their fishing and hunting grounds by seasons. The area was claimed as a part of the Dutch New Netherland province dating from 1614, where active trading in furs took advantage of the natural pass west, but the Lenape prevented permanent settlement beyond what is now Jersey City.

"Early Europeans who first wrote about these Indians found matrilineal social organisation to be unfamiliar and perplexing. ... As a result, the early records are full of 'clues' about early Lenape society, but were usually written by observers who did not fully understand what they were seeing."

Hopi

The Hopi (in what is now the Hopi Reservation in northeastern Arizona), according to Alice Schlegel, had as its "gender ideology ... one of female superiority, and it operated within a social actuality of sexual equality." According to LeBow (based on Schlegel's work), in the Hopi, "gender roles ... are egalitarian .... [and] [n]either sex is inferior." LeBow concluded that Hopi women "participate fully in ... political decision-making." According to Schlegel, "the Hopi no longer live as they are described here" and "the attitude of female superiority is fading". Schlegel said the Hopi "were and still are matrilinial" and "the household ... was matrilocal".

Schlegel explains why there was female superiority as that the Hopi believed in "life as the highest good ... [with] the female principle ... activated in women and in Mother Earth ... as its source" and that the Hopi "were not in a state of continual war with equally matched neighbours" and "had no standing army" so that "the Hopi lacked the spur to masculine superiority" and, within that, as that women were central to institutions of clan and household and predominated "within the economic and social systems (in contrast to male predominance within the political and ceremonial systems)", the Clan Mother, for example, being empowered to overturn land distribution by men if she felt it was unfair, since there was no "countervailing ... strongly centralized, male-centred political structure".

Iroquois

The Iroquois Confederacy or League, combining five to six Native American Haudenosaunee nations or tribes before the U.S. became a nation, operated by The Great Binding Law of Peace, a constitution by which women retained matrilineal-rights and participated in the League's political decision-making, including deciding whether to proceed to war, through what may have been a matriarchy or "'gyneocracy'". The dates of this constitution's operation are unknown: the League was formed in approximately 1000–1450, but the constitution was oral until written in about 1880. The League still exists.

In Africa

Akan: Some 20 million Akan live in Africa, particularly in Ghana and Côte d'Ivoire. Many but not all of the Akan still (2001) practice their traditional matrilineal customs, living in their traditional extended family households, as follows. The traditional Akan economic, political and social organisation is based on matrilineal lineages, which are the basis of inheritance and succession. A lineage is defined as all those related by matrilineal descent from a particular ancestress. Several lineages are grouped into a *political unit* headed by a chief and a council of elders, each of whom is the elected head of a lineage — which itself may include multiple extended-family households. Public offices are thus vested in the lineage, as are land tenure and other lineage property. In other words, lineage property is inherited only by matrilineal kin.

Each lineage controls the lineage land farmed by its members, functions together in the veneration of its ancestors, supervises marriages of its members, and settles internal disputes among its members.

The political units above are likewise grouped into eight larger groups called *abusua* (similar to clans), named Aduana, Agona, Asakyiri, Asenie, Asona, Bretuo, Ekuona and Oyoko. The members of each *abusua* are united by their belief that they are all descended from the same ancient ancestress. Marriage between members of the same *abusua* is forbidden. One inherits or is a lifelong member of the lineage, the political unit, and the *abusua* of one's mother, regardless of one's gender and/or marriage. Note that members and their spouses thus belong to different *abusuas*, mother and children living and working in one household and their husband/father living and working in a different household.

According to this source of further information about the Akan, "A man is strongly related to his mother's brother (wTfa) but only weakly related to his father's brother. This must be viewed in the context of a polygamous society in which the mother/child bond is likely to be much stronger than the father/child bond. As a result, in inheritance, a man's nephew (sister's son) will have priority over his own son. Uncle-nephew relationships therefore assume a dominant position."

"The principles governing inheritance stress sex, generation and age — that is to say, men come before women and seniors before juniors." When a woman's brothers are available, a consideration of generational seniority stipulates that the line of brothers be exhausted before the right to inherit lineage property passes down to the next senior genealogical generation of sisters' sons. Finally, "it is when all possible male heirs have been exhausted that the females" may inherit.

Certain other aspects of the Akan culture are determined patrilineally rather than matrilineally. There are 12 patrilineal Ntoro (which means spirit) groups, and everyone belongs to their father's Ntoro group but not to his (matrilineal) family lineage and *abusua*. Each patrilineal Ntoro group has its own surnames, taboos, ritual purifications, and etiquette.

A recent (2001) book provides this update on the Akan: Some families are changing from the above *abusua* structure to the nuclear family. Housing, childcare, education, daily work, and elder care etc. are then handled by that individual family rather than by the *abusua* or clan, especially in the city. The above taboo on marriage within one's abusua is sometimes ignored, but "clan membership" is still important, with many people still living in the *abusua* framework presented above.

Tuareg

The Tuareg (Arabic:ØæÇÑÞ, sometimes spelled Touareg in French, or Twareg in English) are a Berber ethnic group found across several nations in north Africa, including Niger, Mali and Algeria. The Tuareg are *clan*-based, and are (still, in 2007) "largely matrilineal". The Tuareg are Islamic, but mixed with a "heavy dose" of their pre-existing beliefs including matrilineality.

Tuareg women enjoy high status within their society, compared with their Arab counterparts and with other Berber tribes: Tuareg social status is transmitted through women, with residence often matrilocal. Most women could read and write, while most men were illiterate, concerning themselves mainly with herding livestock and other male activities. The livestock and other movable property were owned by the women, whereas personal property is owned and inherited regardless of gender. In contrast to most other Muslim cultural groups, men wear veils but women do not. This custom is discussed in more detail in the Tuareg article's clothing section, which mentions it may be the protection needed against the blowing sand while traversing the Sahara desert.

Serer

The Serer people of Senegal, the Gambia and Mauritania are patrilineal (*simanGol* in Serer language) as well as matrilineal (*tim*). There are several Serer matriclans and matriarchs. Some of these matriarchs include Fatim Beye (1335) and Ndoye Demba (1367) —

matriarchs of the Joos matriclan which also became a dynasty in Waalo (Senegal). Some matriclans or maternal clans form part of Serer medieval and dynastic history, such as the Guelowars. The most revered clans tend to be rather ancient and form part of Serer ancient history. These proto-Serer clans hold great significance in Serer religion and mythology. Some of these proto-Serer matriclans include the *Cegandum* and *Kagaw*, whose historical account is enshrined in Serer religion, mythology and traditions.

In Serer culture, inheritance is both matrilineal and patrilineal. It all depends on the asset being inherited — i.e. whether the asset is a paternal asset — requiring paternal inheritance (*kucarla*) or a maternal asset — requiring maternal inheritance (*den yaay* or *-een yaay*). The actual handling of these maternal assets (such as jewellery, land, livestock, equipment or furniture, etc.) is discussed in the subsection Role of the Tokoor of one of the above-listed main articles.

Guanches

The Berber inhabitants of Gran Canaria had developed a matrilineal society by the time the island was conquered by the Spanish. The power of the Guanarteme (king) was based on the link with Atidamana, the legendary Queen that unified the island some centuries before the conquest. The women of the family passed down the legitimacy of the monarchy, to the point that when the island surrendered, the natives handed over a young girl to the conquistadors, since she was the sole inheritor of the royal legitimacy.

In Asia

Minangkabau: In the Minangkabau matrilineal clan culture in Indonesia, a person's clan name is important in their marriage and their other cultural-related events. Two totally unrelated people who share the same clan name can never be married because they are considered to be from the same clan mother (unless they come from distant villages). Likewise, when Minangs meet total strangers who share the same clan name, anywhere in Indonesia, they could theoretically expect to feel that they are distant relatives. Minang people do not have a family name or surname; neither is one's important clan name included in one's name; instead one's given name is the only name one has.

The Minangs are one of the world's largest matrilineal societies/cultures/ethnic groups, with a population of 4 million in their home province West Sumatra in Indonesia and about 4 million elsewhere, mostly in Indonesia.

The Minang people are well-known within their country for their tradition of matrilineality and for their "dedication to Islam" — despite Islam being "supposedly patrilineal". This well-known accommodation, between their traditional complex of customs, called adat, and their religion, was actually worked out to help end the Minangkabau 1821-37 Padri War. This source is available online.

As further described in the same online source, their (matrilineal) *adat* and their Islam religion each help the other to avoid the extremes of some modern global trends: Their strong belief in and practice of *adat* helps their Islam religion to *not* adopt a "simplistic anti-Western" version of Islam, while their strong belief in and practice of both Islam and *adat* helps the Minangs to limit or avoid some undesired effects of modern global capitalism. The Minangkabau are a prime example of a matrilineal culture with female inheritance.

China

Originally, Chinese surnames were derived matrilineally, although by the time of the Shang Dynasty (1600 to 1046 BCE) they had become patrilineal. The Chinese character for "surname" (ÓY) still contains a female radical (sY), suggesting its matrilineal etymology.

Archaeological data supports the theory that during the Neolithic period (7000 to 2000 BCE) in China, Chinese matrilineal clans evolved into the usual patrilineal families by passing through a transitional patrilineal clan phase. Evidence includes some "richly furnished" tombs for young women in the early Neolithic Yangshao culture, whose multiple other collective burials imply a matrilineal clan culture. Toward the late Neolithic period, when burials were apparently of couples, "a reflection of patriarchy", an increasing elaboration of presumed chiefs' burials is reported.

Relatively isolated ethnic minorities such as the Mosuo (Na) in southwestern China are highly matrilineal, and use matrilineal *family names*, i.e., matrinames.

ViÇt Nam

Most ethnic groups classified as "Montagnards (Austronesian and Austroasian)" are matrilineal. On North Vietnam, according to Alessandra Chiricosta, the legend of Âu Cõ is said to be evidence of "the presence of an original 'matriarchy' ... and [it] led to the double kinship system, which developed there .... [and which] combined matrilineal and patrilineal patterns of family structure and assigned equal importance to both lines."

India

Of communities recognised in the national Constitution as Scheduled Tribes, "some ... [are] matriarchal and matrilineal" "and thus have been known to be more egalitarian." Several communities in South India practiced matrilineality, especially the Tiyyas and Nair (or *Nayar*) in the state of Kerala, and the Bunts and Billava in the states of Kerala and Karnataka. The system of inheritance was known as Marumakkathayam in the *Nair* community or Aliyasantana in the *Bunt* and the Billava community, and both communities were subdivided into clans. This system was exceptional in the sense that it was one of the few traditional systems in western historical records of India that gave women some liberty and the right to property.

In the matrilineal system, the family lived together in a tharavadu which was composed of a mother, her brothers and younger sisters, and her children. The oldest male member was known as the *karanavar* and was the head of the household, managing the family estate. Lineage was traced through the mother, and the children belonged to the mother's family. All family property was jointly owned. In the event of a partition, the shares of the children were clubbed with that of the mother. The karanavar's property was inherited by his sisters' sons rather than his own sons. Amitav Ghosh has stated that, although there were numerous other matrilineal succession systems in communities of the south Indian coast, the Nairs "achieved an unparalleled eminence in the anthropological literature on matrilineality".

The Marumakkathayam system is not very common in Kerala and Karnataka these days for many reasons. Society has become much more cosmopolitan and modern. Men seek jobs away from their hometown and take their wives and children along with them. In this scenario, a joint-family system is no longer viable. But conceivably, there might still be a few tharavads that pay homage to this system.

Malaysia

A culture similar to the *Minangkabau's*, above, is present in Negeri Sembilan, Malaysia, ever since West Sumatrans settled there in the 14th century.

In Oceania

Some oceanic societies, such as the Marshallese, the Trobrianders, the Palauans, the Yapese and the Siuai, are characterized by matrilineal descent. The sister's sons or the brothers of the decedent are commonly the successors in these societies.

Matrilineal Identification Within Judaism

Matrilineality in Judaism is the view that people born of a Jewish mother are themselves Jewish. The conferring of Jewish status through matrilineality is not stated explicitly in the Torah, though Jewish oral tradition maintains this was always the rule, and adduces indirect textual evidence. In biblical times, many Israelites married foreign women, and their children appear to have been accepted as Israelite without question; the Talmud understands that the women in question converted to Judaism.

In the Hellenistic period, some evidence indicates that the offspring of intermarriages between Jewish men and non-Jewish women were considered Jewish; as is usual in prerabbinic texts, there is no mention of conversion on the part of the Gentile spouse. On the other hand, Philo of Alexandria calls the child of a Jew and a non-Jew a *nothos* (bastard), regardless of whether the non-Jewish parent is the father or the mother.

The Mishnah (Kiddushin 3:12) states that, to be a Jew, one must be either the child of a Jewish mother or a convert to Judaism. The Talmud (Kiddushin 68b) derives this law from the Torah. The relevant Torah passage (Deut. 7:3-4) reads: "Thy daughter thou shalt not give to his son, nor shalt thou take his daughter to thy son. For they will turn away thy son from following me, that they may serve other gods."

With the emergence of Jewish denominations and the modern rise in Jewish intermarriage in the 20th century, questions about the law of matrilineal descent have assumed greater importance to the Jewish community at large. The heterogeneous Jewish community is divided on the issue of "Who is a Jew?" via descent; matrilineal descent still is the rule within Orthodox Judaism, which also holds that anyone with a Jewish mother has an irrevocable Jewish status, and matrilineal descent is the norm in the Conservative movement. Since 1983, Reform Judaism in the United States of America officially adopted a bilineal policy: one is a Jew if either of one's parents is Jewish, provided that either (a) one is raised as a Jew, by Reform standards, or (b) one engages in an appropriate act of public identification, formalizing a practice that had been common in Reform synagogues for at least a generation. Karaite Judaism, which includes only the Tanakh in its canon, interprets the Torah to indicate that Jewishness passes exclusively through the father's line.

Feminist Relationship

According to Kanchana N. Ruwanpura, "Sri Lanka .... is highly regarded even among feminist economists for the relatively favourable position of its women, reflected [in part] in the ... matrilineal and bilateral inheritance patterns and property rights", although she argued for caution in interpreting Sri Lanka's "gender-based ... achievements and/or matrilineal communities" and wrote that matrilineality coexists with "patriarchal structures and ideologies", which are influenced by "the main religious traditions, Buddhism, Hinduism, and Islam", even while "repressive cultural practices ... [may not be] pervasive" and "Sri Lankan women are surely not constrained by classical patriarchy". She wrote that "feminists have claimed that Sri Lankan women are relatively well positioned in the South Asian region". She also wrote that, on the other hand, feminists have criticized a view of women's lives in Sri Lanka, *e.g.*, because in accordance with "village practices and folklore ... young women raped (usually by a man) are married-off/required to cohabit with the rapists!" She wrote that "female-heads have no legal recourse" from "patriarchal interests".

According to her, "some female heads possessed" "feminist consciousness" and "the economic welfare of female-heads depends upon networks that mediate the patriarchal-ideological nexus, although the distinctions and similarities of the ethnically-based experiences of female-heads provide a sound basis for a coherent feminist perspective."

She wrote that

> *"in many cases female-heads are not vociferous feminists ... but rather 'victims' of patriarchal relations and structures that place them in precarious positions.... [while] they have held their ground ... [and] provided for their children".*

She wrote that

> *"in a shift from economic to non-economic forms of support .... feminists would no doubt wish to observe a significant shift in attitudes reflecting progressive and accommodating values towards female-heads, [but] this is not taking place on any scale in these communities."*

Bibliography

Alain, Touraine: *Return of the Actor*, University of Minnesota Press, Minneapolis, 2203.

Asad, Talal: *Genealogies of Religion*, Johns Hopkins University Press, Baltimore, 1993.

Bell, Daniel: *The Coming of Post-Industrial Society*, Harper Colophon Books, New York, 1974.

Buller, Cornelius A.: *The Unity of Nature and History in Pannenberg's Theology*, Rowman & Littlefield, Lanham, Maryland, 1996.

Burr, Vivien: *An Introduction to Social Constructionism*, Routledge, London, 1995.

Clarke, Peter B.: *The Oxford Handbook of the Sociology of Religion*, Oxford University Press, Oxford/New York, 2009.

Craig R. Prentiss: *Religion and the Creation of Race and Ethnicity*, NYU Press, New York, 2003.

Dave Elder-Vass: *The Reality of Social Construction*, Cambridge University Press, New York, 2012.

Davie, Grace: *Predicting religion: Christian, Peculiar & alternative Future*, Ashgate Publishing, New York, 2003.

Errington, Shelly: *Meaning and Power in a Southeast Asian Realm*, Princeton University Press, Princeton NJ, 1989.

Fitzgerald, Timothy: *Discourse on Civility and Barbarity*, Oxford University Press, New York, 2007.

Foucault, Michel: *The Birth of the Clinic: an archaeology of medical perception*, Tavistock, London, 1977.

Frier, Bruce W.; Bagnall, Roger S.: *The Demography of Roman Egypt.*, Cambridge University Press, Cambridge, UK, 1994.

Fuchs, Christian: *Internet and Society: Social Theory in the Information Age*, Routledge, New York, 2008.

Gellner, Ernest: *Legitimation of Belief*, Cambridge University Press, Cambridge, 1974.

Giddens, Anthony: *Modernity and sef-identity: self and society in the late modern age*, Polity Press, Cambridge, 1991.

Harvey, Graham: *Indigenous Religions: A Companion*, Cassell, London and New York, 2000.

Josephson, Jason Ananda: *The Invention of Religion in Japan*, University of Chicago Press, Chicago, 2012.

Joyce, Rosemary A. & Susan D. Gillespie: *Beyond Kinship: Social and Material Reproduction in House Societies*, University of Pennsylvania Press, 2000.

Kant, Immanuel: *Religion and Rational Theology*, Cambridge University Press, 2001.

Lenski, G.: *Human Societies: An Introduction to Macrosociology*, McGraw-Hill, New York, 1974.

Lévi-Strauss, Claude: *The Way of the Mask*, University of Washington Press, Seattle, 1982.

McMullin, Neil: *Buddhism and the State in Sixteenth-Century Japan*, Princeton University Press, Princeton, N.J., 1984.

Monaghan, John; Just, Peter: *Social & Cultural Anthropology*, Oxford University Press, New York, 2000.

Radcliffe-Brown, A.R., Daryll Forde: *African Systems of Kinship and Marriage*, KPI Limited, London, 1950.

Seely Brown, John; Duguid, Paul: *The Social Life of Information*, Harvard Business School Press, New York, 2000.

Smith, E. Gene: *Among Tibetan Texts: History and Literature of the Himalayan Plateau*, Wisdom Publications, Boston, 2001.

Smith, Wilfred Cantwell: *The Meaning and End of Religion*, Harper and Row, New York, 1978.

Tillich, P.: *Theology of Culture*, Oxford University Press, London, 1959.

Timothy, Fitzgerald, *The Ideology of Religious Studies*, Oxford University Press, New York, 2000.

Weber, Max: *The Protestant Ethic and the Spirit of Capitalism*, Los Angeles, Roxbury Company, 2002.

Webster, Frank: *Theories of the Information Society*, Routledge, Cambridge, 2002.

Webster, Frank: *Theories of the Information Society*, Routledge, London, 2002.

Williams, Paul; Tribe, Anthony: *Buddhist Thought: A complete introduction to the Indian tradition*, Routledge, Cambridge, 2000.

Wilson, Bryan: *Religion in Sociological Perspective*, Oxford University Press, Oxford, 1982.

Wolf, Eric: *Europe and the People Without History*, University of California Press, Berkeley, 1982.

Index

❑❑❑